ROMANTIC ESCAPE

Designing the Modern
Guest House III

ROMANTIC ESCAPE

Edited by Wendy Perring

Designing the
Modern Guest House III

CONTENTS

6 / Preface

8 / Project Case Studies

Oceanside Guest House

10 / **Shuimo Chanjing Lake View Holiday Inn**

16 / **Haitian Zuoshe Guest House**

22 / **Munwood Lakeside**

30 / **Manshausen Island Resort**

36 / **Mangiabove Guest House**

42 / **Namaste Suites**

50 / **Vacation House in Euboea**

Mountainside Guest House

58 / **The Bivou**

66 / **Dengfeng Qingjing Lanshan Courtyard**

72 / **Joyful Boutique Hotel**

78 / **Qingyan Guest House**

84 / **Cave House**

90 / **Septuor**

98 / **My Fairytale Villas**

104 / **Sargent Residence**

110 / **Tainaron Blue Retreat**

118 / **Watermill on the Crag**

124 / **Mazama Ranchero**

Urban Guest House

130 / **Bushe Hotel**

138 / **Shanshui Boutique Hotel**

144 / **Twisting Courtyard**

150 / **Rare Yard**

158 / **LIBERTINE LINDENBERG**

164 / **One House**

170 / **iii_house**

178 / **Florida home with a relaxed patina**

184 / **Quaperlake Street**

192 / **Štajnhaus**

200 / **The New Road Residence**

Rural Guest House

208 / **Warborne Farm – The Long Barn**

214 / **Mr Yao's house #1**

220 / **Hacienda Sac Chich, Casa de Maquinas – Casa Sisal**

226 / **Mr Yao's house #30**

232 / **Can Guix**

238 / **The Relais La Leopoldina**

244 / **Cherry Orchard Residence**

250 / **MOOYARD-II**

256 / **Spanish Mission-Style Guest House**

260 / **The Ibiza Campo House**

266 / **Vacation House in South Peloponnese**

274 / **Dune House**

280 / **Doris Home**

286 / Index

PREFACE

Wendy graduated from the University of Edinburgh in 1996 with Distinction and was Scottish Young Architect of the Year in 1995. She was a founding director of Perring Architecture and Design. PAD studio was established in 2013.

Having undertaken a Postgraduate Teaching course at UEL in 1999, Wendy has been actively involved in education and teaching at numerous institutions. She is a part time studio teacher at Portsmouth University, a visiting critic at Arts Institute Bournemouth and private Tutor for Oxford Brookes University.

In 2016 Wendy joined Design South East (DSE) as a panel member and has chaired the RIBA Awards South Region. Wendy is a trustee of and actively involved with SPUD, a local arts charity specializing in public engagement, and educational arts programmes. SPUD regularly engages in community consultation where major public arts and urban improvements are proposed. Ensuring those local voices are heard through proper consultation can make a major contribution to social cohesion and the future sustainability of communities. Wendy has written critiques and provided commentary for numerous architectural journals and books including the Architects Journal, the RIBA Journal and a new book which will be published in the spring 'Aalto – Utzon – Fehn: Three Paradigms of Phenomenological Architecture' by Roger Tyrell (Routledge 2018).

Guest houses can provide spaces' in which to escape the everyday. Due to budget and spatial limitations, guest houses are often restrained, offering pared back accommodation with only the essentials on offer. On occasion, the guest houses can deliver opulent and luxurious spaces, more indulgent than their associated permanent dwelling; offering the inhabitant an opportunity to leave normality.

In the UK alone, the number of guest annex buildings being constructed or converted has risen by 20% in the last two years alone. The guest house, can accommodate more than the occasional visiting friend; children are staying at home longer; elderly parents can be accommodated; and it has become a socially accepted and lucrative source of earning additional income, where the quirkier the space, the more in demand it becomes.

The typical guest house project site is a challenging mix of constraints including existing buildings and landscape features. To arrive at a clever solution requires creativity and lateral thinking. As a result, the guest house's unique typology provides a test bed for new ideas; as a transient place never permanently occupied. In this sense, one can afford to be more playful, more adventurous and to push the boundaries of what one may normally expect.

The projects contained in this book vary considerably in scale, style and situation. Many involve thoughtful re-use of existing buildings, some are available for public occupation and some are private. All are unique.

Reflecting upon my own experience in designing several guest houses invokes feelings of joy. Every time that PAD studio approaches a guest house project we attempt to understand the place in which we are working and reveal buildings that engage in a dialogue with the landscape. Hopefully, the end result is a narrative, a story about place, people and materials. Our aim is that this narrative, the experience of staying in the guest house's that we design will be an enriching experience. We hope the memories made will be inspiring and will cause a ripple effect as the visitors return to their own stories, and homes.

Our brief for the Warborne Farmstays was to provide accommodation for paying guests within self-contained apartments sited around a communal courtyard. Located on an award winning organic farm in the New Forest National Park, England, the property was a collection of redundant Georgian farm buildings.

Should they wish to, guests can engage in farm life, picking vegetables, attending to farm animals and explore the New Forest, and local coastline. Our clients were adventurous, quirky and fun. The buildings were textured, rural and simple in layout. The budget was tight but the aspiration high. We collaborated closely with the contractor, designing and making elements as required during the process.

We incorporated materials that were found on the farm, such as old stable stalls as space dividers. Old metal roofing was oiled to become wall cladding and metal windows were fitted with mirrored glass and used in the rooms. Many furniture items were bespoke, made to maximize the space available. Secret loft spaces were created for children and we wanted the experience for guests to be fun, honest and appropriate the building's heritage.

The narrative resulted from a close understanding of client, place and history. The project now offers a place where new memories can be forged and the normal everyday can be left far behind. PAD studio believes architects have a responsibility to act as storytellers, telling stories through the medium of three-dimensional space. The plot is built through layering of history, context and relationships. These layers inspire us and provide design direction as we formulate them into an architectural proposal which illustrates a dialogue between all the elements.

Like the projects exhibited in this book, we hope that visiting one of our buildings will be a life-enriching experience where the narrative provides a better understanding of place. This is what all great buildings embody and how special places to call 'home' are made.

Wendy Perring

Managing Director – MA Arch (Edin.) Dip Arch (Dist) RIBA

Project Case
Studies

Location /
Lijiang, Yunnan, China

Area /
17,222 square feet
(1600 square meters)

Architecture and design /
Yang Ying

Photography /
Mu Tou

Text /
Yoli Zhang

Shuimo Chanjing Lake View Holiday Inn

Shuimo Chanjing Lake View Holiday Inn, which is a high-end boutique guest house located at the lakeside of Lugu Lake, is the result of the designer's painstaking efforts over three years.

Before construction, the site hosted an old, ruined building, a local Muleng house, which was horizontally stacked with a series of square logs. It was dilapidated, as it had been deserted for a long time.

The design for the new inn—over a total building area of 17,222 square feet (1600 square meters)—deconstructed the existing structure of the old edifice and created a set-back building. The interior space uses modern Hui-style design, embraces Chinese style, stresses beauty of symmetry, and blends well with the natural landscape.

This guest house has three floors, the building area of which decreases successively from the first floor to the third floor. The wharf and the private garden are located on the first floor and have an excellent lighting and ventilation effect, which create a private mansion for guests.

The designer built a glasshouse to keep out wind and rain as well as to make indoor plants thrive. Modern Hui-style design inside shows harmonious and smooth lines, and neat and orderly layouts. The central lobby has its own symmetric axis, with scripts and paintings hanging on pilasters on both sides of the lobby, showing a deep artistic conception. There are several ancient trees in the central lobby. Sparse and scattered flowers and trees make a beautiful picture.

This guest house has 12 rooms, which are arranged symmetrically along the central axis, balanced and harmonious. These rooms show a world of Zen; people can sit on the futon to meditate or sip tea. Noble orchids are echoed by the clean lake and distant mountains. Natural landscapes blend with each other and form a whole.

Additionally, the rooms use wooden, hollowed-out partition screens to optimize the visual effect of space, which gives the spaces a certain degree of privacy and creates a sense of serenity and elegance. Alternatively, they are decorated with carved patterns, delicate and dynamic. From 'arhat' beds and large terraces in rooms, people can overlook the beautiful scenery of Lugu Lake and get closer to nature.

01 / Entrance to guest house
02 / External view of garden near lake
03 / Lobby area

1. Guest room
2. Tea house
3. Washing room
4. Rest area
5. Water view
6. Open area
7. Wooden bridge
8. Bar
9. Cigar bar
10. Storage room

04 / Outdoor balcony
05 / Bedroom
06–07 / King-sized room with view of lake

Third-floor plan

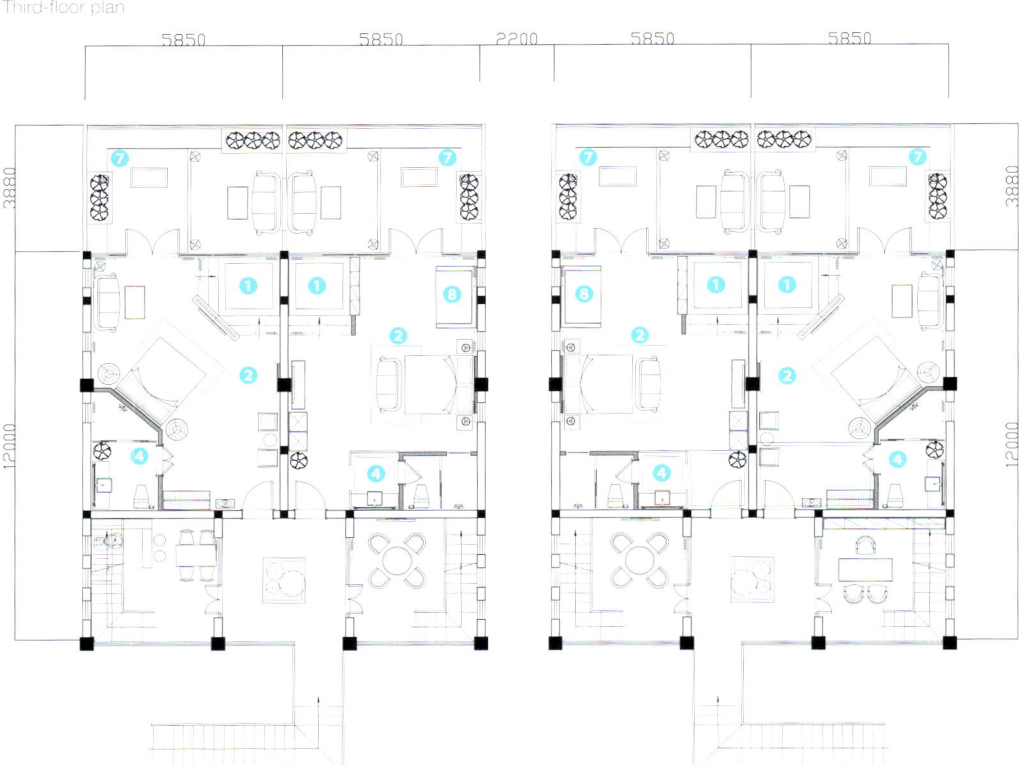

Second-floor plan

1. Bathtub
2. Guest room
3. Study room
4. Toilet
5. Sinks
6. Shower
7. Terrace
8. Arhat bed

14 Oceanside Guest House

08 / Atrium
09 / View of lobby
10 / Duplex suite
11 / Lake view from French window

Location /
Wenzhou, Zhejiang, China

Architecture and design /
Yan Lefeng

Composition /
1 building, 8 bedrooms

Photography /
Xu Ninglong

Haitian Zuoshe Guest House

There is a solitary house on an island of Dongtou District of Wenzhou in Zhejiang Province. Many years ago, the owner of this house moved stones by hand to build it. Years later, the children grew up and left the island, leaving the grandfatherlandlord and a dilapidated house behind.

However, it came as a shock six months later when the dilapidated house was transformed into a guest house. A shabby stone house in most people's eyes, the designer saw a Santorini-style white hotel between the blue sea and the clear sky. He successfully transformed the stone house into a waterfront guest house with a resort-style ambiance.

There are three swimming pools outside the guest house, one of which extends out to face the sea; another clinging to the cliff. At night, romantic lights are lit, creating the perfect setting for a summertime pool party. The guest house comprises a lobby with a bar counter, a dining hall and a coffee bar on opposite sides, and an open kitchen inside. Guests who book the whole guest house can cook for themselves.

The rough texture and snow-white color of the paint outlines the Santorini flavor. Old door planks are transformed into tables, with a row of booths set along windows. People can sit on cushions with feet up, enjoying the scenery and sipping tea.

The guest house has eight rooms: Hearing Tidewater, Feeling Mists, Meeting Sea, Staring Billows, Keeping Fish, Watching Sand, Riding Waves, and Appreciating Clouds. The owner, who has a passion for literature and art, named the rooms poetically.

Offering a simple, clean, northern-Europe style, each room is decorated by artworks. People can relax in the sunshine, listening to the sound of the waves, and read their favorite books. The balconies offer a beautiful spot where people can take in the views at dawn or sunset, offering added appeal for guests.

01 / Building façade
02 / Entrance to building

03–04 / Outdoor leisure area
05 / Indoor space
06 / Guest room

07 / Sideboard at corner of stairs
08 / Plush chair
09 / Window next to bed
10 / Outdoor bathtub

11-12 / Bedroom

Location /
Dali, Yunnan, China

Area /
10,764 square feet
(1000 square meters)

Architecture and design /
IDO (Init Design Office)

Cooperation unit /
Chongqing Hexin Architectural Design Institute Co., Ltd.

Photography /
Archi Exist Photographer

Munwood Lakeside

Munwood Lakeside is one of the two design hotels recently designed by IDO (Init Design Office) in Dali, Yunnan province. Located beside Erhai Lake, it is an original farmhouse that's been expanded and reconstructed, expanding from 3229 square feet (300 square meters) to 10,764 square feet (1000 square meters).

Simply-design-style as starting point

IDO's consistent design principle—refuse fashion and popular design methods and skills—try to offer simple and direct solutions and create appropriate architecture. As an attempt of contemporary vernacular, the designers should try to make the building really belong to the site.

A building belonging to the site

• Layout: Controlling the scale, break up the whole into parts and slope roofs echo surrounding farmhouse.

• Boundary: The stone walls, being served as a boundary, make the relationship between the hotel and the surrounding neighbors not only different, but also connected.

• Multi-level public space design: The most difficult part of design was to cross the front road to enjoy the Erhai Lake. The relationship between the building and the road is difficult to deal with, so a half-sinking public space was designed to make a link. Space below the partition can make a psychological link with the water, while the platform built on the space established a more direct relationship with the Erhai Lake. This platform used the steel structure, which was quite different from the main body. The elevation was reduced to establish a close relationship with the same floor ground. The building on the right side of the platform was open for two reasons. For one, to make the stream line below always feel part of the spacious outdoors; for another, seen from the road, to make it look more ethereal and light, unlike the surrounding houses, which were very thick.

• Diversity of the guest room design: There are 13 guest rooms, each with a unique landscape, connecting directly with the site. Ten different rooms were designed to create a variety of experiences.

• Relationship with the original house: The transition between the new and old houses was designed naturally; it was very direct in the processing of structure and spatial function; and it was continued in the form.

01 / Surrounding landscape and architecture
02 / Courtyard

Axonometric drawing

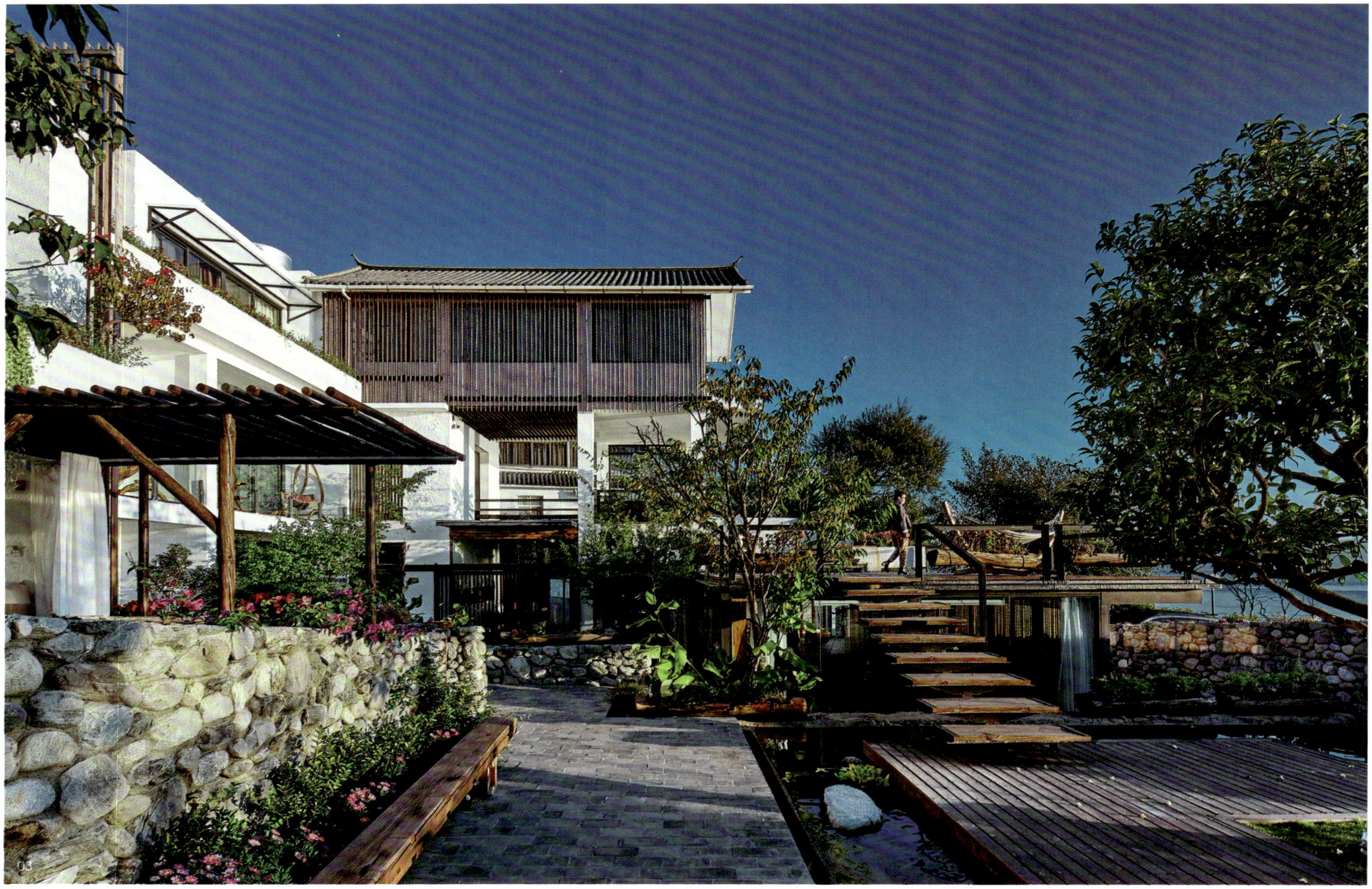

03-04 / Courtyard
05 / Grey space
06 / Pool between sunken study and stone wall

Third-floor plan

Second-floor plan

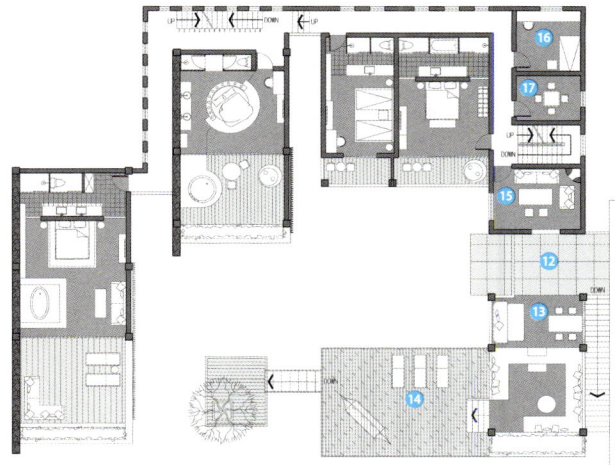

First-floor plan

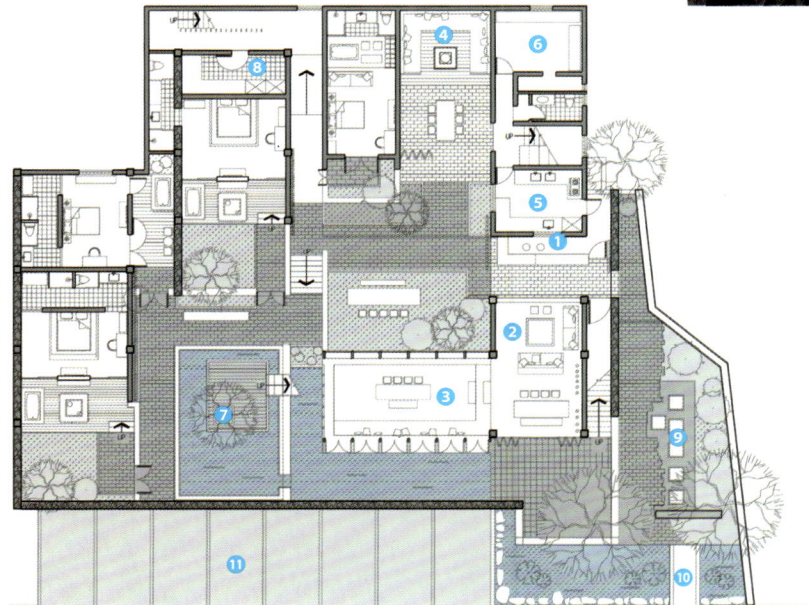

① Reception area
② Lounge
③ Sunken study
④ Fire pit
⑤ Kitchen
⑥ Warehouse
⑦ Old tea tree
⑧ Car wash
⑨ Exhibition area of water reuse system
⑩ Bridge at entrance
⑪ Outdoor parking space
⑫ Glass ground
⑬ Lounge room
⑭ Outdoor platform
⑮ Tea room
⑯ Staff lounge
⑰ Chess room
⑱ Warehouse

07 / Lobby and sunken study
08 / Sunken study
09 / Reception area in lobby

Section of guest room

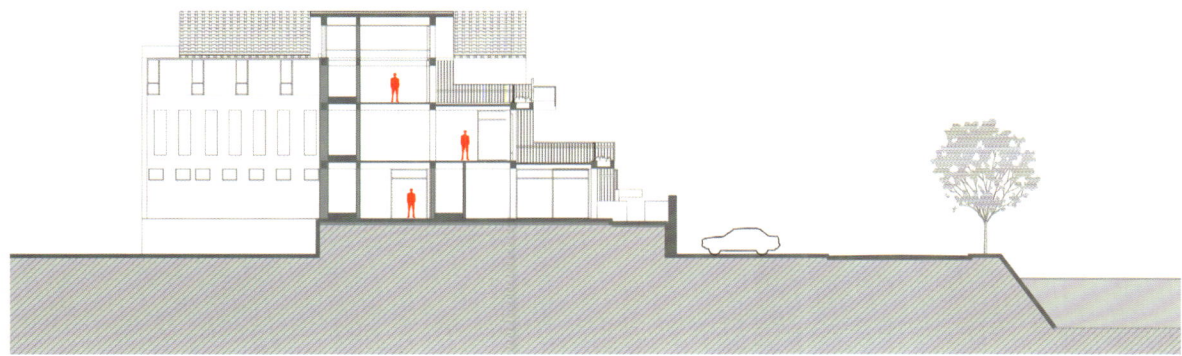

Section of sunken study

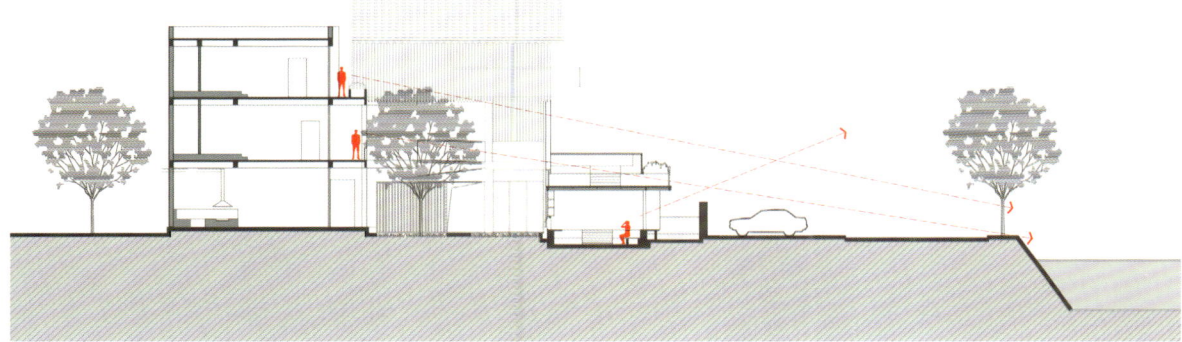

10–11 / View from one guest room
12 / Chinese fire pit

Location /
Manshausen Island, Steigen, Norway

Area /
355 square feet (33 square meters)

Architecture and design /
Snorre Stinessen / Stinessen Arkitektur

Photography /
Siggen Stinessen, Steve King

Manshausen Island Resort

Conceptually the shelter has the same basic form and function as a cave or protected overhang; a secure and comforting retreat from the wild nature outside.

The market analyses established the need to accommodate two to four people in each cabin, a comfortable bathroom, a small kitchen, and sufficient storage space. The main design idea was to create small cabins that would offer a high level of comfort to the visitor and at the same time truly showcase the nature and natural elements outside. The shape of the building attempts to underline the earthbound foundation at the rear and the cantilevered exposure towards the view at the front.

The cabins were designed to offer guests shelter and comfort while, at the same time, underlining the dramatic experience of the elements outside—the sea, landscape, changing lights, weather, and different seasons. Above all, the design endeavored to fulfill the functional requirements of the guests, with ample space for luggage and clothing/equipment, a comfortable bathroom, and a kitchen and dining area. The cabins accommodate two to four people, or a family of five. The master bed is positioned in the main room, slightly withdrawn from the floor-to-ceiling windows, to enable the visitor an around-the-clock experience of the outside elements, while still being comfortably sheltered.

The local climate and remote location dictated a limited season for building—weather permitting. Additionally, the resort needed a fixed opening date and the building season was also high season for potential guests. Thus, it was decided to prepare as much as possible during wintertime and limit the construction period at the island to a minimum. Transportation and logistics ruled out prefabricated modules, but pre-cut and prefabricated building elements would be within the size and weight limits.

The shelter design endeavored to make a minimum environmental impact with the use of massive-wood construction, and the construction was planned taking into account the logistical restrictions. Massive wood plates were also ideal for pre-cut and prefabrication. The main construction of one shelter was set up as a prototype at the factory for inspection and adjustments before finalization, packaging, and shipment. Total assembly time at the island was five to six weeks in difficult weather conditions.

01–02 / Perched above old quarry

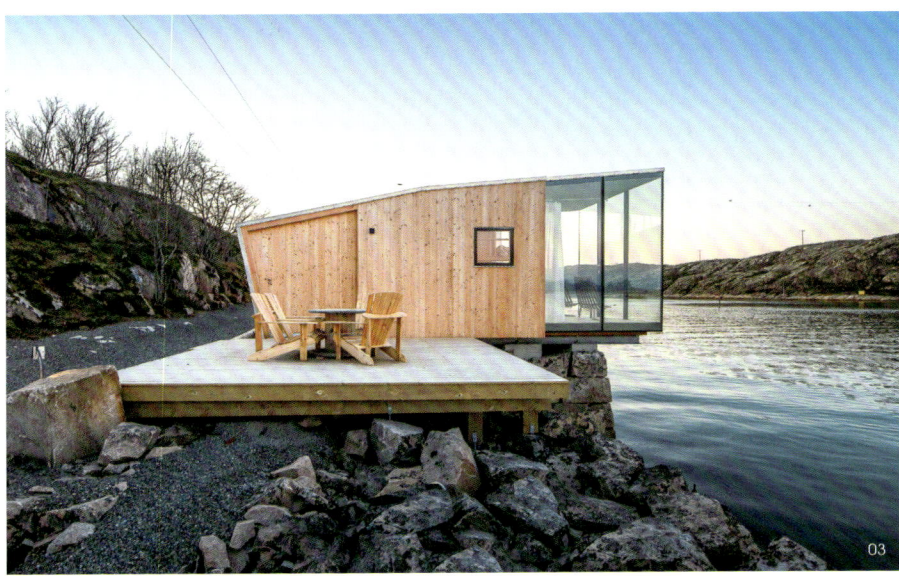

03 / Cabin with private terrace
04 / Covered entrance providing practical shelter
05 / Comfortable reading area facing water
06 / Northern lights outside living room

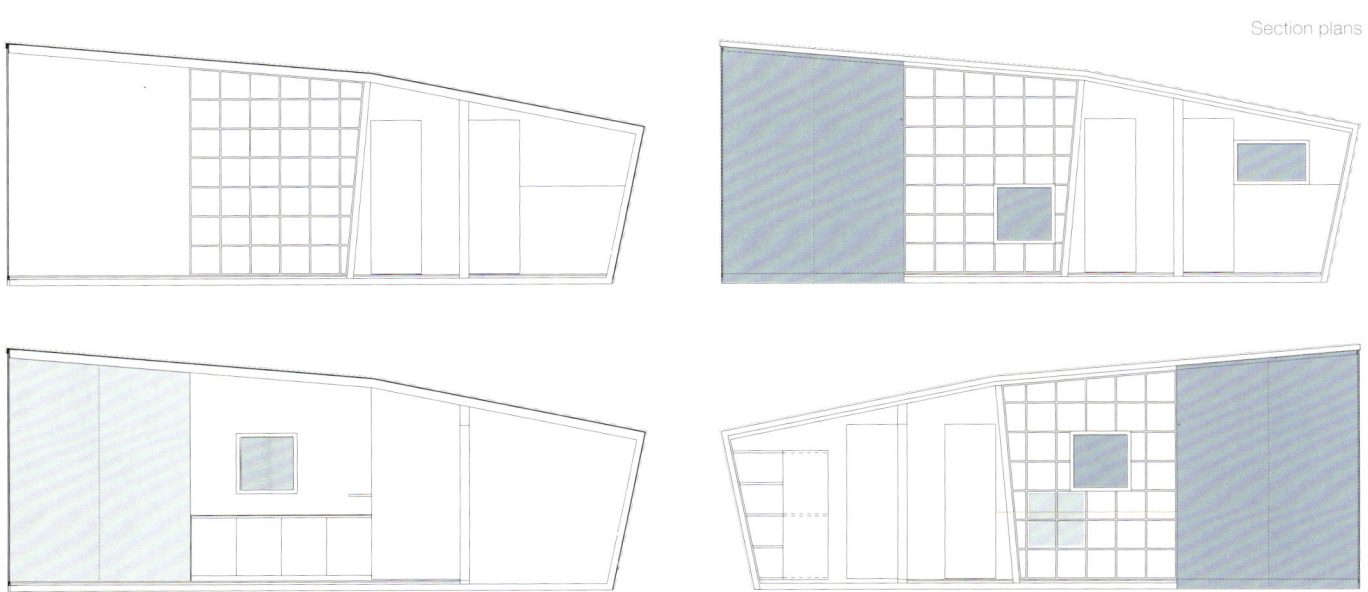

Section plans

07 / Room divider doubling as table
08 / Custom-designed kitchen
09 / Room with view
10 / Main bed next to shelves

34 Oceanside Guest House

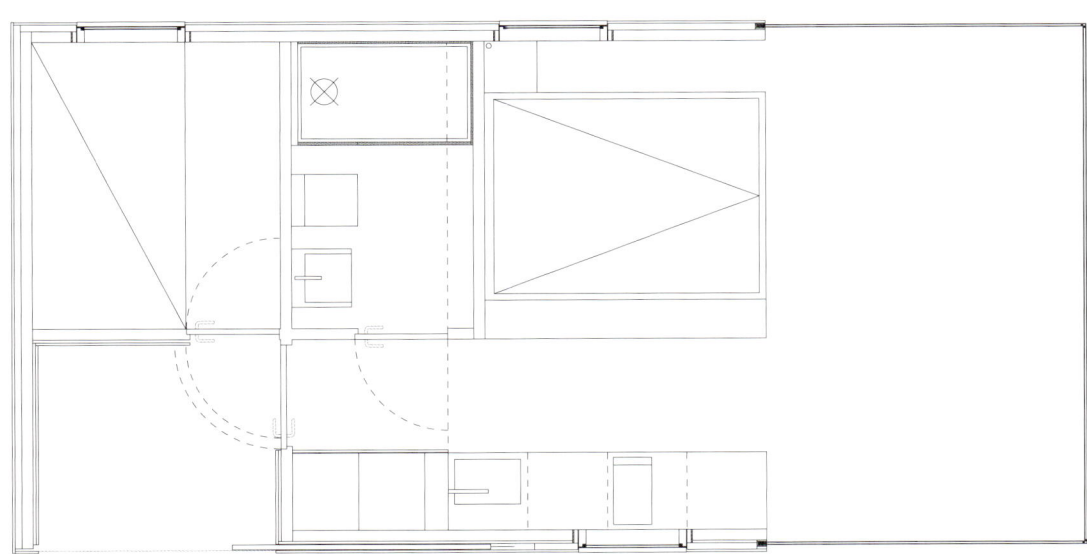

Floor plan

Location /
Ragusana, Italy

Area /
6458 square feet
(600 square meters)

Architecture and design /
Valentina Gianpiccolo and
Giuseppe Minaldi

Photography /
Antonio Principato

Mangiabove Guest House

Mangiabove is a homely tourist residence immersed not only in the Ragusana countryside, characteristic for its dry white stone walls that demarcate the surrounding pasture lands and farmlands, but it is also situated near the coastline. Built in solid stone, like all the rural buildings in the area, Mangiabove still retains its original planimetric and volumetric composition: an 'L' with an east/west (double level) axis for the houses and to the east a north/south (one level) axis for the stables and warehouses that surround the courtyard and its central stone well.

A wooden truss ceiling was put up in the common room, given the size of the environment, using the traditional cane-mesh technique of plaster casting, which has excellent insulation properties. The exposed stone, along with some original stone inserts and niches for the shelter of the animals, were kept where possible, even in the interior of the houses.

The double height of the east/west orientation block was used to create a new level, accessible not only from the inside but also independently from the outside. This was done by creating new balconies and a new staircase facing north. The first is a concrete ramp, covered in cultured marble, in correspondence with the breakfast room, and the second is a metal ramp, in correspondence with the stone structure, so as not to weigh down the visual. The accommodation units are seven in total, equipped with kitchens and bathrooms, living area, and master bedrooms. Three of these are connected to the upstairs bedrooms, which have private bathrooms and terraces.

The roofs of the houses are made of wood, with beams, planks, insulating layers, and Sicilian titles. The ceilings are of a gray light blue color so as to recall the color of the sky, and at set intervals the color is broken up by the white of the beams and the white of the lime plaster of the walls. White and blue colors and different geometric patterns were selected for the layout of the various rooms.

01 / Courtyard
02 / Tropical garden with view of Mediterranean sea
03 / Infinity pool overlooking countryside

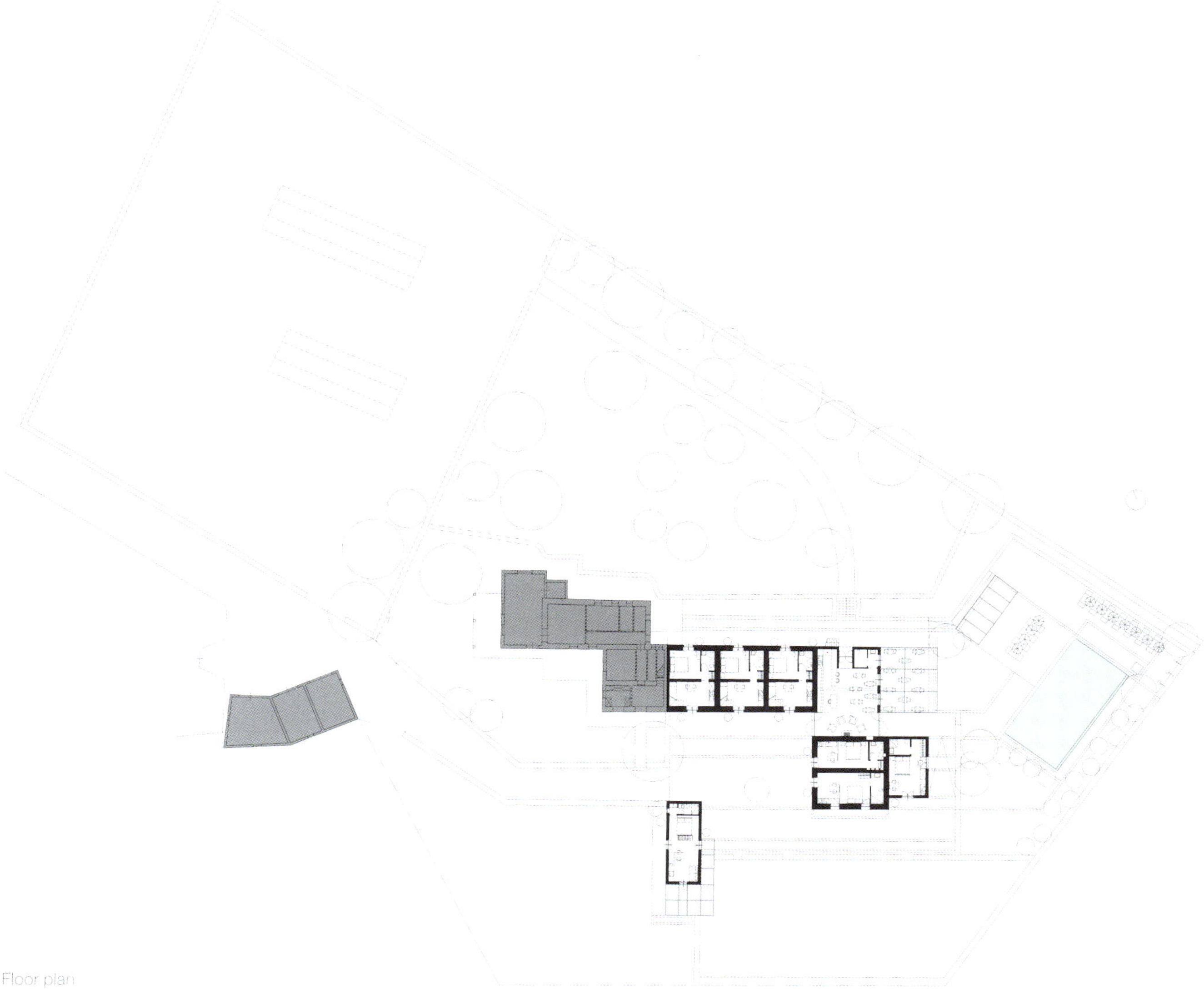

Floor plan

04 / Green and shady breakfast area
05 / Baroness Suite
06 / Mangiabove's living room
07 / Barn renovated into kitchen

08 / Quartara
09 / Timpa
10 / Balcony outside

Location /
Oia, Santorini, Greece

Area /
1722 square feet
(160 square meters)

Architecture and design /
Elias Apostolides, Maria
Chatzistavrou, Lime Deco

Photography /
George Fakaros

Namaste Suites

The guest house is located at the most photographed part of Oia at the cliffside overlooking the Aegean and the caldera, right below The Church of the Resurrection. The original cave-homes dating from 1900 were joined as one building of 1722 square feet (160 square meters) and renovated by the architect Elias Apostolides. The building material contains pozzolan, which has great strength and insulative properties.

The architect treated the cave as a work of art using details of the native architecture, but also influences from Italy and the East. The interiors reminisce of a sculpture, in which man intrudes with particular finesse. The flooring is covered with black and white Naxos marble and wood.

The décor fully respects the particular architecture of the space, completing and showing the individual elements, giving the visitor the feeling of a pleasant luxury residence with positive energy influence. That's why the name of the residence is Namaste Suites, which means 'I bow with gratitude to your positive energy and welcome you.'

Lime Deco office of Chatzistavrou Maria took the lead in the decoration, in light of an excellent collaboration and chemistry with the owners. Natural materials such as bamboo, straw, linen, marble, stone, and metal were used in their natural shades of gray and beige.

The main room consists of the primary living room with an auxiliary kitchenette. Down a small staircase, there is an old cistern that is shaped like a reading and relaxation area with a comfortable bamboo armchair. There are two bedrooms, the largest of which is inside the cave and the other is smaller with a window overlooking the Caldera view.

The interior room has its own lounge-desk, walk-in wardrobe, and a spacious bathroom with a free-standing bathtub. The two rooms share an outdoor Jacuzzi, while a lounge overlooks the caldera through the unique marble window, which is a trademark of the house.

01 / Caldera and sea view
02 / Cave houses of Namaste Suites
03 / Patio with jacuzzi

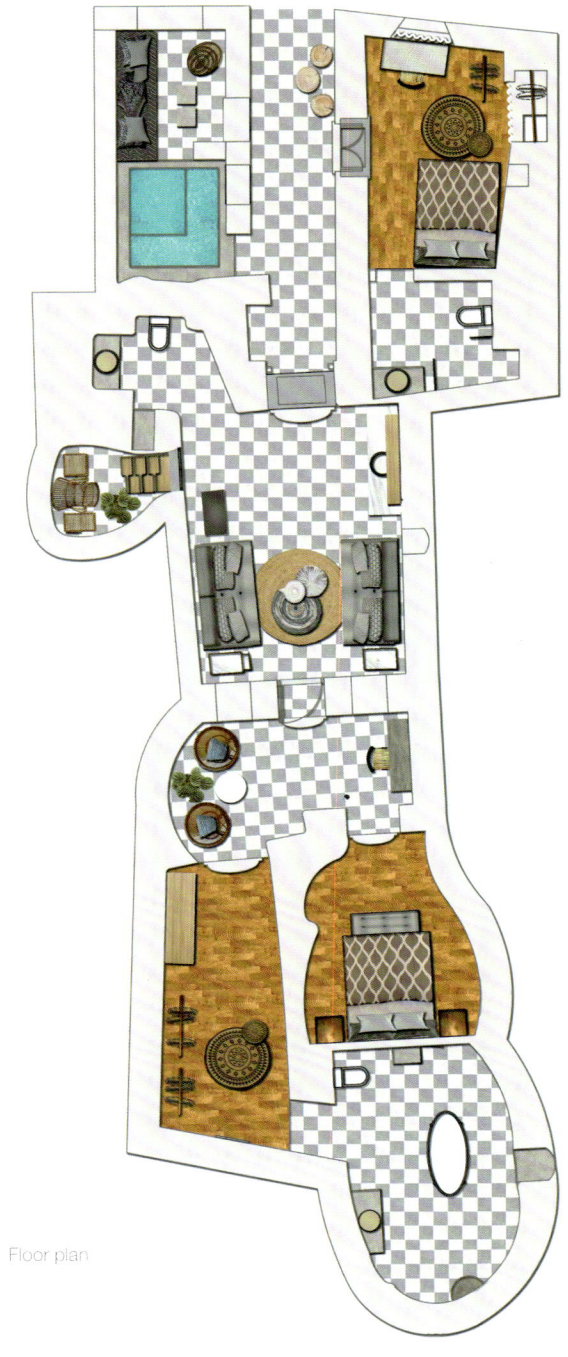

Floor plan

04 / Main corridor viewing sea
05 / Jacuzzi area
06 / Reading corner in house
07 / Jacuzzi with window and sea view

08 / Living room with kitchen
09 / Inside master bedroom
10 / Old cistern with bamboo armchair

11 / Master bedroom
12 / Bathroom with tub
13 / Guest bathroom

48 Oceanside Guest House

14 / Spare bedroom
15 / Spare bedroom with caldera view

Location /
Chronia, Euboea, Greece

Area /
3391 square feet
(315 square meters)

Architecture and design /
GEM Architects

Photography /
Costas Vergas

Vacation House in Euboea

The complex consists of four separate buildings: the main house with a two-story stone volume and three single-floor guest houses, which are situated in an inclined olive grove overlooking the gulf of Evia. They were all placed on the north upper side of the lot, following the landscape's morphology and giving the overall impression of a small settlement.

The volumes of the house interweave with the olive grove and become an integral part of the landscape. The volumes meander among the trees, creating small sheltered courtyards that enjoy privacy and beautiful sea views.

The thick inclined walls are inspired from the local Monastic architecture. At the same time, these walls created by a tectonic geometry create a distorting cubicle language, which tries to bind together tradition with abstraction.

Everything works to create a bio-climatic complex. No air-condition is needed due to the thick walls, good insulation of the terraces, and the adaption to the microclimate of the olive grove. Small courtyards shaded by the trees work as buffering zones from the sun and heat. Rainwater is collected and reused for watering the garden.

Materials used are simple and minimalist: concrete floors and roofs and dark-gray custom-made metal frames contrast to the white walls. Concrete stucco on the bathroom walls creates a sense of primitivism. A minimalist and ascetic language is expressed in a modern contemporary way, a language with many affinities to Greek culture.

The existing landscape is treated with respect. The design process reads the messages from the microcosm—the neighborhoods of earth, rocks, and trees—and adapts to its polymorphic nature. The end the constellation of houses looks like it is part of this nature. A swimming pool with a dining area and a resting area are situated at a lower level of the steep lot. A small path connects the houses to the pool plateau, with the sea beyond.

01 / Building and surrounding landscape
02 / Side of building

Site plan

52   Oceanside Guest House

03 / Entrance to building
04 / Swimming pool
05–06 / Outdoor lounge of guest house at night

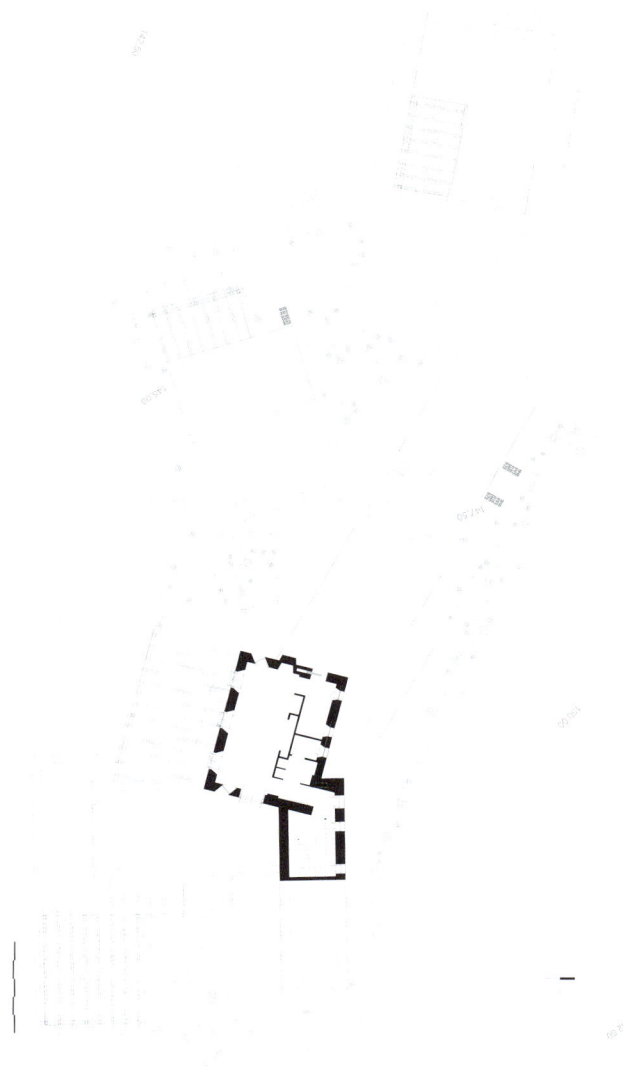

First-floor plan

07 / Kitchen on first floor
08 / Outdoor dining room
09 / Indoor kitchen and dining room

10 / Indoor living room
11 / View of living room from entrance

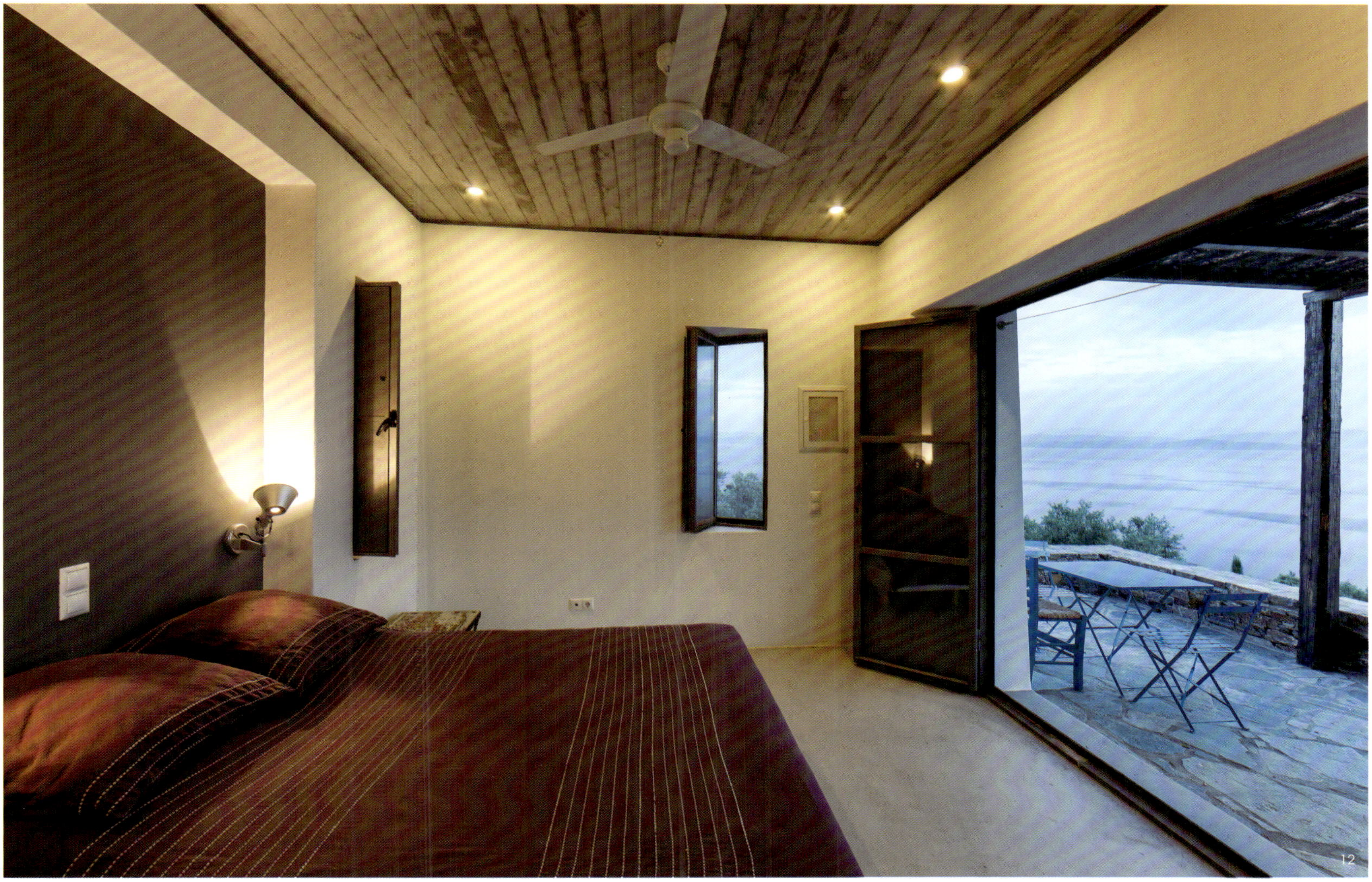

12

13

14

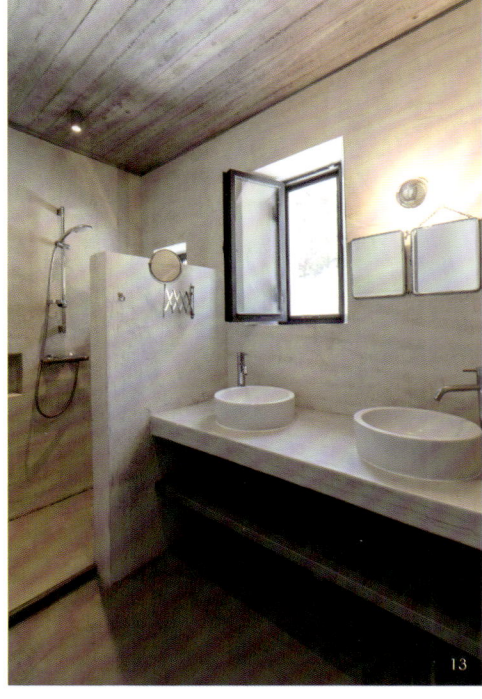

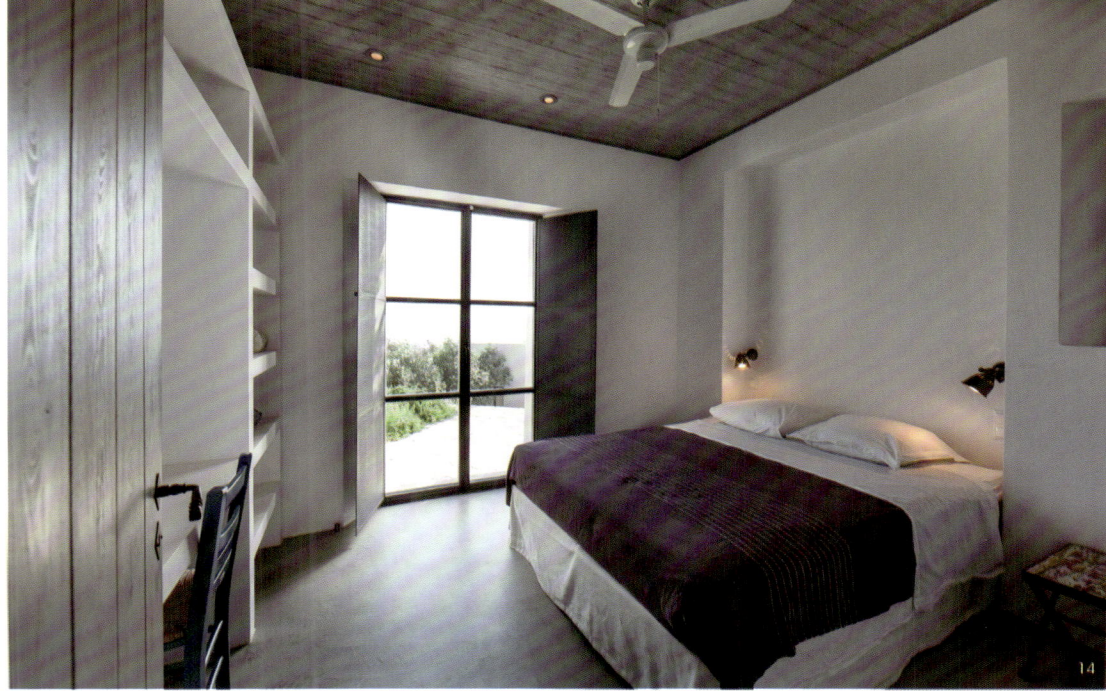

12 / Bedroom with ocean view
13 / Bathroom
14 / Bedroom

Location /
Lijiang, Yunnan, China

Area /
9042 square feet
(840 square meters)

Architecture and design /
Chow I-Shin

Photography /
Shin Nakamura

The Bivou

The Bivou, located at Lijiang, a World Heritagelisted city, was transformed from two old folk houses in Shuhe Ancient Town to a guest house with 16 rooms and two farmhouse gardens. The simple concept was to design a guest house that retained its originality while also providing new standards in comfort and style.

To merge with local history and the 100-yearold culture, and also keep the ecology sustainable, the designer remained faithful to the local roots in the design process by learning typical building techniques from villagers to achieve the sustainable development of the community. The plans incorporated bamboo flooring and super-efficient LED lighting inside, as well as solar panels and insulated glass to provide renewable thermal energy for all rooms, ensuring high-quality comfort.

Meanwhile, the design team integrated unique design elements into the Bivou, so that their design concept could penetrate into each space, rivalling the designs of hotels in Shanghai and New York. The hall and dining room of the Bivou are simple, natural but distinctive, preserving the basic framework of the old buildings, yet providing advanced facilities. The amenities are modern and household items are mainly white to create a clean atmosphere. The carpet on the ground adds comfort and luxury.

The Bivou has rooms with distinctive designs, suites surrounded by lush gardens, and well-equipped

villas suitable for small families. The farm in the west offers the best portrayal of the changing farmland outside, while the yard in the east hosts the flowers of Yunnan. Guests staying in the villas can enjoy the quiet solitude in the private garden where the azaleas and camellias grow.

01 / Panorama of guest house
02 / Entrance to building

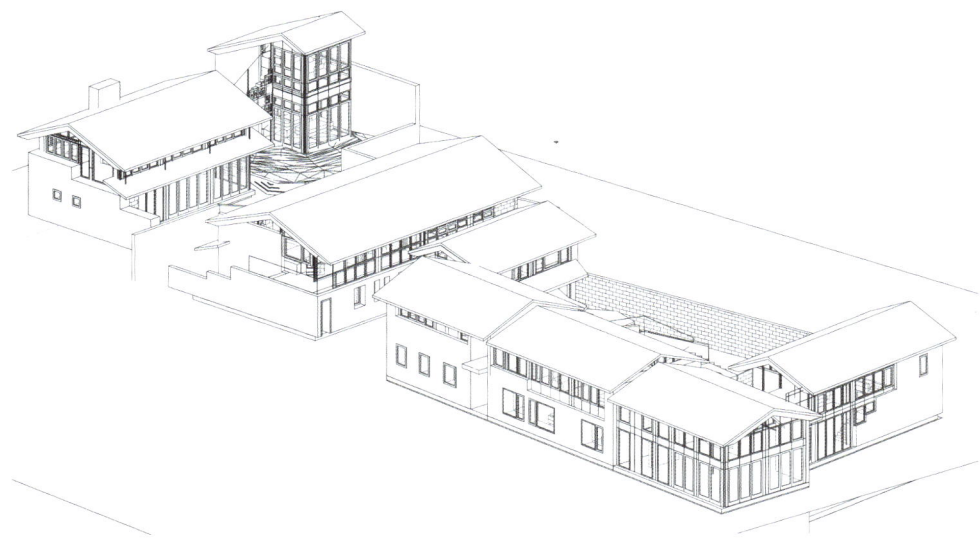

Top-down orthogonal view of north side

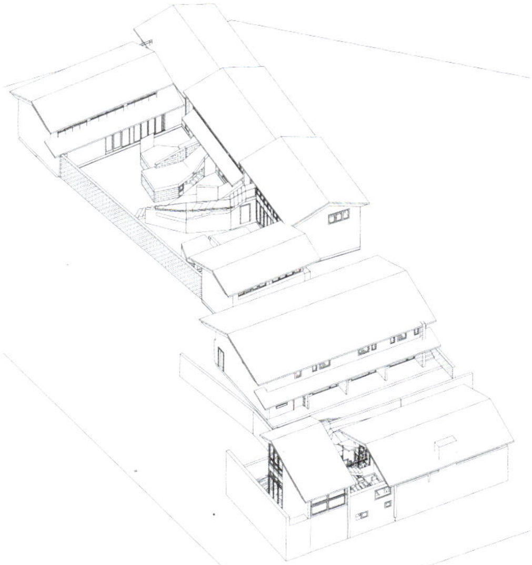

Top-down orthogonal view of south side

03 / Corner of building
04 / Courtyard
05 / Study

60　Mountainside Guest House

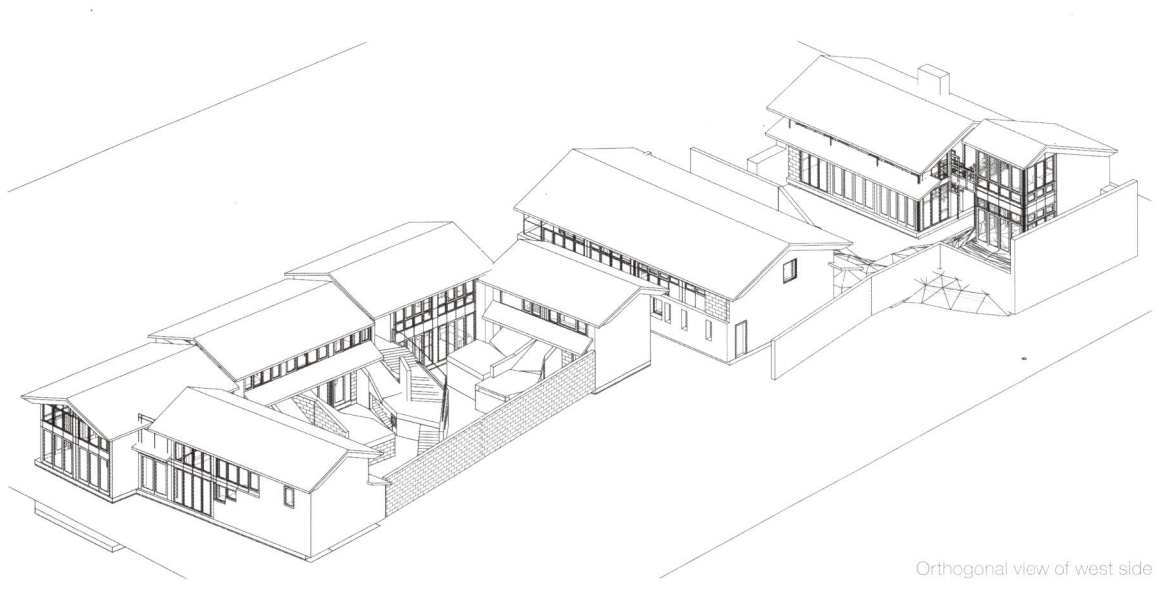

Orthogonal view of west side

61

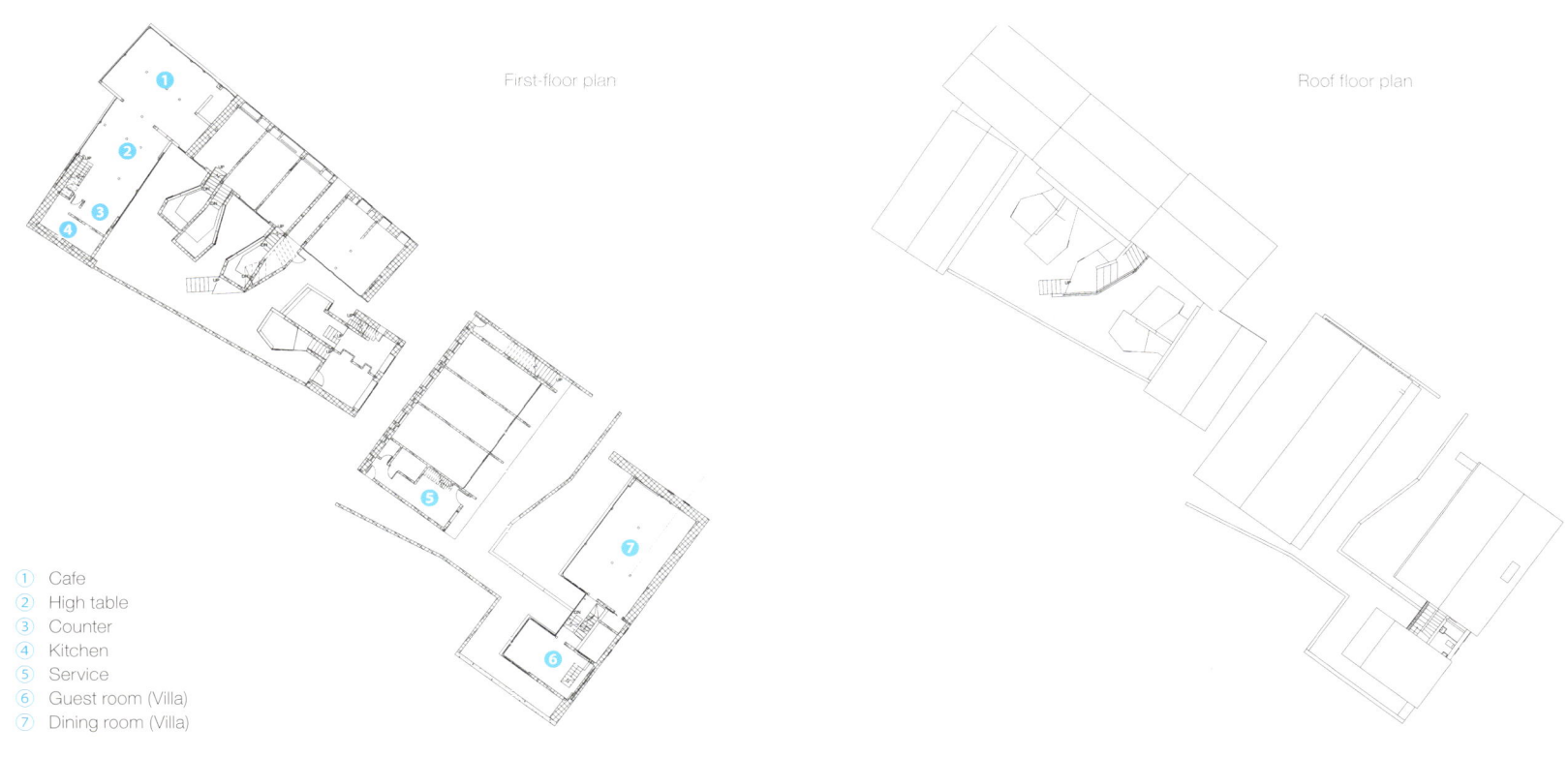

First-floor plan

Roof floor plan

① Cafe
② High table
③ Counter
④ Kitchen
⑤ Service
⑥ Guest room (Villa)
⑦ Dining room (Villa)

06 / Bedroom
07 / Bathroom
08 / Lounge

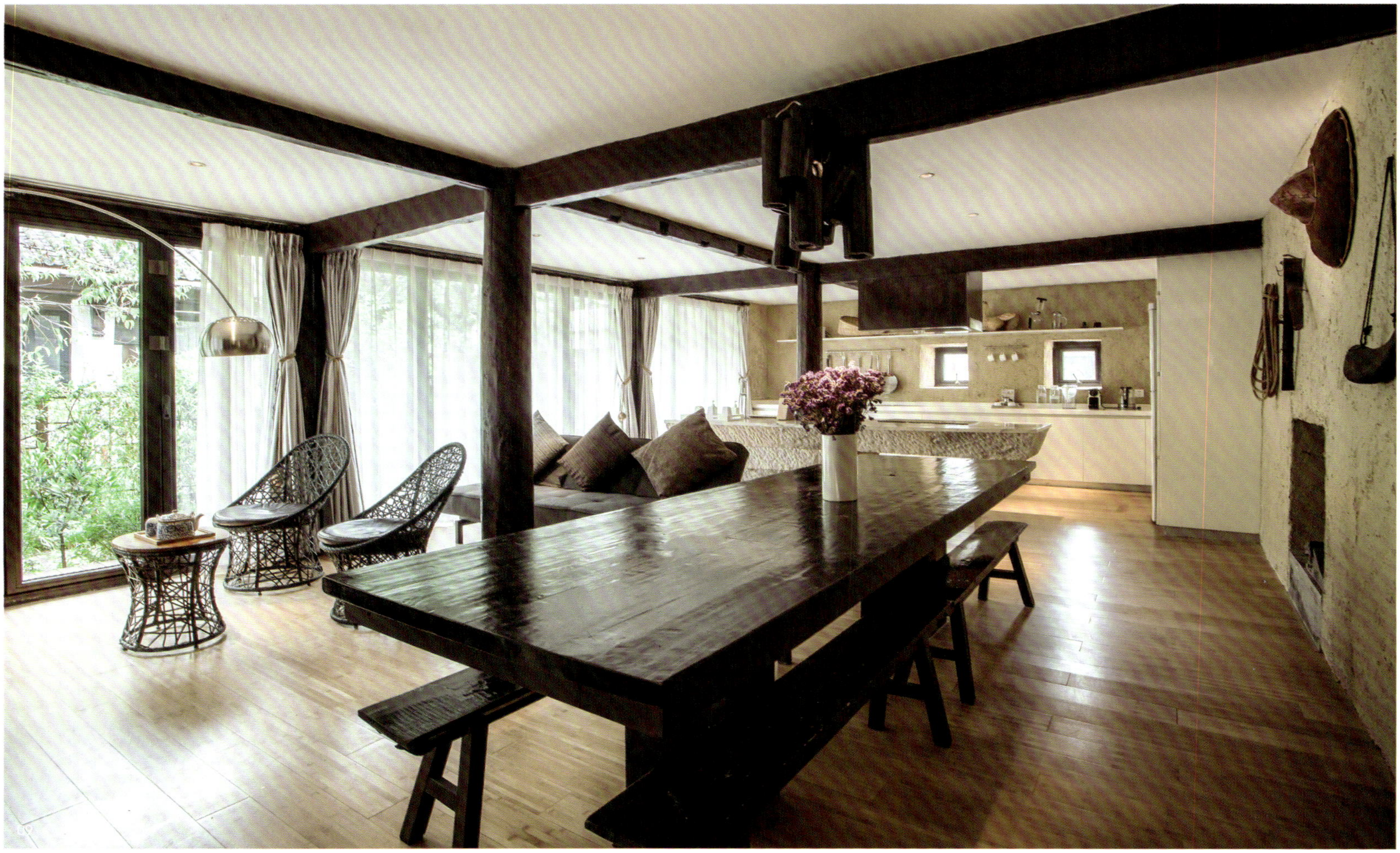

09

10

11

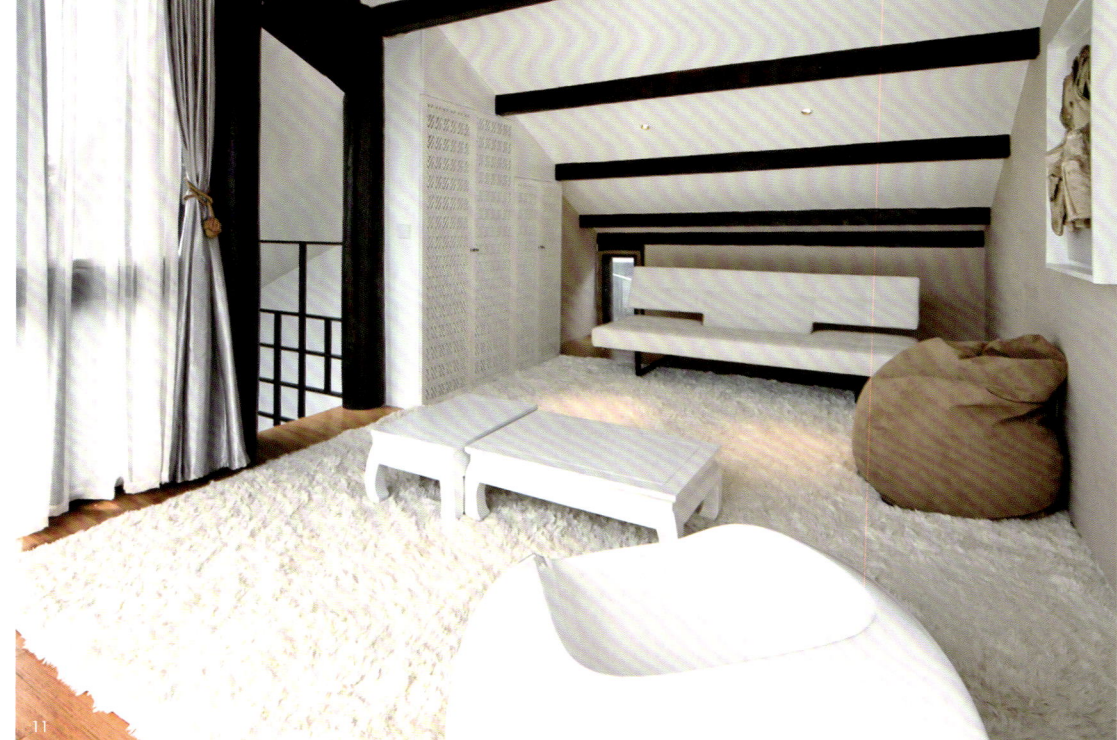

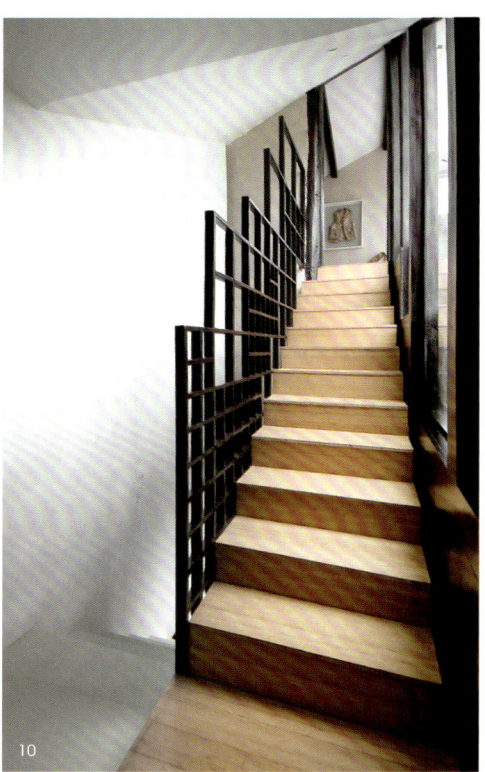

09 / Villa lounge
10 / Stair
11 / Lounge
12 / Bedroom
13 / Porch outside of bedroom

Location /
Dali, Yunnan, China

Area /
12,917 square feet
(1200 square meters)

Architecture and design /
Chen Bo, Zhong Yun

Photography /
Fang Zheng

Dengfeng Qingjing Lanshan Courtyard

Dengfeng Qingjing Lanshan Courtyard was restored and reconstructed in the style of an ordinary Bai House in Shaxi Ancient Town. The overall design of the project was accomplished by young designers—Pu Lieping (a famous artist of Chinese character culture) and his design team. The renovation of the whole courtyard follows the principle of 'restoring old structures with old structures,' proposed by Huang Yinwu, and the new Chinese style is used to add and continue the vitality of the whole courtyard in the scheme of reconstruction.

In the process of restoring old houses, the designers retained the old elements. In addition to replacing some of the decaying wood beams, wood rafters, wood purlins, and damaged tiles, they retained the main frame structure and most of the materials to retain and restore the historical appearance, which offers the trace of time.

In addition to respecting history, they also accommodated new ideas. The spatial and functional layout of the rooms was redesigned according to people's current living habits and needs under the premise of respect for local folk customs. Therefore, during the restoration, the designers elevated the existing roof as a whole and added independent bathrooms to improve the livability of space.

The new rooms and kitchens in the courtyard were planned and designed in respect for local customs and habits, and all construction was carried out in accordance with traditional structures, materials, and techniques. Traditional construction was engaged by using local craftsmen, adapting the designs as necessary to incorporate age-old methods and modern requirements and styles in regard to window lattices, furniture, and other elements. All the woodwork used solid wood as the raw materials, among which window lattices were made of beech wood, the dark brown part of furniture was made of walnut, and the light-colored part was made of Manchurian ash.

As for the surface treatment of materials, the designers use wood wax oil and tung oil to show traditional Chinese woodwork more completely and in more detail, as well as to present the concept of environmental protection and sustainability.

01 / Panorama of guest house
02 / Courtyard
03 / Night view of courtyard

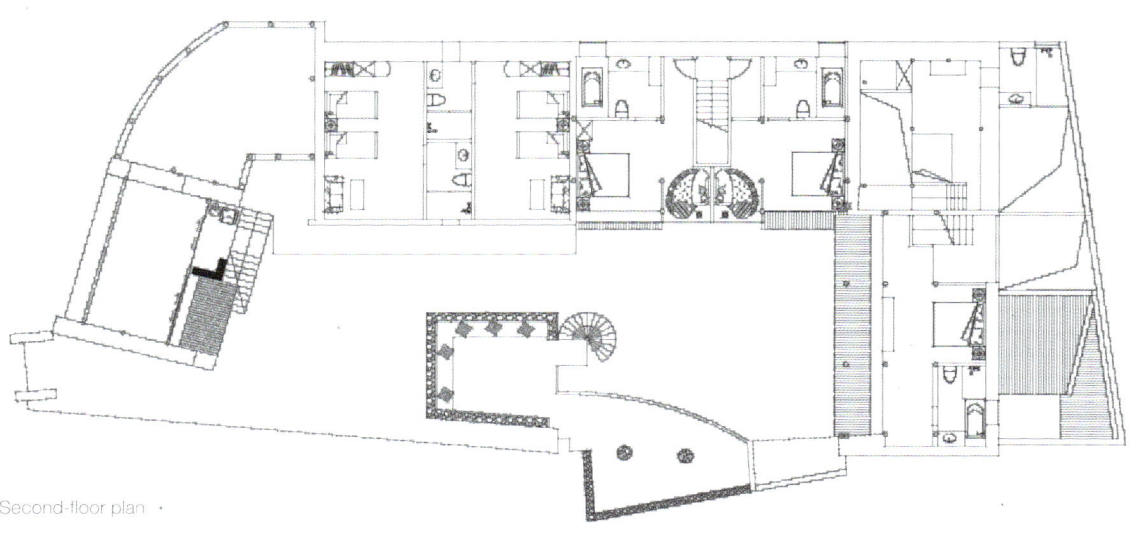

Second-floor plan

First-floor plan

04–05 / Night view of corridor in courtyard
06 / Top-down night view of whole courtyard
07 / Tearoom

08 / King-sized room with view of mountain
09–10 / Part of king-sized room with view of mountain

11 / King-sized room with courtyard
12 / Toilet of the family suite
13 / King-sized room with window

Location /
Wenzhou, Zhejiang, China

Area /
32,292 square feet
(3000 square meters)

Architecture and design /
Lv Kunpeng

Photography /
Ingallery

Joyful Boutique Hotel

The design team of Joyful Boutique Hotel hope to achieve their good desires to return and live in the countryside by transforming the village. The hotel is located at Taishi Village in Yongjia County. Most buildings in this village are "China's European-style" buildings that are quite common but not ideal for use—they are large in size but can't be put to good use. Many spaces are still unused. In front of the hotel is a nursing home out of use, which is also a 'China's European-style' building. The designer thinks this beautiful Chinese village along the Nanxi River should use an architectural form that is more suitable for this land, therefore, he decides to take advantage of local materials to make a significant change on the architectural appearance.

The design team removes the south wall to build a nice plank road through rice fields. Two existing rooms are merged into one. Though this will reduce the number of rooms by half, they still does so in view of the living quality of rooms. As a result, rooms become larger and more comfortable. Large French windows provide enough lighting as well as a wider vision, from which people can look at the distant scenery on the bed. The balcony of each room is separated so that guests can enjoy themselves without interference. Besides, water features are added to make landscapes vivid; on the southeast of this hotel is a large infinity swimming pool.

The transformed Joyful Boutique Hotel has 27 rooms, two of which are villa suites. The hotel has an open lawn in its yard. The removal of south wall gives people a wider vision. Additionally, the design team adds three swimming pools for the hotel. Joyful Boutique Hotel consists of three detached buildings. The first floor of No. 1 Building is a public area including a lobby, a dining hall, a banquet hall, a kitchen and offices. Rooms are on the second to fourth floor. No. 2 Building is a building of rooms. No. 3 Building is a villa.

The existing traditional hedge garden is transformed into lawns to provide a wider vision so that people can see the distant scenery in rooms; to offer an open area so that guests living in this hotel can sit on the grass to enjoy the sunshine and nature. The lobby uses old wooden roof and glass on the side of building to increase lighting; the ground is designed with splicing materials; the door that is pieced together with old planks—both front and back—seems to be very decorative; furniture and decorations that are got from Nepal increase some exotic charms; the long table made by experienced carpenters is plain but profound; the fire burning in the fireplace on one side keeps the entire hall warm. The dining hall reserves the existing marble floor; dining tables are made with old wood on site and fitted with colored pillows and cushions, which makes the atmosphere here more lively. The candles on the ceilings throughout the dining hall is one of the most amazing elements, flicking like stars in the sky. The multi-functional room has a sloping roof with planks on the top and walls made with recyclable red bricks. At the center of the room is a fireplace. In winter, the burning fire made by people can warm the entire hall. Moreover, the design team reinforces the windows and puts cushions and pillows in the room. In the afternoon sun, life suddenly becomes slothful.

The large infinity swimming pool and rice fields are near at hand. The swimming pool is made of white terrazzos. It is both time-consuming and power-wasting, but spotlessly white and smooth. Except for the tea table, other areas are elevated so that people can look at the scenery beyond the window on the bed. Floors and walls are decorated with old planks; TVs can be pulled out to adjust directions and angles. Natural and local building decoration materials are used whenever possible: red bricks and old planks that are removed from old buildings, pebbles from Nanxi River, old ship plates, battens, bamboo, sleepers out of service, withered trees and so on. These materials enrich visual and tactile senses—people can touch and feel the difference of materials: warm wood, rough cement and sleek bamboo with irregular arrangements, all of which is to provide the most simple accommodation experience for lodgers.

01 / External view of guest house
02 / Guest house at night

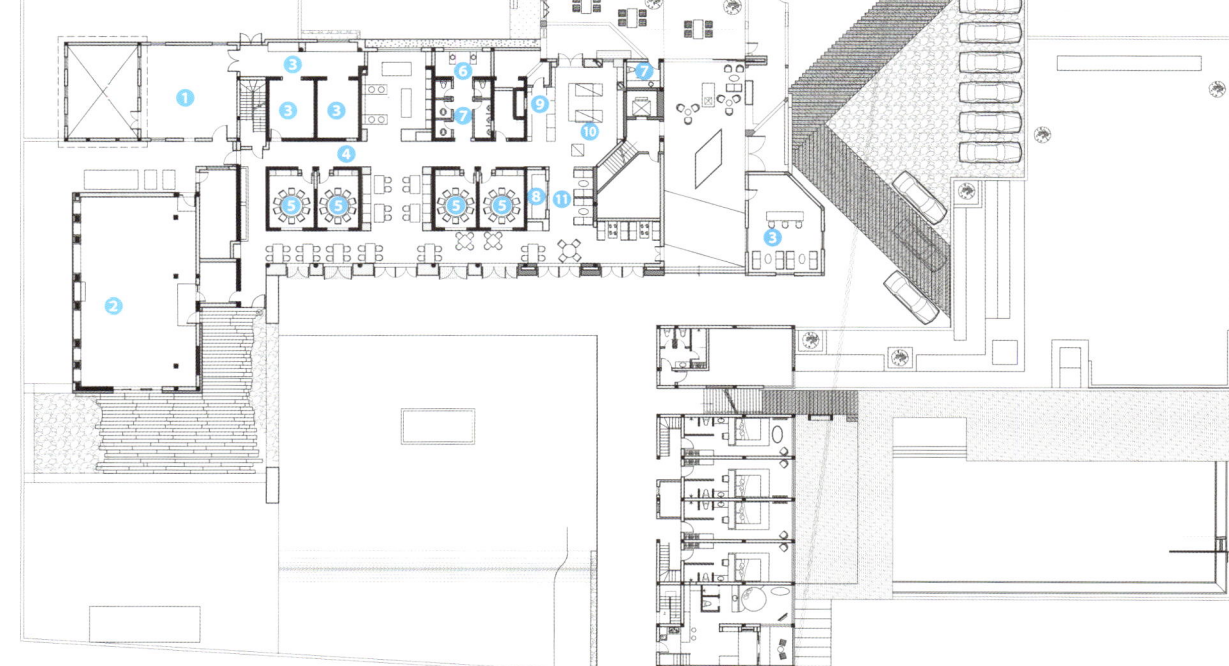

Site plan

① Kitchen
② Banquet hall
③ Office
④ Aisle
⑤ Private room
⑥ Bathroom
⑦ Toilet
⑧ Liquor store
⑨ Cash register
⑩ Vegetable display hall
⑪ Dining area

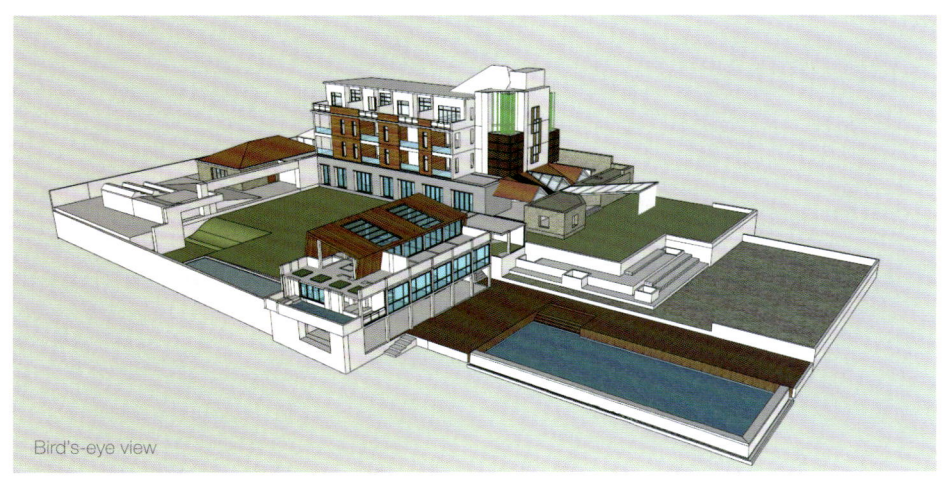

Bird's-eye view

03 / Infinity pool
04 / Hammock next to pool
05 / Door made of planks pieced together

06 / Dining hall of guest house
07 / Sightseeing platform

08 / King-sized room with view of rice field
09 / Rice field in front of hotel
10 / Outdoor hot tub

11 / Spa suite
12 / Handmade decoration
13 / Heated spa pool

Qingyan Guest House

Location /
Moganshan, Zhejiang, China

Area /
25,833 square feet (2400 square meters)

Architecture and design /
Lin Weiping Interior Design Co., Ltd

Photography /
Liu Ying

Qingyan Guest House is located on an open area of Xiantan Village at the foot of Moganshan. At the very beginning, it was just a local farmhouse resort, which had been operated for 14 years under the name of Biwu Mountain Villa.

The redesign of the guest house embraced simplicity. Bamboo elements and soft modern furnishings work well with the natural environment to create a warm and homely atmosphere. From the structural reinforcement of the old house to underfloor heating, every facet was considered. The redesign abandoned redundant elements and integrated itself into landscapes.

The dining hall is on the first floor of the guest house and its walls are covered with bamboo, which has a strong decorative effect and highlights the distinctive vegetation of Moganshan. On the second and third floors are the bedrooms, which are decorated with bamboo and wood-grain furniture. Painted trails of ink on the walls create a simple and natural atmosphere offering a sense of sleeping among dim, misty bamboo groves and seas of clouds. Beside the French window is the balcony, where people can enjoy the wild jungle outside. Bluestone walls, an original cabinet, and a dressing table made of bamboo and planks create an elaborately decorated bathroom.

With several historical stone benches and water jars on the ground, the exterior decoration of Qingyan Guest House is simple and honest without any artificial polish, showing the original ecology specific to the farmhouse. There is also a backyard, which is a paradise for children because they can play on the large lawn and build their dream castles in the sandpit.

01 / Swimming pool
02 / Exterior view

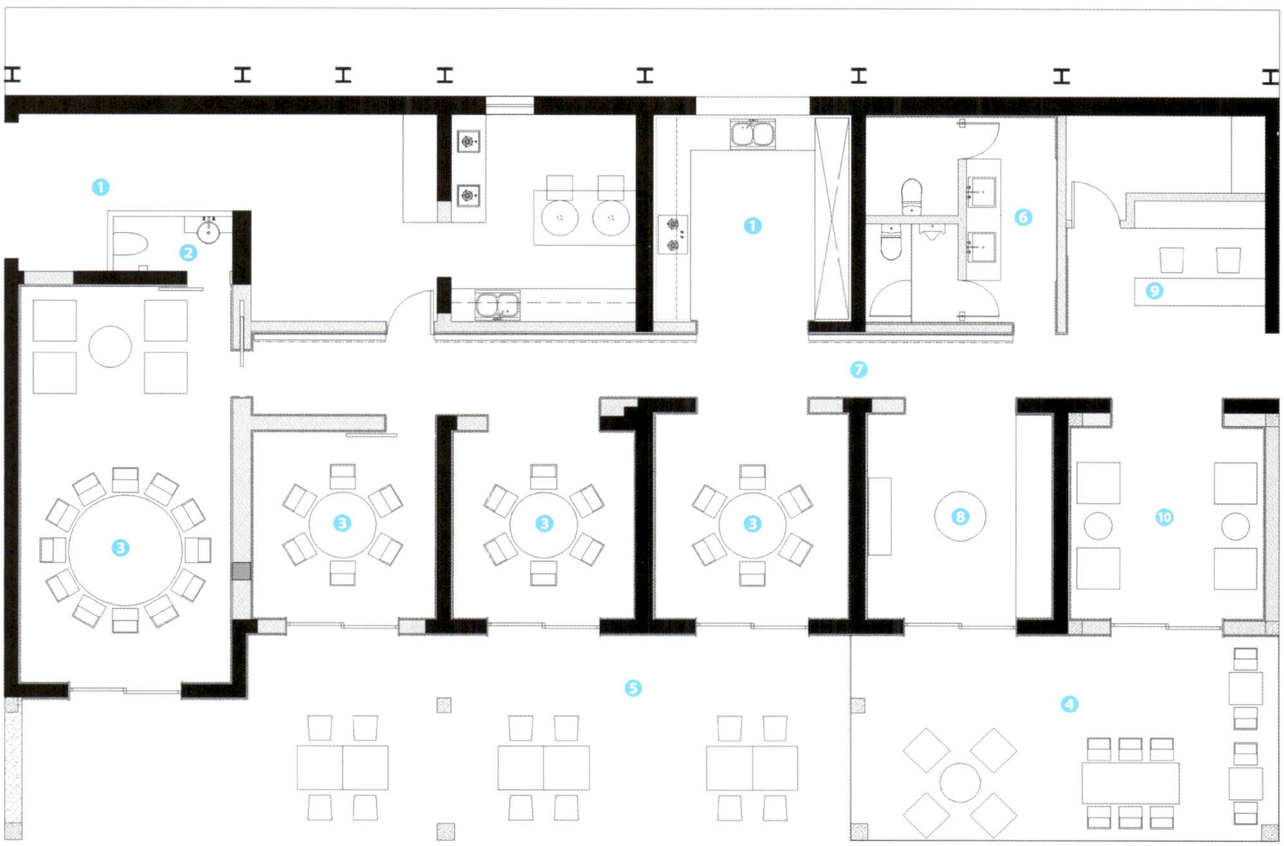

① Kitchen
② Secondary bathroom
③ Balcony
④ Leisure area
⑤ Outer corridor
⑥ Washroom
⑦ Passage
⑧ Living room
⑨ Reception area
⑩ Public area

First-floor plan

79

1. Jiuyue Room
2. Lingyin Room
3. Zhuxi Room

Second-floor plan

80 Mountainside Guest House

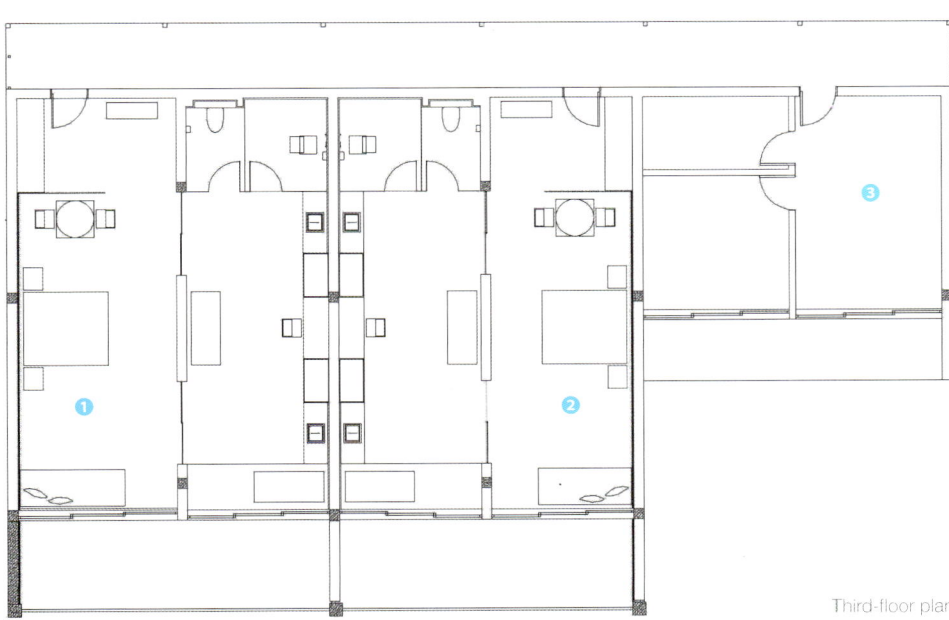

① Rufeng Room
② Queyun Room
③ Linen room

Third-floor plan

03 / Outdoor area between first floor and second floor
04 / Stairs
05 / Reception area

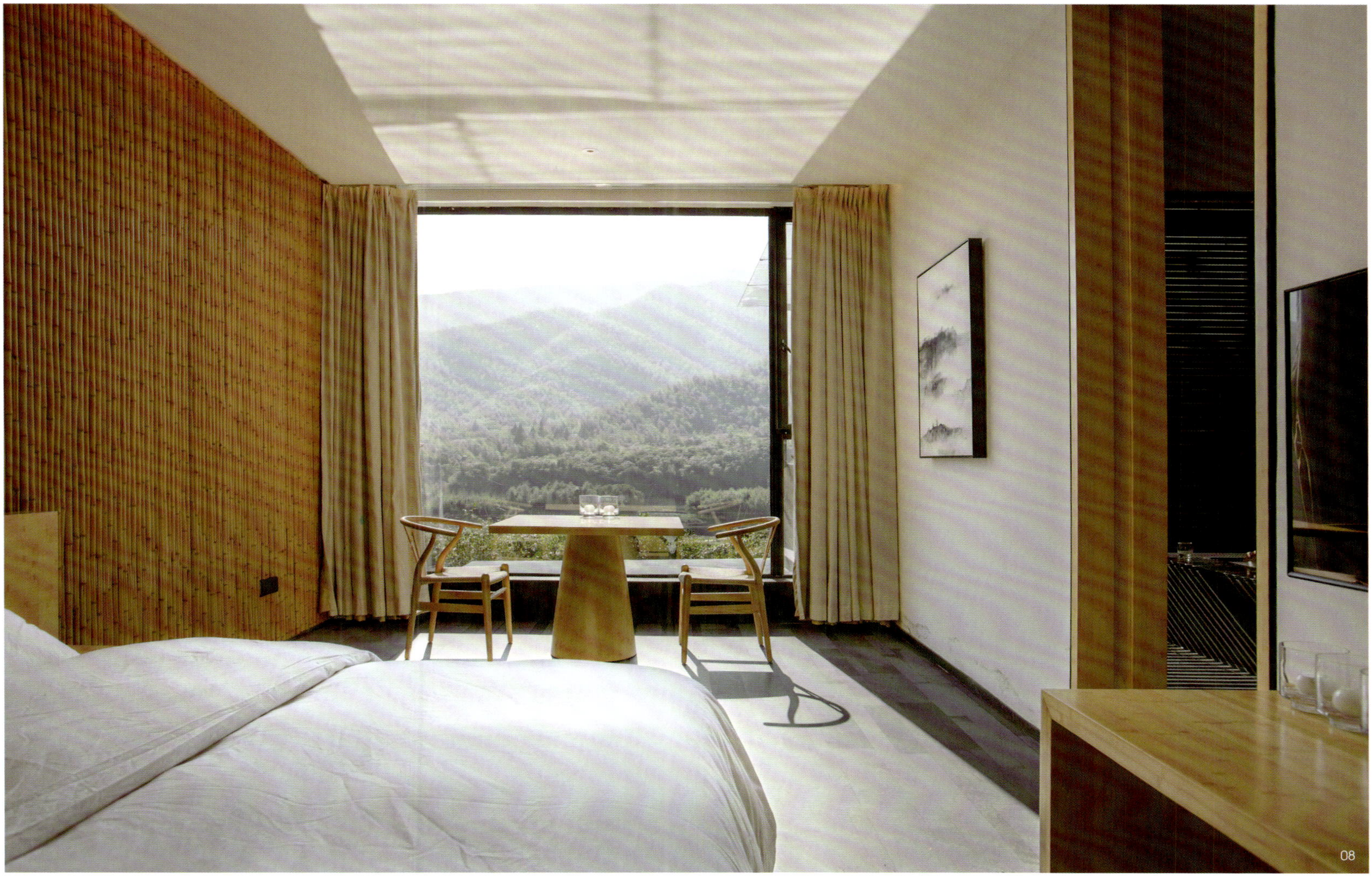

08

09

10

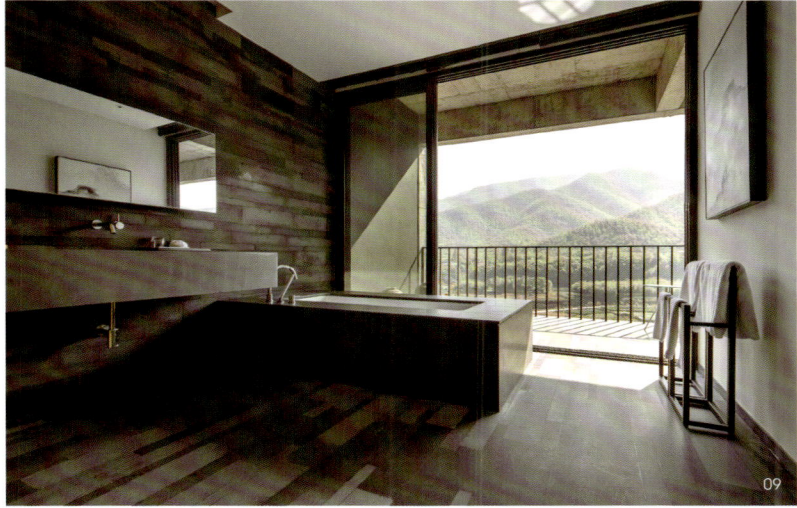

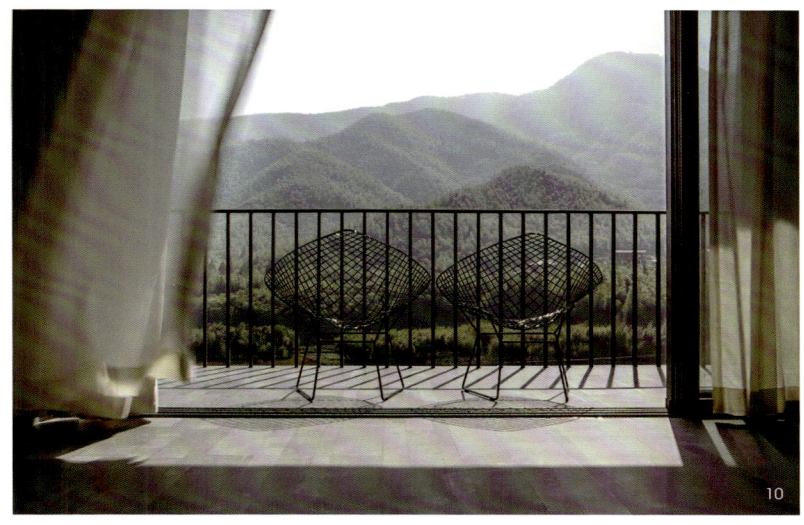

06 / Lingyin standard room
07 / Rufeng bathroom
08 / Zhuxi king-sized room
09 / Queyun bathroom
10 / Balcony

Cave House

Location /
Sierra Morena, Córdoba, Spain

Area /
1119 square feet (104 square meters)

Architecture and design /
UMMO Estudio

Photography /
David Vico

Cave House sits in the foothills of Sierra Morena in calcarenite stone terrain. The slightly sloping strata gives rise to various geological formations native to the area, among these are caves, which resulted from the quarrying that supplied Cordoba with stone for centuries. Historically, the product of these hollows in the rock emerged when livestock watchmen used them as small shelters. Today, they have been rehabilitated to form rural housing and accommodate new countryside activities.

Within this dialogue, the designers created a new spatial experience that manages to value the tectonic nature of the area through the use of new architectural elements: clean and quiet volumes, bright and ample spaces, use of stone materials for the flooring, such as concrete and marble, glass openings to the south to conjure natural light, and handcrafted wooden furniture to give warmth to the cave house.

The façade of the cave house is joined to a series of vernacular building structures rooted in the traditional use of the farm and can be found across a 32,292-square-foot (3000-square-meter) garden located within a 9.3-hectares (23-acre) estate, dedicated to ecological agriculture bearing crops of beets and garlic and fruit trees of different autochthonous varieties.

A path leads people to the terrace of the cave house and invites guest inside the interior of the earth, from the bottom of a descending staircase to a level height from which they can enjoy and contemplate the surroundings and the richness of the abundant nature. Acting as the preface to the cave itself, this introductory space acquires a particular importance as the juncture between the exterior and the interior, showing a contrast between the strength of the stone and the lightness of simple and discrete architecture that adapts to the existing form of the hollow, allowing one to go deep inside and create a refuge.

Access into the interior of the cave house is like entering an unexpected space full of unknown sensorial nuances, where silence prevails and takes on a fleeting role before eyes that can marvel at the lighting effects cast upon the stone and the distinct materials used to shape the space, all of which is accompanied by the sensation of thermal conditions preserved year round within the entirety of this massive cave and of which are independent from exterior climatic conditions during cold winter months and hot summers.

Unlike similar spaces executed in caves, which are typically designed with a single entry into a windowless interior as a result of direct excavation of the land, the particularity of this cave house can be found in the bedroom, where the presence of a wide opening to the exterior faces east, capturing the morning light while at the same time providing a healthy dose of cross ventilation, renewing the air in all the rooms.

With a keen awareness of the high value of the natural space and with an intention to cause the least possible impact on the walls and ceiling of the natural stone, the project was designed with a multifunctional floor capable of responding to the distinct needs of the accommodation. This element, executed through polished concrete acting as artificial stone, creates a dialogue with its surroundings, drawing near to its limits but without ever touching, while at the same time creating a distribution of the various facilities, enabling them to reach the necessary points required. The flooring acts as a vertical division in the bathroom as it rises to create the only sector that is differentiated inside the cave, providing intimacy while changing the chromatic hue of its finish.

As a gesture of respect towards the natural, direct contact between the pre-existing materials and the newly added elements was avoided to the extent possible; however, in places in which it was required, the rehabilitation attempted to opt for materials in a natural state with a presence well-suited to the atmosphere of the cave in each of its variables.

Master plan

01 / Façade

02 / Outside overview
03 / Entry
04 / Living room
05 / Coffee area

Section plan

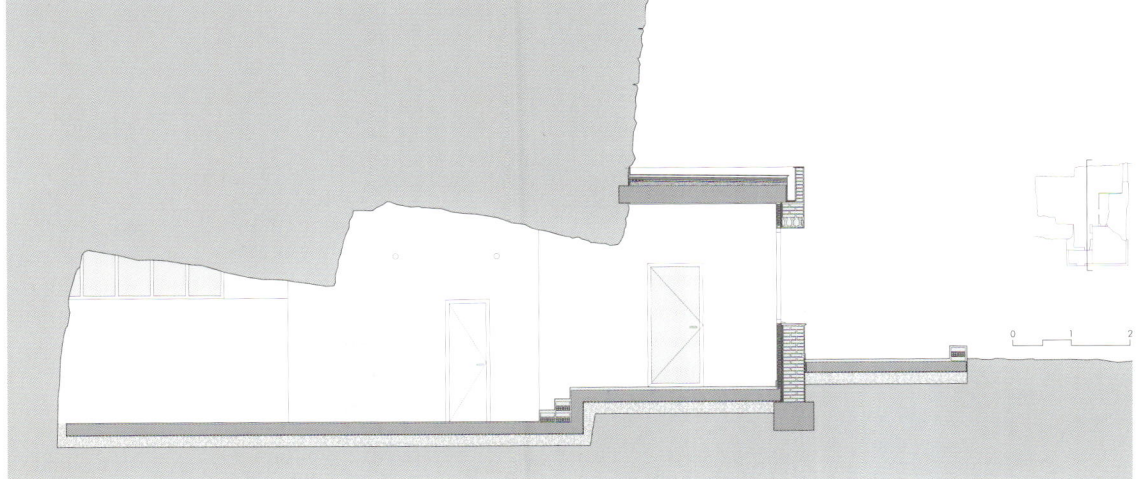

Main plan

1. Terrace
2. Kitchen
3. Living area
4. Bedroom
5. Bathroom

0 1 2   5

06 / Interior

88 Mountainside Guest House

07 / Custom furniture design
08 / Bathroom
09 / View from bathroom
10 / Dinning area

Location /
Deqing, Zhejiang, China

Area/
6942 square feet
(645 square meters)

Architecture and design /
Temp Architects

Photography /
Temp Architects

Septuor

Located in the Zhejiang Province, a valley of Deqing is quiet and covered with lush bamboo groves. Due to its close proximity to Yangtze Delta Plain, this area is a destination for urban residents to take holidays. It is here that the Septuor guest house is situated, providing seven rooms constructed at the site of an old folk house.

The peninsula-shape site is nestled under a mountain, near a river, surrounded by beautiful landscape, which was the site of the original house. The design had an inserted-beam timber structure as the main body, with double height and a sloping roof. Apart from the portico at the front, the other three sides were enclosed with 15-inch (380-millimeter) thick loam walls. The internal space—which housed two brothers and their families—was very compact.

To create spacious and comfortable guestrooms, the architect modified the framework first, re-dividing the six compact living spaces into four rooms. The wooden pillar previously hidden in the partition is exposed in the guestroom, implying the former use of the space. New reinforced concrete structures are parallel to the wooden structures to accommodate guestrooms, toilets, and public spaces. The top space of the coffee house and dining hall can be used as the private garden for the guestroom on the second floor.

The architect built another room in the backyard. Its circular plane makes the most of the irregular shape of the site; an ear-shape partition was used inside the room, matched with a tapered skylight and pale-gold coatings, creating a fluid, mysterious atmosphere.

Additionally, the architect abandoned the public corridor system in the old house, taking advantage of the site and new volume, and connecting the guestrooms by several independent paths to establish a direct relationship between the guest house and nature.

The dislocation of framework blurs the affiliation between parts and the whole and provides multiple ways of perception. The original height difference and paths on the site were also preserved and integrated into the circular system on the ground floor, where guests are able to stroll freely. In such a relatively narrow plot, Septuor realized an unobstructed and very private resting experience.

01 / Front view across creek
02 / Side view in creek

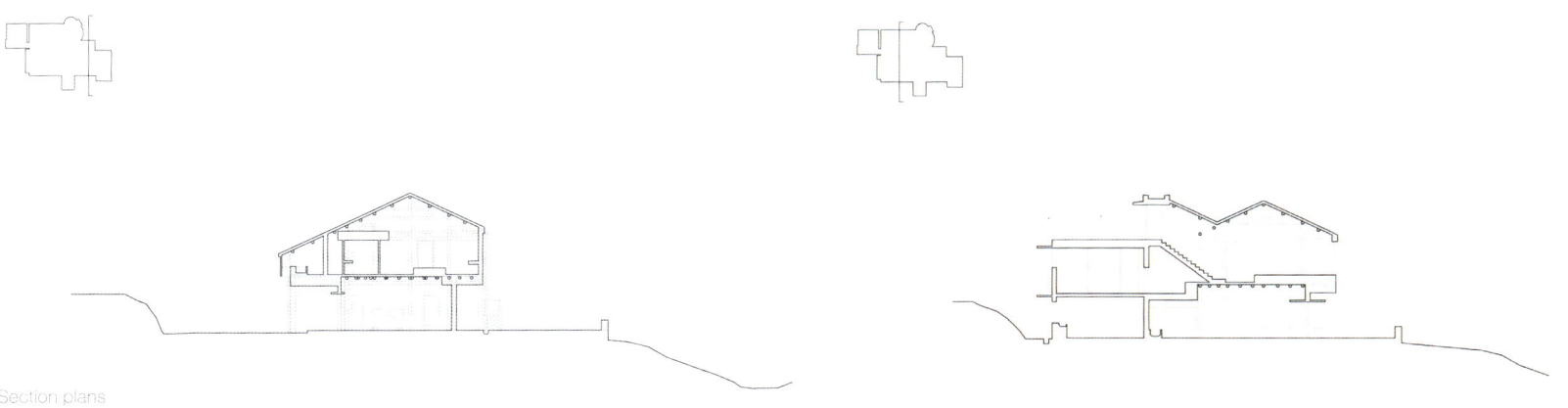
Section plans

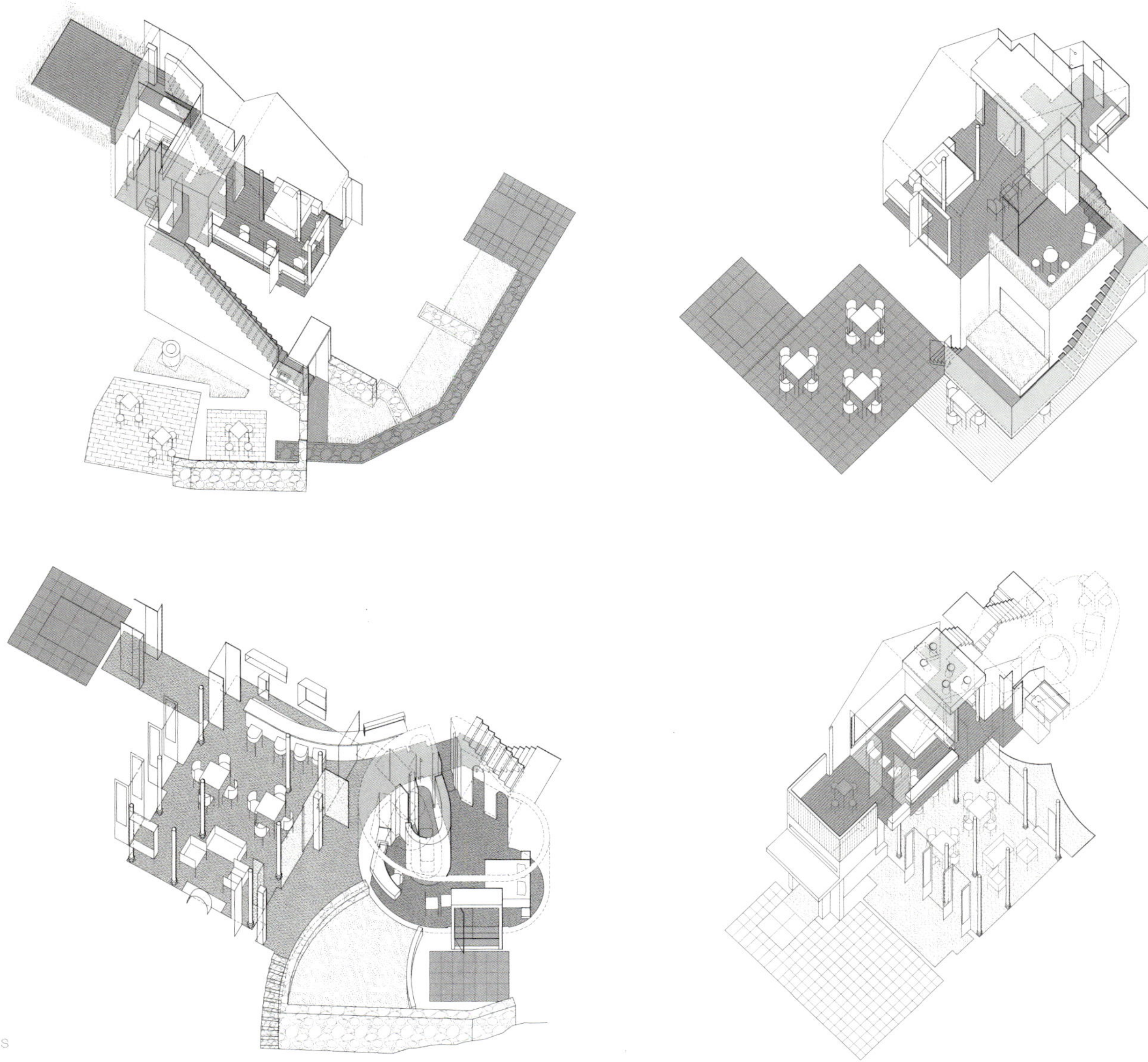

Axonometrics

03 / Terrace above room
04 / Entrance courtyard
05 / Interior view of cafe

06 / Interior view of room 7

Third-floor plan

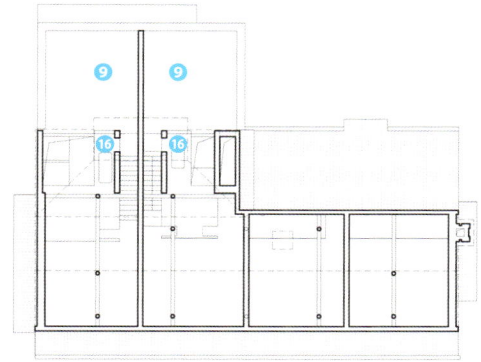

Roof plan

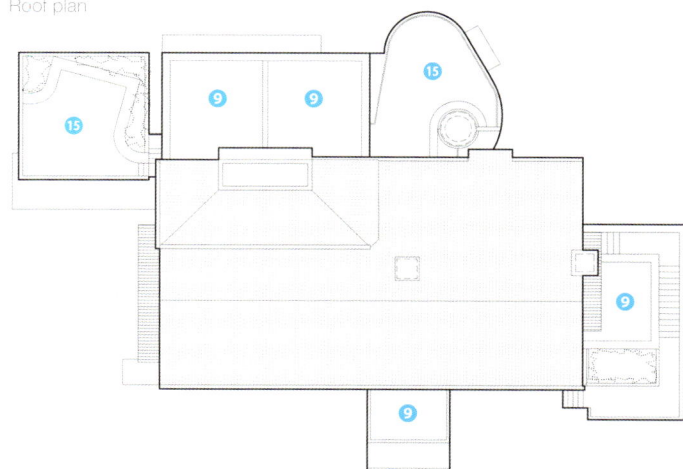

Second-floor plan

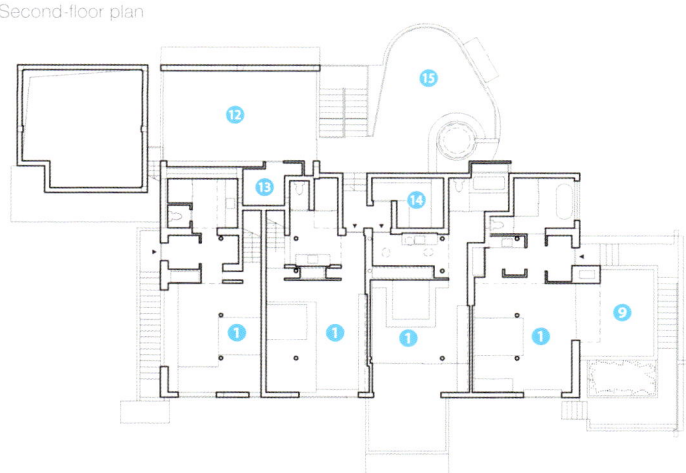

① Guest room
② Entrance lobby
③ Hallway
④ Cafe
⑤ Public toilet
⑥ Kitchen
⑦ House of landlord
⑧ Southern public terrace
⑨ Garden for guest room
⑩ Eastern public terrace
⑪ Public terrace for cafe
⑫ Meeting and dining space
⑬ Storage room
⑭ Linen room
⑮ Public terrace
⑯ Bathroom for guest room

First-floor plan

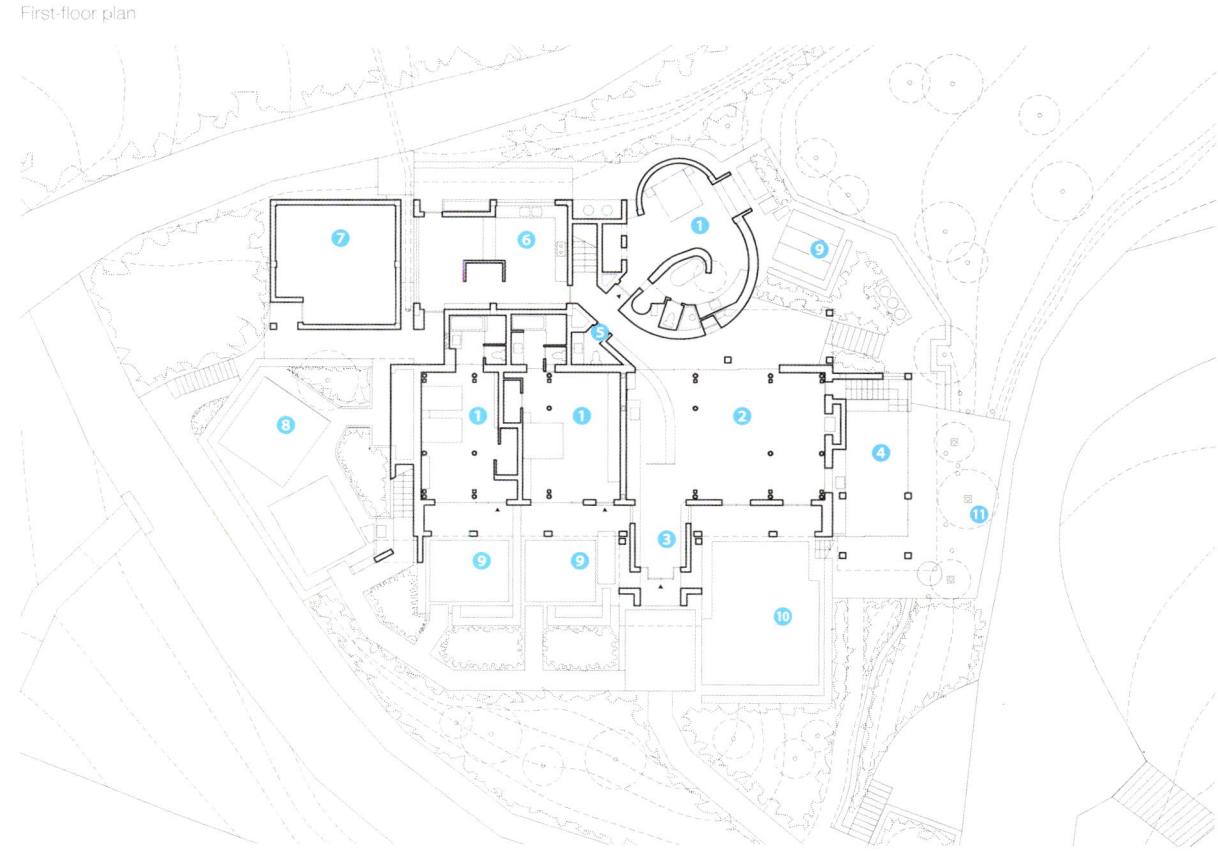

95

96 Mountainside Guest House

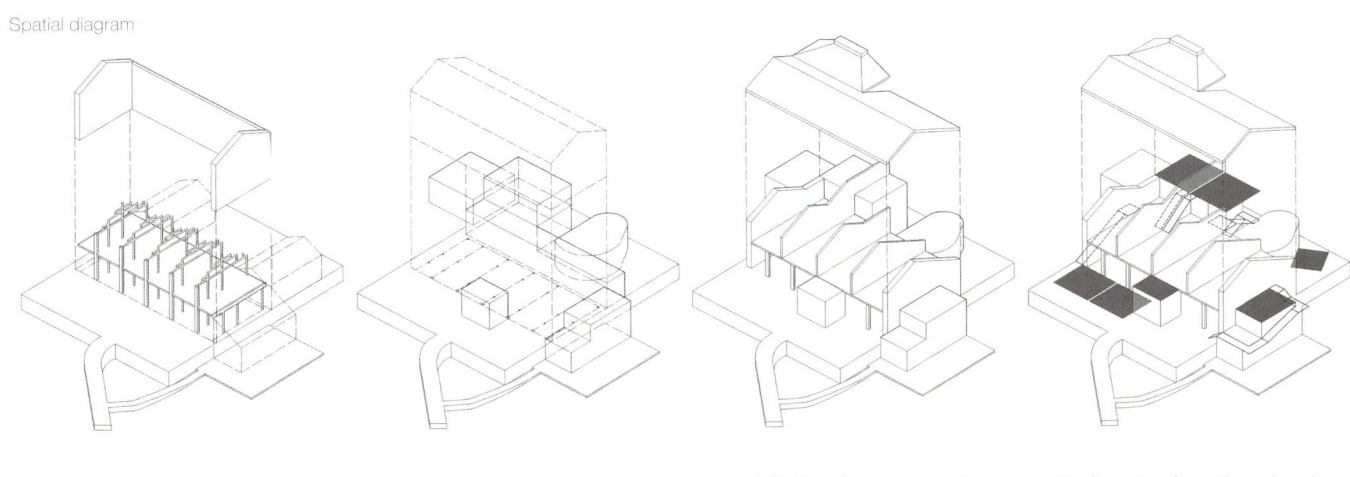

Spatial diagram

Structure of original layout   New volumes   Redefinition of space and roof   Configuration for paths and gardens

07 / Interior view of room 4
08 / Interior view of room 3
09 / Interior view of toilet in room 4
10 / Interior view of room 4

Location /
Vonitsa, Greece

Area /
8611 square feet
(800 square meters)

Architecture and design /
Maria Chatzistavrou,
Lime Deco

Photography /
Louisa Nikolaidou

My Fairytale Villas

This guest house is located in Vonitsa among green surroundings on the south side of Amvrakikos Gulf, Greece. In an olive grove with a variety of trees such as pomegranate, lemon, and orange trees, the boldness of nature became a reference point in the decoration of the house. Stone and wood dress the remodeled old building, which consists of an open-plan ground floor with living room, kitchen, and washing room and a floor with the bedrooms and main bathroom.

On the ground floor and almost level to the surrounding patio, there is a spacious dining room with wood and metal, with shades of gray used in the living room to balance the intensity of the materials. Antiques from the family collection decorate the room, including a wooden trunk used as a coffee table. Chandeliers with clear crystal add glamor to the space. The curtains are unobtrusive, allowing undisturbed outside views.

The kitchen, separated from the living area by a towering arch, ends in Paso dressed in wood. The kitchen bench is solid oak, the cupboards oak veneer, and the dining table has the rustic appearance of untreated wood pieces. The ground floor washing room has been dressed with cement mortar, composed of natural materials such as stone sink, the granite bench, and bronze items.

In the master bedroom, the mood is enhanced through wooden carvings and ambient lighting with an impressive mirror of old cut tiles and small pieces of wood, while the children's bedrooms are more simplistic and playful. The central corridor is lit by upturned metal buckets. Off the balcony of the first floor is a living room and a dining table to enjoy the views of the Amvrakikos Gulf, while an easy opening pergola makes it possible to use the balcony all day long.

01 / View of main villa
02 / Living room area with fireplace
03 / Dining room
04 / Pool view

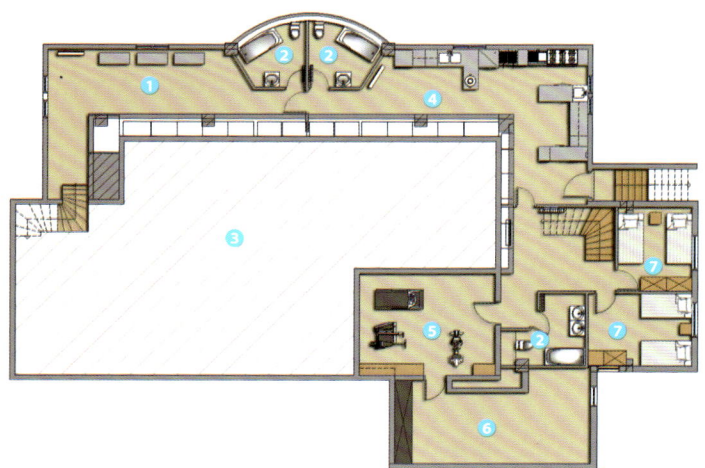
Basement floor plan

First-floor plan

① Storage
② Bathroom
③ Concrete foundation
④ Professional kitchen
⑤ Gym
⑥ Boiler room
⑦ Staff bedroom

① Kitchen entrance
② Kitchen
③ Calmness Room
④ Dining room
⑤ Joy Room
⑥ Balcony
⑦ Living room
⑧ Hallway
⑨ Main entrance
⑩ Bathroom
⑪ Serenity Room

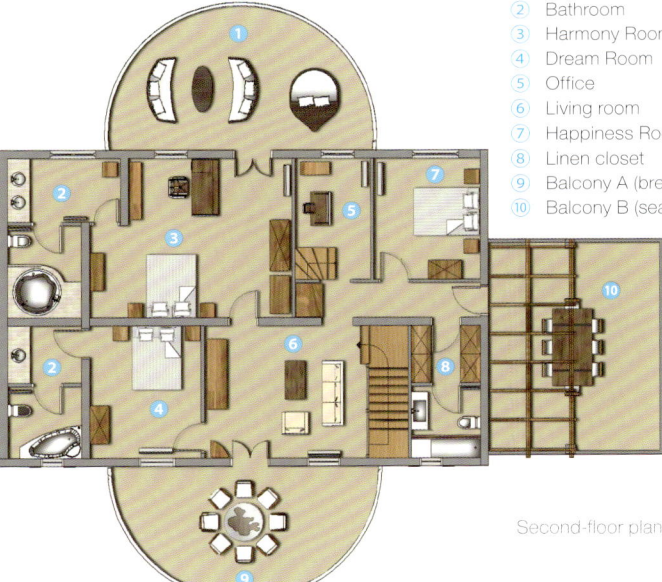

- ① Balcony C, sea and pool view
- ② Bathroom
- ③ Harmony Room
- ④ Dream Room
- ⑤ Office
- ⑥ Living room
- ⑦ Happiness Room
- ⑧ Linen closet
- ⑨ Balcony A (breakfast)
- ⑩ Balcony B (sea view)

- ① Bathroom
- ② Enthusiasm Room
- ③ Shared living room
- ④ Optimism Room

Second-floor plan

Third-floor plan

05 / Kitchen on first floor
06 / Office
07 / Second-floor living room
08 / Guest room with en-suite bathroom and balcony

09 / Childrens' bedroom on third floor
10 / Master bedroom
11–12 / Balcony with dining table
13 / Spa in master bathroom
14 / Master bedroom bathroom

Location /
Queenstown, New Zealand

Architecture and design /
Hyndman Taylor Architects Ltd.

Photography /
Simon Devitt

Sargent Residence

This holiday home in an exclusive subdivision in Queenstown makes its mark amidst gabled pitches through a collection of shifting single-pitched forms designed to mimic the rising backdrop of the Remarkables Mountain Range while also providing an intimate connection with the landscape from inside. Clad in cedar, these changing forms meander down the hill, effectively cutting into it and wrapping around a central courtyard, sunken behind a sloping garden.

'Right from the get-go our clients wanted something different, yet still in keeping with the alpine feel as the sub-division guidelines require,' said architect Erin Taylor of Hyndman Taylor Architects. Their response was to use a collection of interlinked single-pitch forms with a dynamic relationship to the alpine context. Viewed against the backdrop of the Remarkables, these forms shift and stagger up incrementally with the direction of the mountain face. Conversely, from the top of the site, the roof pitches shift into opposing directions, channeling views and entry.

The entrance pulls you into a long corridor that opens entirely to the views through a glazed link on the north-western aspect. On one side of this upper floor is the guest wing, which sits perched above the courtyard and opens out onto the north-facing top garden. Further along is the family's sleeping quarters, where the internal spaces profit from the high pitches. These light- and view-filled spaces are enhanced by playful patterns, textures, and lighting.

'A rock garden cut away from the envelope provides a well-considered natural outlook for the north-east-facing kids' bedroom. The house accommodates a range of adaptable breakout areas for the various occupants to retreat to, essential in a home that often caters to large groups,' explained Erin.

A double-height atrium-style window lights the way as one descends into the main lower living area. At the bottom is a kitchen that opens to the outdoor living space and a dining area that steps down to a sunken lounge. Those enjoying alfresco dining by the outdoor fire can effectively see over the living room couches to the view beyond, while being screened from the prevailing southerlies. The entire southern face of this level is a glazed panorama, welcoming plenty of natural light. In contrast to these glazed walls, high level shuttered peepholes and clerestory windows scattered throughout the house offer small vignettes into the landscape.

To the left at the bottom of the staircase is a sunken library that leads to yet another guest bedroom, the en-suite of which doubles as the powder room at the bottom of the stairs. This characterizes the way the house is compiled; a series of cleverly interlinked spaces of discovery—that can be comfortably excluded as group sizes demand—inspired by and connected to the rugged surroundings.

01

01 / Building façade
02 / Panorama

03 / Outdoor dining space
04 / Courtyard landscape
05 / Small library leading to guest bedroom

05

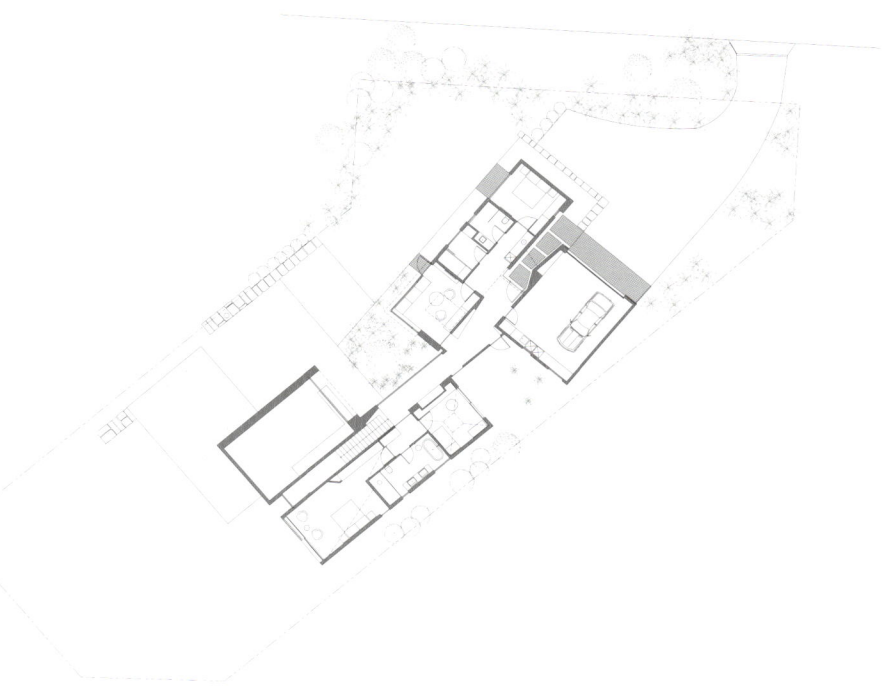

Second-floor plan

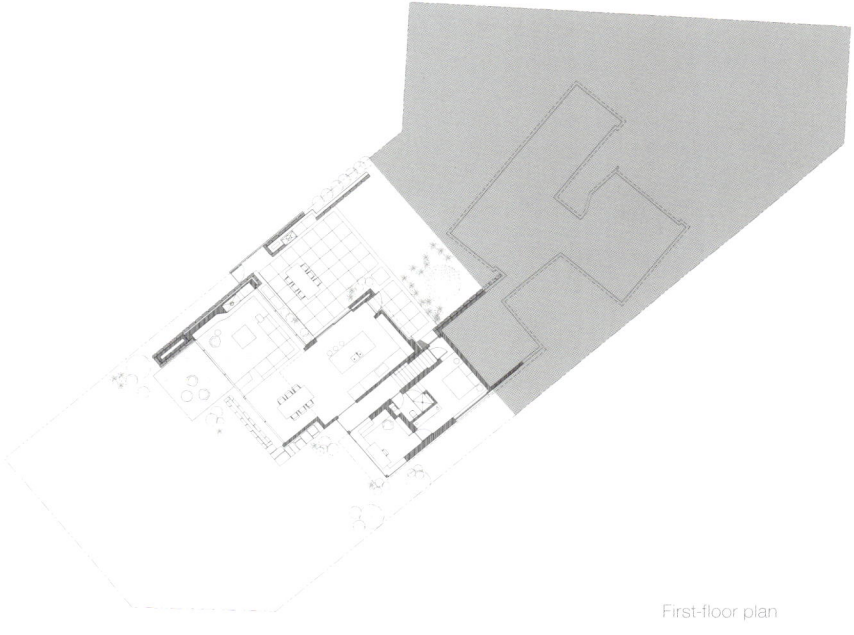

First-floor plan

107

06 / Bedroom
07 / Panoramic window
08 / Bathroom

09 / Living room on first floor
10 / Dining area by French window in living room

Location /
Vathia, Mani, Greece

Area /
2056 square feet
(191 square meters)

Architecture and design /
Kostas Zouvelos + Kassiani Theodorakakou

Photography /
George Messaritakis

Tainaron Blue Retreat

The towers, these imposing tall and narrow prisms, are the most stubborn and absolute expression of Mani building. On the outskirts of the settlements, the *'xemonia'* were erected in order to defend or expand the land property. They served to control, exclude, or drive out the opponents, but also to transfer the pressure from the main settlement to new territories.

Tainaron Blue Retreat is a representative sample of traditional *xemonia* of the South. The tower—now transformed into a small guest house—faced a similar construction, which had also been a strong fortified complex. Both together, they controlled the road to the area around Tainaron. The war tower was built on solid ground and rocks known as 'rizomies,' at a strategic spot that offers an amazing view of the sea and the hinterland.

The restoration of the traditional building solved form issues in relation to the old texture of the masonry, so that the final look of the tower gives the impression of a building that emerges from the rock, upon which it is founded. The grouting internally and externally was done with real *'kourasani'* or Roman mortar (a combination of Thermic soil, ceramic powder, lime, and a special shade of river sand) and minimum amount of cement, which enhances the static adequacy of the masonry and ensures durability.

The conversion of the tower into a guest house had to overcome considerable difficulties. The reason was the need for a high degree of adaptation to the specific characteristics of the regional architecture and at the same time the demand for accommodation in rooms with modern aesthetic perception. The four floors, with their relatively limited interior spaces that comprise of three bedrooms with bathroom and shared kitchen, breakfast, and reception space, are organized along a vertical axis, allowing guests to have the unique experience of moving through narrow openings ('waterfalls'), wooden stairs, or rocks protruding from the walls and arches ('steps').

As the formation of the exterior spaces had to ensure minimum interference, the addition of a water surface area was adapted to the specific environment and respected the topography of the landscape, resulting in an even and unified set of buildings and space with intensity and character.

01 / Building façade
02 / Gate at entrance

03 / Guest house and surrounding landscape
04 / Outdoor swimming pool
05 / Outdoor leisure area

Site plan

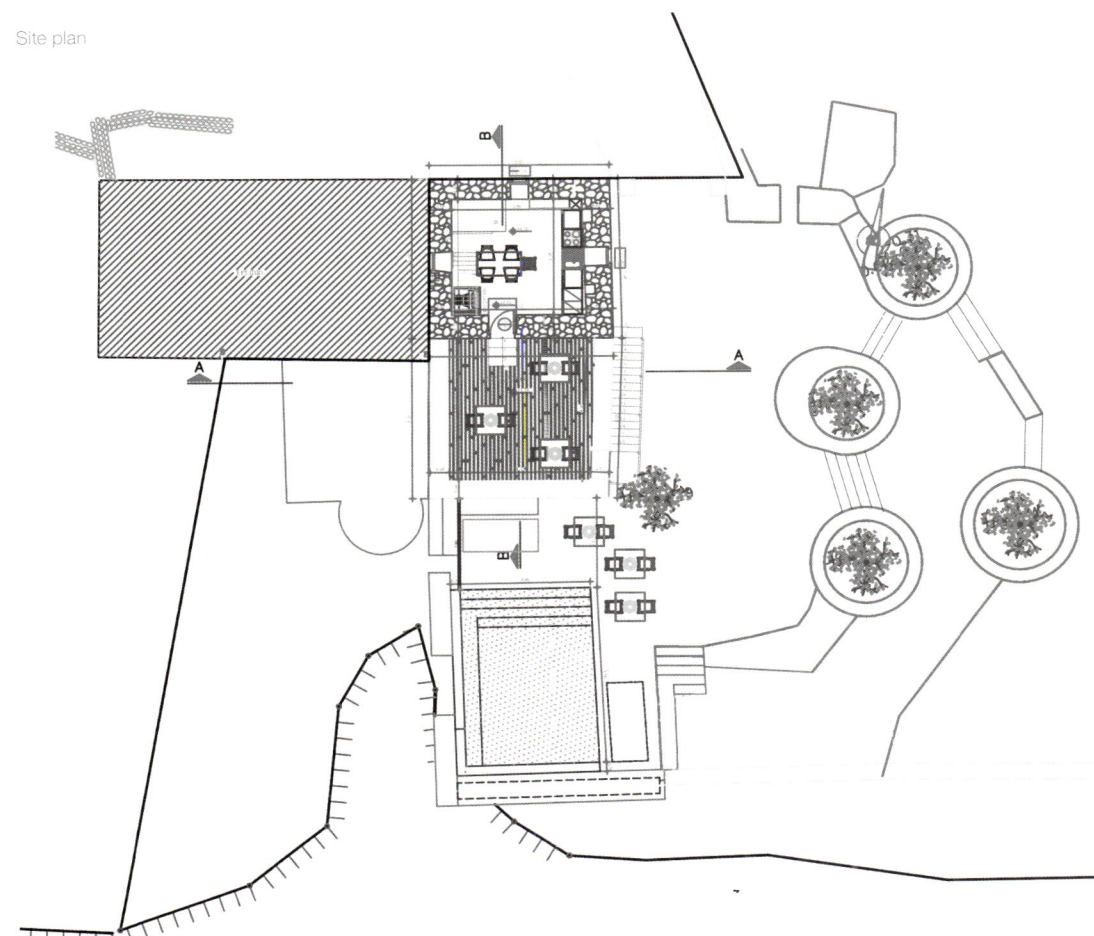

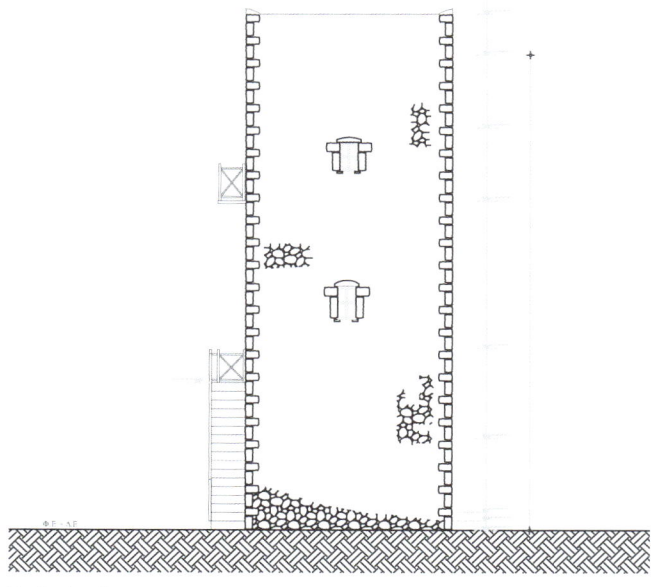

North elevation

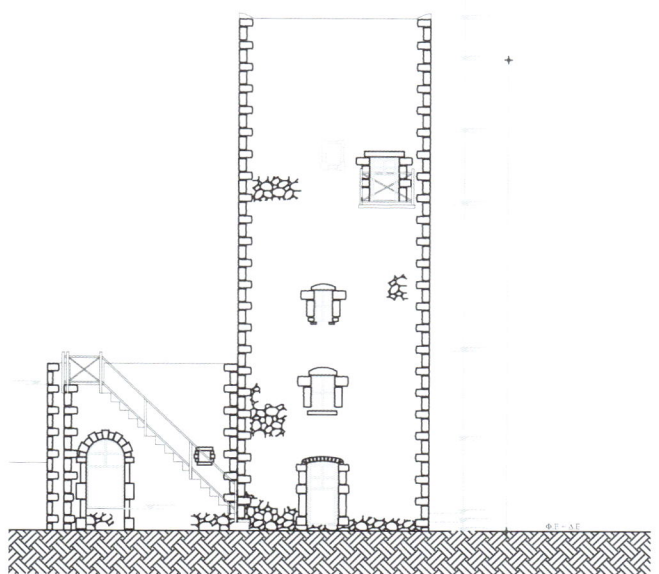

East elevation

06 / Outdoor dining area at night
07 / Outdoor swimmming pool at night
08 / Outdoor couch
09 / Kitchen
10 / Stairs

114   Mountainside Guest House

Sections

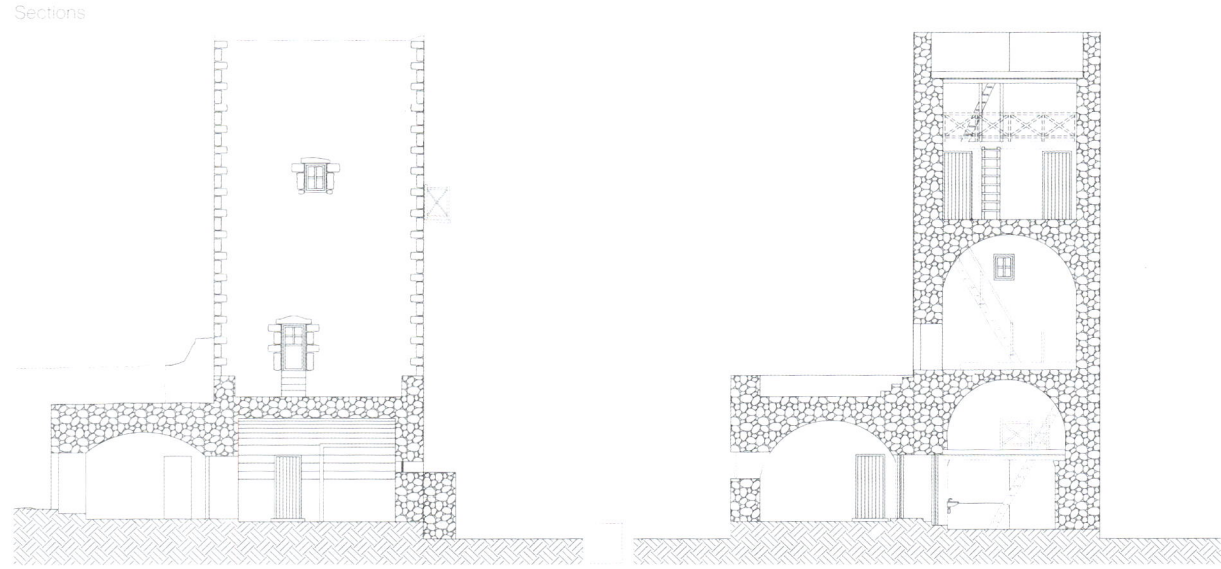

11 / View of bedroom interior
12 / Bathroom in bedroom
13–16 / Bedroom

116   Mountainside Guest House

Location /
Ponte de São Simão, Portugal

Area /
592 square feet
(55 square meters)

Architecture and design /
Bruno Lucas Dias

Photography /
Hugo Santos Silva

Watermill on the Crag

Downstream, just a few miles from the spring of the Alge Creek, two imposing cliff faces appear, massive walls ripped by the creek and time alike.

The Crags of Saint Simon are imposing indeed, and of unmatched beauty. Refreshed by the crystal-clear waters of the creek and its distinctive vegetation, they bestow upon the place a magical feeling of peace and tranquility, where nature and humankind become one. The sound of the running water and birds and the solemnity of the rock faces provide those enjoying the location with an unforgettable encounter with nature.

One hikes down the path, once opened by the strength of bare arms with the help of a mule, to set off on a journey through time, finding at the feet of the crags, where creek and margins blend, an old inactive watermill and an oven that used to bake bread with the wheat and corn flour straight from the grindstones.

This local lodging project was born out of the respect of the existing language, and aims to re-qualify the constructions and their context, faithfully respecting, as much as possible, its past use.

The development was cost-limited, aiming to maximize the reuse of existing elements of the mill. Therefore, the project was focused on a resolution of the interior, by using a single-material covering: pinewood, one of the natural elements of the region.

External interventions are limited to window frames (replaced by new double-glazed wooden frames) and thermal improvements to the roof. Internal spaces are drawn per their function, their lighting, and with a purpose of well-being. Four distinct spaces were created: rest, hygiene, meals, and leisure. The combined result is increased thermal comfort of the building and better potential for its use.

The target audience is of middle or upper-middle socioeconomic class, both nationals and foreigners. This is a place of refuge, for blending with nature, with the comfort and expectations of modern living.

01 / Main entrance
02 / Exterior view

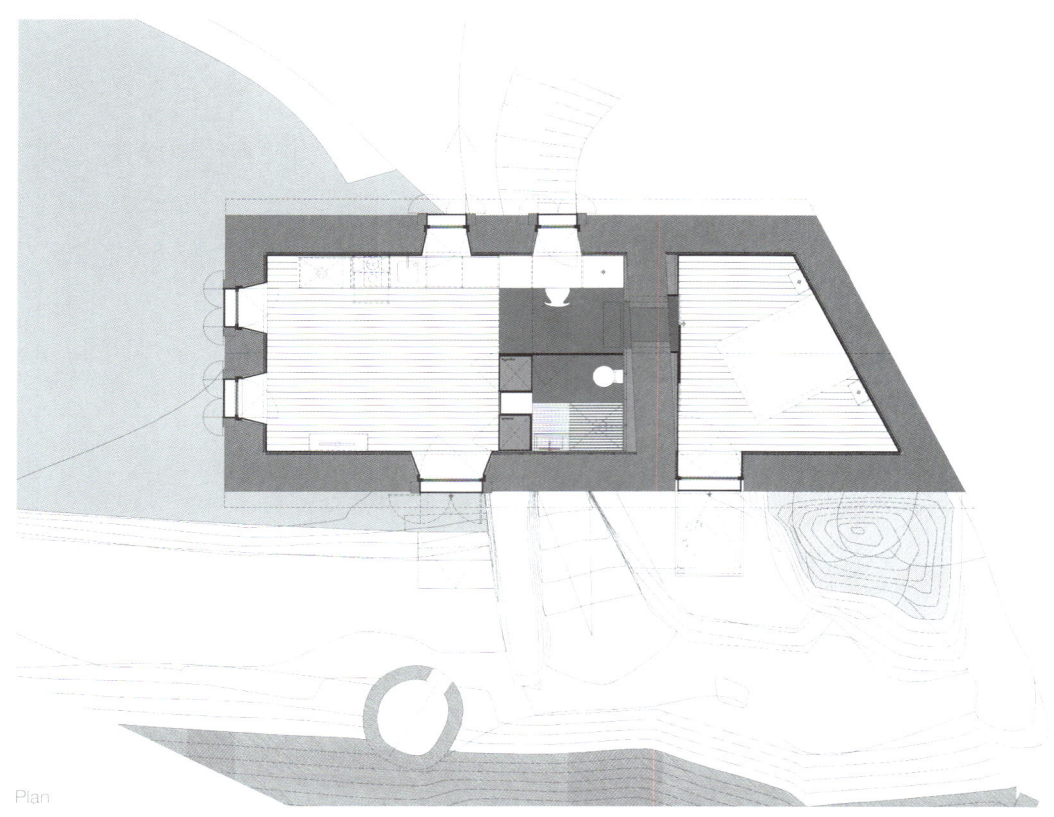

Plan

03 / Interior view
04 / Kitchenette
05 / Door to outside
06 / Recreation area

07–08 / Bedroom

Sections

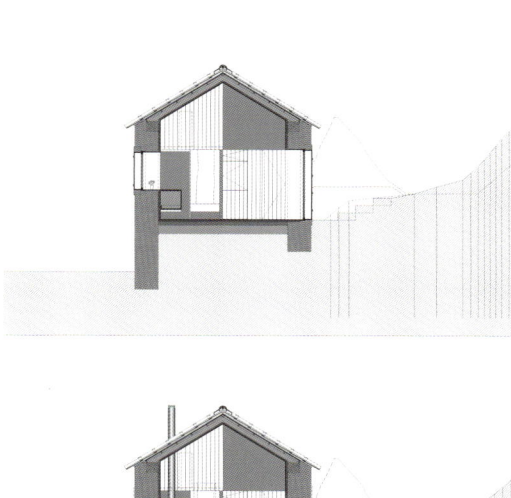

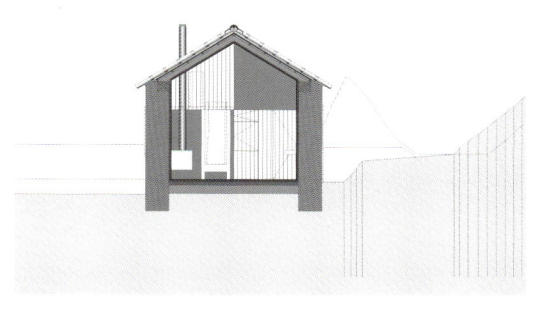

Elevations

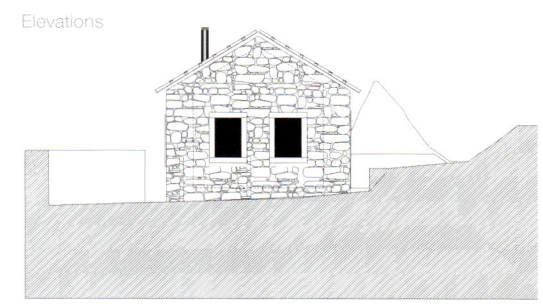

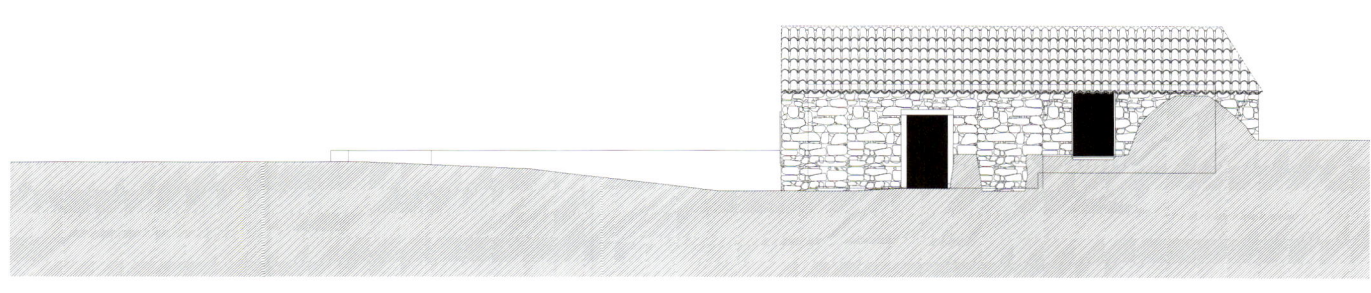

Location /
Mazama, Washington, United States

Area /
1600 square feet (149 square meters)

Architecture and design /
CAST Architecture, Tim Hammer

Photography /
CAST Architecture, Stefan Hampden

Mazama Ranchero

Nestled at the edge of a subalpine meadow in the upper Methow Valley, the Ranchero is a base camp for year-round outdoor adventure and a social hub for gatherings of friends and family.

The plan emphasized simplicity, abundant natural light, and a strong connection to the surrounding peaks and adjacent aspen grove. The public wing features an open floor plan with an expansive patio that sets the stage for relaxation and socializing. The deep veranda, oversized entry, and ski wax room provide family and guests a functional landing zone between activities. The private wing offers a master suite with an extra day bed, a ship's berth-inspired bunk room, and peaceful getaway nooks.

A simple material pallet focuses on highly durable, low-maintenance solutions such as Cor-ten steel siding, aluminum clad windows and a concrete skirt that protects the structure's base during the winter snowpack and spring snowmelt cycle. Mild steel and color-embedded fiber cement panels clad the interior walls for a durable, paint-free finish. Crisp white aluminum ceiling panels reflect light into the home and help blur the line between the indoors and outdoors. The home features regionally crafted custom-finish details, casework and furnishings throughout.

The home is designed to take advantage of passive solar heat gain in the winter while minimizing solar heat gain in the summer. Built at a modest scale with super insulated walls and ceilings, energy efficient windows and systems, the home is intended to minimize energy consumption. Low VOC finishes, concrete floors, and a heat recovery ventilator insure clean and healthy air.

01 / Front view of architecture
02 / Side view of architecture

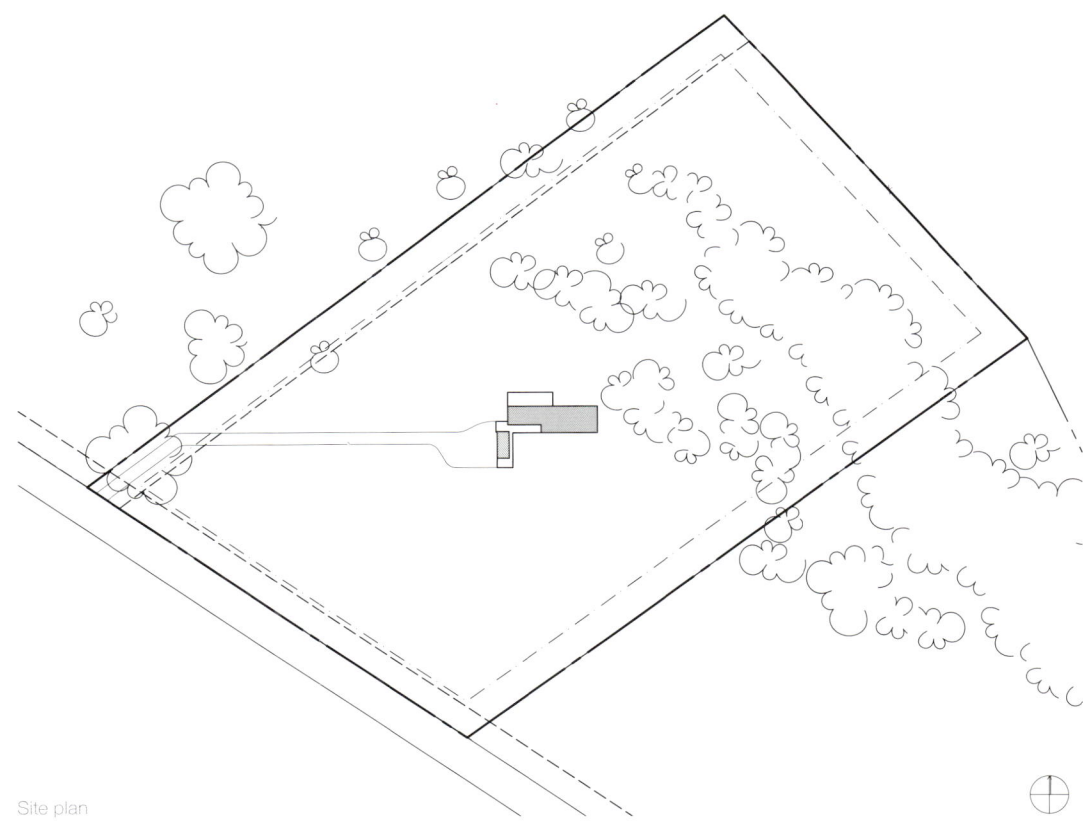

Site plan

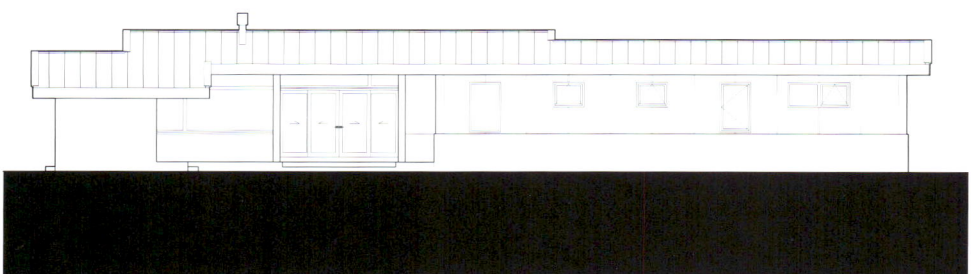

South elevation

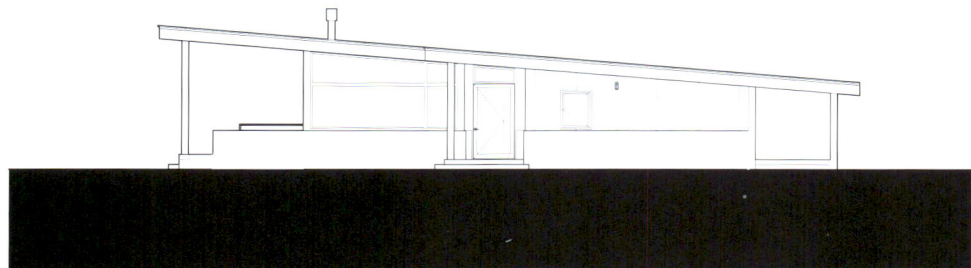

West elevation

03 / Living room
04 / Dining room
05 / Dining room interior

North elevation

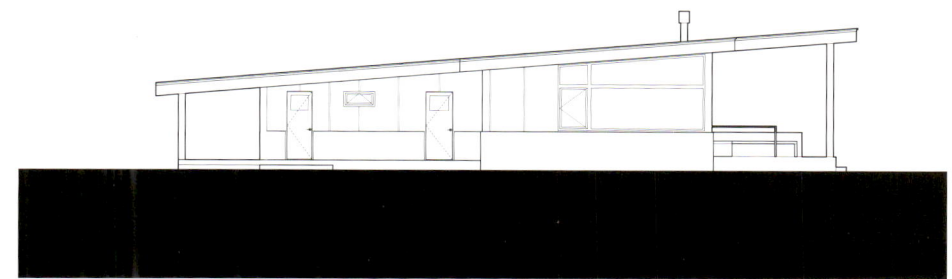

East elevation

Floor plan

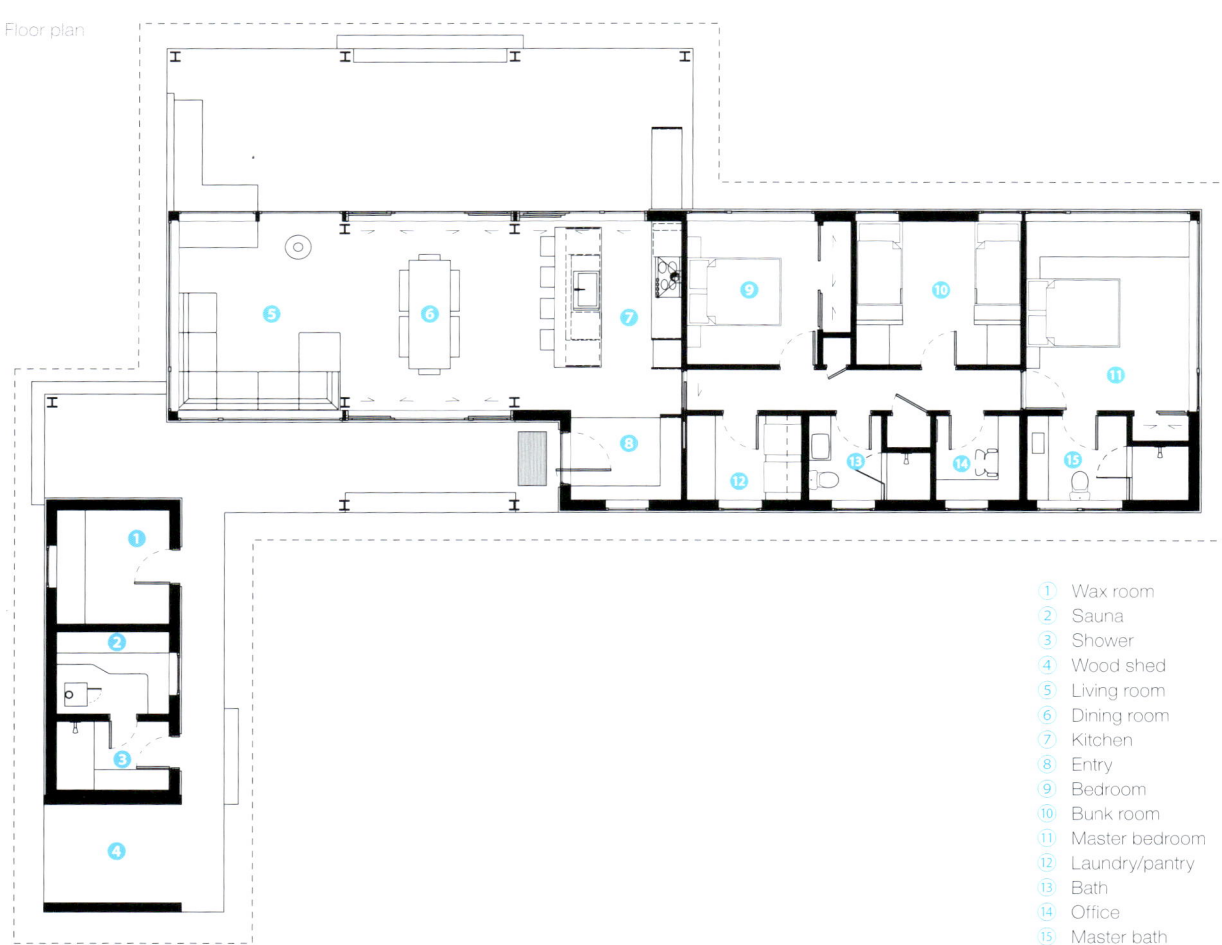

① Wax room
② Sauna
③ Shower
④ Wood shed
⑤ Living room
⑥ Dining room
⑦ Kitchen
⑧ Entry
⑨ Bedroom
⑩ Bunk room
⑪ Master bedroom
⑫ Laundry/pantry
⑬ Bath
⑭ Office
⑮ Master bath

06 / Bedroom
07 / Multi-person bedroom

Location /
Huangshan, Anhui, China

Area /
8611 square feet
(800 square meters)

Architecture and design /
Zhu Shouyao

Photography /
Xiong Wei,
Duan Chenguang

Bushe Hotel

A concept of geography and culture, Bushe Hotel—located in Tunxi District, Huangshan, Liyang—is an integration of modern design set among ancient Hui-style buildings.

Hui-style buildings are effectively preserved in this region and renovated to keep and maintain the original appearance and ancient style, which offers a miniature, concentrated display of the Hui cultural model. The surrounding buildings and facilities are upgraded and improved, and lots of new stylish buildings are built. The guest house sits among the old and new.

Bushe Hotel was designed by renowned designer Zhu Shouyao, who had lived in Huizhou for four years and had a profound and original understanding on Huizhou culture. When designing Bushe Hotel, he didn't use traditional elements of Hui-style buildings, but refined and regrouped traditional elements in a modern, simple, and stylish manner.

The overall design of the hotel draws on three main colors of Hui-style buildings—black, white, and gray; old wooden objects removed from old houses are widely used as materials to process and regrouped in order to create a comfortable, simple, natural, and profound effect.

The entrance hall doesn't use the traditional design of reception desks, but, rather, a tea room with a larger area. The background avoided using complex elements; a lot of blank space and bold style creates a quiet, artistic conception full of Zen wisdom.

The balcony on the second floor makes the most of the space, light, and shadow, using four French windows to establish a dining hall. Sunlight shows levels of light and shadow and a sense of rhythm through the windows. Whether sun, rain, or snow, dining guests can feel warm and relaxed in this space.

Simultaneously, the designer integrated the hostess's enthusiasm for literature, poetry, art, flowers, and plants into the design of the hotel by designing an open-air garden full of flowers and plants, as well as a small, bright book house with black tiles outside the dining hall.

This hotel has 10 rooms. The designer strove to create comfortable rooms with simple lines, soothing colors, ample lighting, and natural materials. The use of old wood, bamboo, black iron and other special materials shows the designer's ingenuity greatly.

The room designs have a lot of highlights: in the street-side room, guests standing by the balcony or window can see old streets in Liyang Ancient town, small bridges over the flowing stream, white walls, black tiles and intoxicating night views. Some rooms use Japanese tatami-style structures to create a sense of comfort and warmth for people in a smaller space.

Asymmetric pendant lamps and pictures embody the designer's pursuit of innovation and subversion. The largest suite—called Bushe—is a duplex room, the floors and walls of which are made of the most primitive wood, with ceilings made of natural bamboo. All the rooms on the third floor have sloped roofs. Simple windows and elegant walls reflect the concept of an unassuming and elegant living space.

01 / Building façade
02 / Lobby
03 / Tearoom of Bushe Hotel

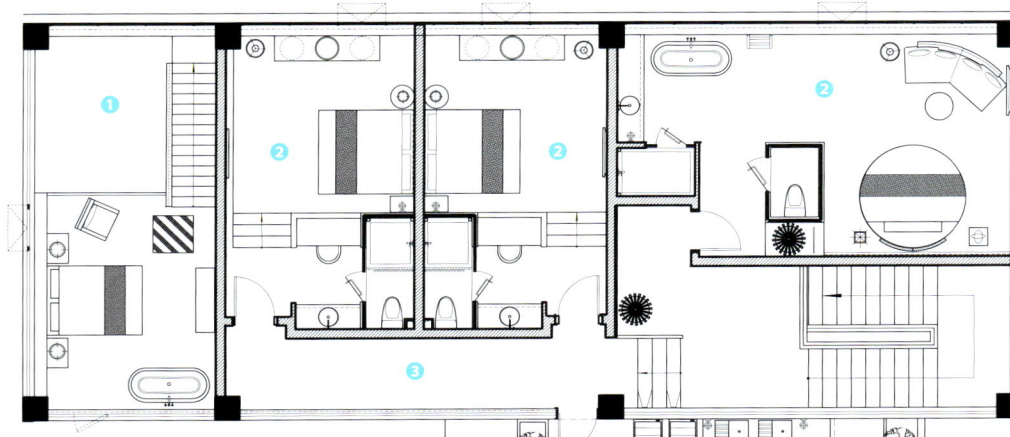

① Courtyard
② Guest room
③ Aisle
④ Terrace

Site plan

04 / Small garden
05 / Living room

06-07 / Living room
08 / Washing area

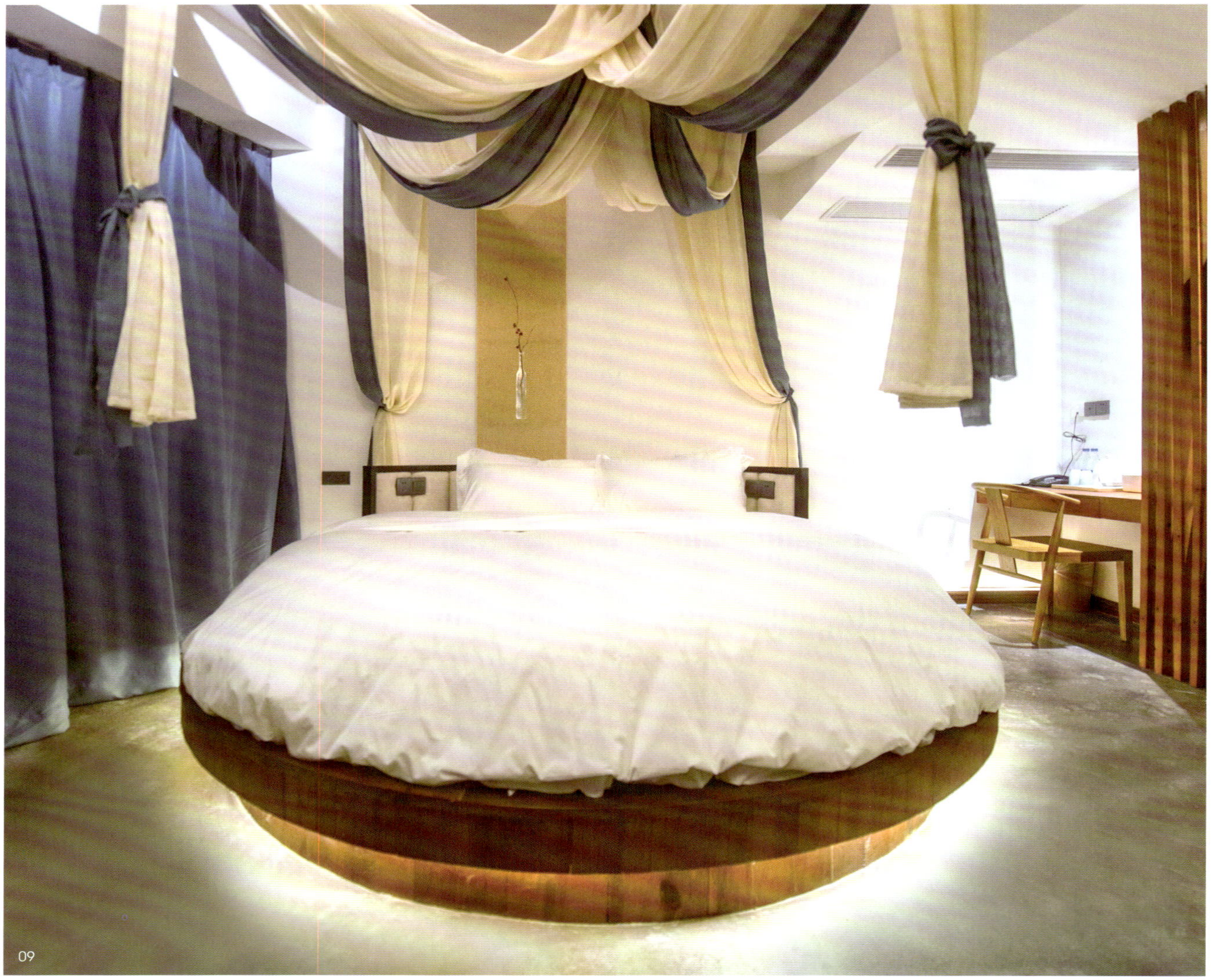

09

10

11

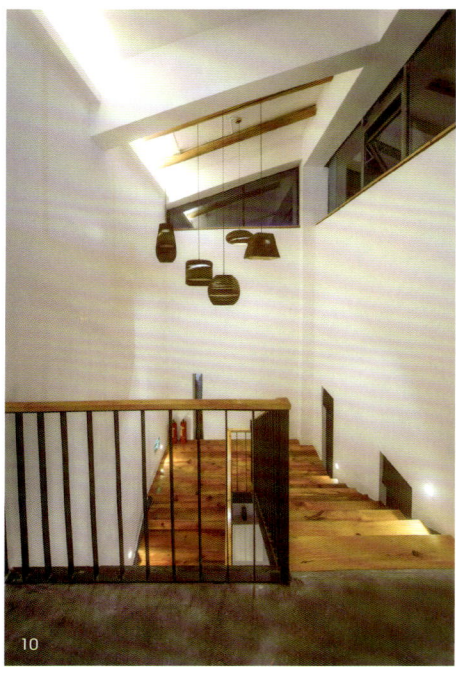

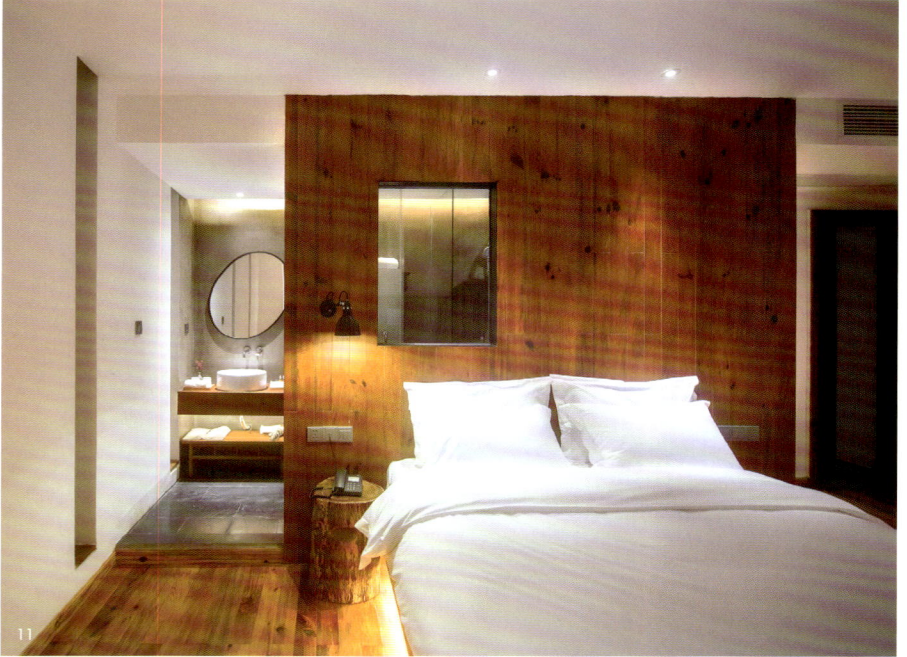

09 / Tingyun Room
10 / Mezzanine on second floor
11–13 / Dexian Room

14 / Liulian Room
15 / Terrace outside guest room

16 / Study
17 / Dining room
18 / Wumeng Room

Location /
Huangshan, Anhui, China

Area /
5382 square feet
(500 square meters)

Architecture and design /
Chen Xi

Photography /
Zhou Yuedong

Shanshui Boutique Hotel

This project is located at the confluence of Shuaishui River, Hengjiang River and Xin' an River on Liyang IN Lane of Tunxi District. Liyang IN Lane preserves Liyang Old Street with a history of 1800 years, which is only separated by a bridge, opposite Tunxi Old Street. Old houses are on the left bank, while bars are on the right bank—tradition and fashion coexist; nearby water goes with far mountains, which forms a harmonious picture.

Viewing the whole building from the lobby entrance, people can find an amazing scene—an old mottled Hui-style house is wrapped by modern steel structures with an irregular geometry of brand-new glass curtain walls. The collision of different materials, architectural forms, and colors forms a delightful contrast and leaves no abrupt impression on people.

In the lobby, wooden pergolas fuse traditional charm into contemporary aesthetics. On the premise of protecting Hui-style old houses, the designer takes modern people's demand for the comfort of life into full account and makes a daring transformation on interior and exterior spaces. Most furniture is made by seasoned native carpenters and is environmentally friendly with distinct characteristics of ancient Huizhou. The tone of the space is elegant and reserved on the whole and the characteristic and modern design makes space gentle and full of modern flavor. This people-oriented design serves functions and hides in buildings cleverly.

Chinese picture-frame partitions in the multi-functional dining hall introduce oriental cultural sentiment into this understated and simple space. The use of integrated lighting zones and bamboo-leaf projection spotlights onto pieces of white cloth create a dreamlike atmosphere.

The designer took advantage of the excellent location of project to ensure that people can enjoy scenery from each room when pushing windows open. The design of indoor rooms is very concise and natural—plenty of timbers fills rooms with simple beauty, and the Chinese implication of hollowed-out wooden partition doors and the use of concrete surface infuse a modern breath into the space.

The designer followed the principle of adjusting measures to local conditions and using local materials, as well as lots of old wood. The overhead loft suite, the sheet wooden stair of which is full of the flavor of era, make use of the structure of the loft to create a unique charm of light and shadow. Double rooms with differences in height don't use simple beds as common rooms do. The minimalist design makes lines of rooms neat; people living in rooms will not have a sense of narrowness.

The people-oriented concept of the designer is fully blended into all design elements and each transformation of old houses reflects the project owners' sincerity into preserving traditional culture treasures.

01 / Building façade
02–03 / Public area of hotel
04 / Study

05 / Multifunctional meeting room and meditation room
06 / Breakfast area
07 / Vegetarian dining room

08–10 / Living room

141

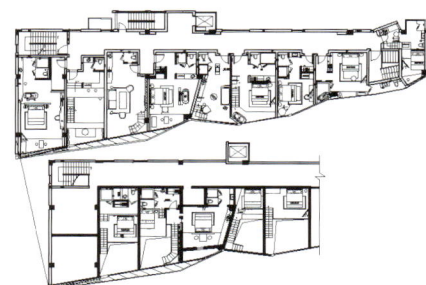
Fourth-floor plan

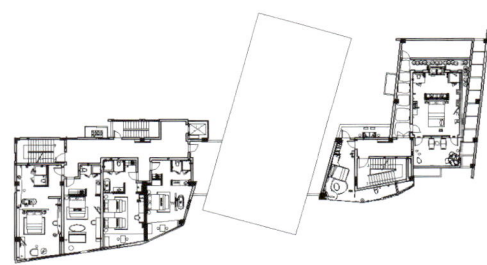
Third-floor plan

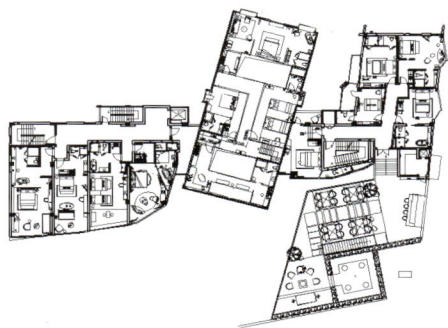
Second-floor plan

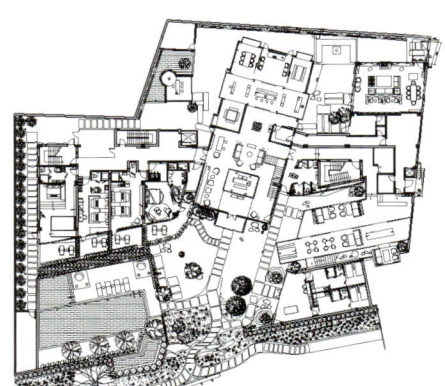
First-floor plan

11 / Lounge in guest room
12–14 / Guest room

143

Location /
Paizihutong, Beijing, China

Area /
1738 square feet
(161.5 square meters)

Architecture and design /
ArchStudio

Photography /
Wang Ning, Jin Weiqi

Text /
Han Wenqiang

Twisting Courtyard

Twisting Courtyard is located in Paizihutong, Dashilar Area, Beijing. It used to be a Siheyuan (courtyard house) with one single entry. The purpose of the improvement was to upgrade the necessary infrastructure needed for modern life, thus turning this traditional courtyard, which mainly served as a residence, into an attractive public space of Beijing Inner City.

Twist within regular layout

The design aimed at getting rid of the solemn and stereotyped impression given by Siheyuan, and creating an open and active living atmosphere. Based on the existing layout of the courtyard, the undulated floor was used to connect indoor and outdoor spaces of different heights. It was extended to the inside of the house, twisting into walls and a roof, thus creating a dynamic connection between the inside and outside space.

What's hidden within the curved wall is necessary auxiliary spaces such as a kitchen, a toilet, and a warehouse; while reception and dining spaces are shown outside the curved wall and connected to the courtyard as a whole. Both indoor and outdoor floors were paved with gray bricks. A hawthorn tree in the courtyard is kept as part of the twisting landscape.

Twist between patterns of utilization

The small yard is mainly used as an urban public space while maintaining the possibility of also being used residentially. The four houses can be rented for public events for purposes such as recreation, meeting, and gathering. Meanwhile, they could be served as a family hostel with three bedrooms.

Integrated furniture was used to enable the flexible switch of space scenes. Furniture boxes were inserted into the existing wood frames of east and west wings. The wood platform with a lifting table hidden inside could be used as a tearoom or bedroom. Bed walls and partitive soft curtains were also used in the main room on the north to meet multiple use requirements.

For the 'Siheyuan' building type, the courtyard is the core of the fun living space. Twisting Courtyard made micro-adjustments to change the temperament of the courtyard space to meet the requirements of multiple uses without changing the existing housing structure, making the traditional courtyard up-to-date and integratable into modern urban life.

01 / Bird's-eye view of courtyard
02 / Nightview

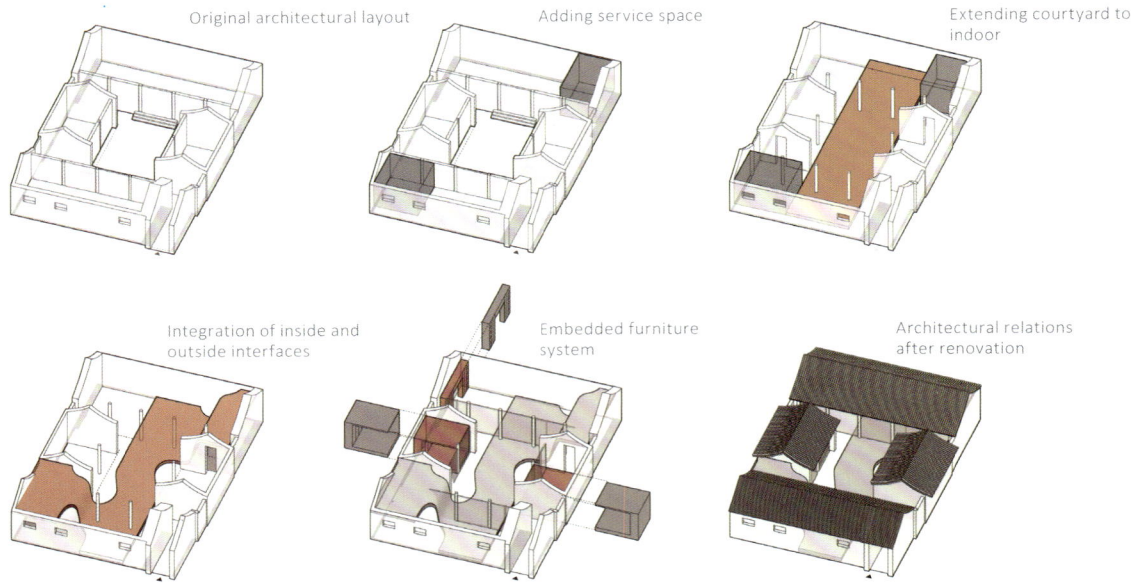

Structural analysis diagram

03 / Entrance
04 / Details

146 Urban Guest House

05 / Main room (bedroom mode)
06 / Main room (relaxation mode)
07 / Kitchen

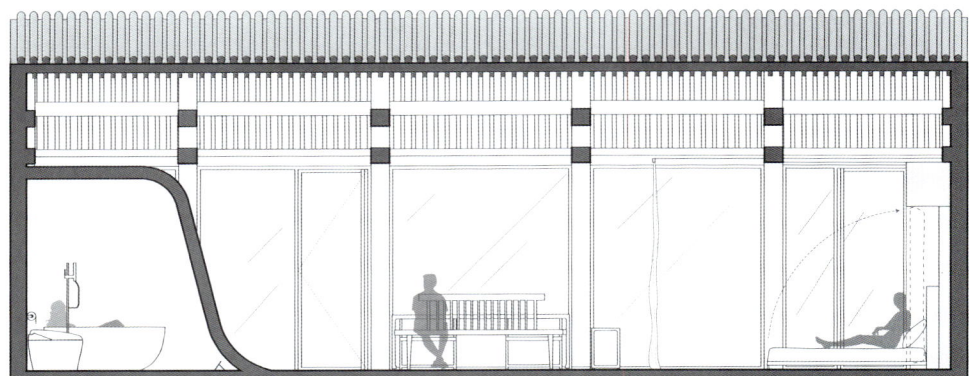
Section

08 / Wing room (bedroom mode)
09 / Wing room (tearoom mode)
10 / Washing room

Plan of housing mode

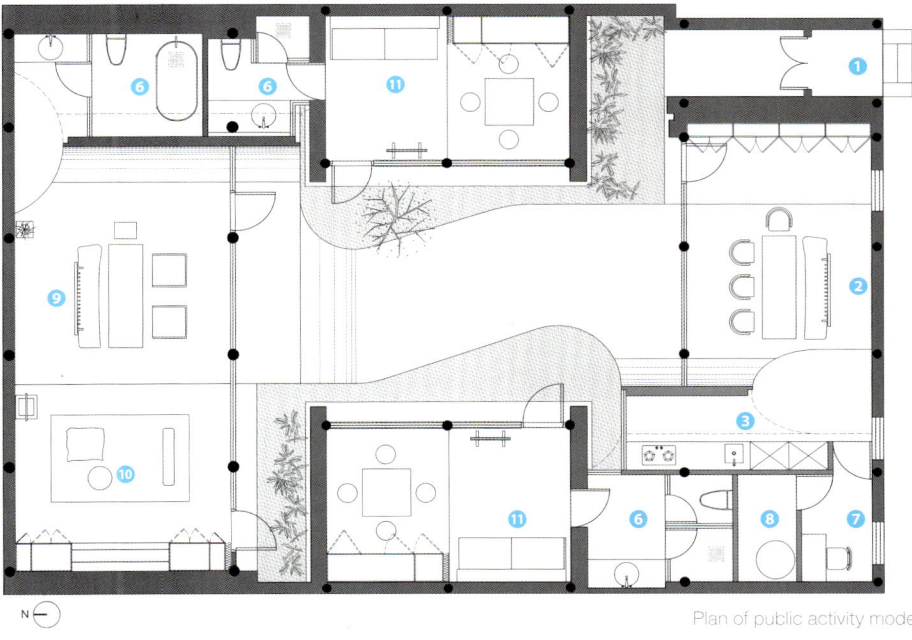

Plan of public activity mode

1. Entrance
2. Dining room
3. Kitchen
4. Tea area
5. Bedroom
6. Restroom
7. Office
8. Equipment
9. Reception area
10. Leisure area
11. Room

Location /
Beijing, China

Area /
2153 square feet
(200 square meters)

Architecture and design /
CCDI Grand Wisdom
Interior Design

Photography /
Lu Fei

Rare Yard

The Rare Yard, located in northwest Beijing at the foothills of Baihujian, is a typical Beijing three-section compound, which stands in a traditional village architecture complex. There is a huge picking garden right beside the west of the rail, which extends to the hillside. Aimed at accommodating three families or groups of 10, the whole building was reconstructed by the designer.

First, the designers reserved the original north room and tore down the east- and west-wing rooms. The main peak of the Yan Mountain ranges, which was previously invisible and could only be seen through the ridge of the roof, can now be appreciated from the west side of the Rare Yard. As local residents live on the west side of the yard, in order to get a relatively broader view of the west mountain and preserve privacy at the same time, the opening was designed toward the east in a U-shape.

The dining room is the combination of south and north rooms, old and new spaces. When the four glass doors fully open, the outdoor platform together with the dining room forms a new space and makes the dining room twice as large, thereby allowing the platform to be used as a part of the space. The huge window is designed to connect the outdoor and indoor space, and thus enable interactions and communications between these two areas.

The stairs are made of toon-tree timber from the old yard. From the spiral stairs leading up to the second floor, people can access the tearoom and tatami area to enjoy tea-tasting activities while viewing the mountains during the daytime and then sleep under the starry sky at night.

The entrance area has two high windows on the top of the doors, which keep the yard's privacy and also enable the two bathrooms to get the nature sunlight. The designer repaired the walls of the two bedrooms, using a cement treatment.

To create a more dynamic space, the bed size was reduced so the floor space would be more generous, while doors were left off the bathroom to create greater connection inside the bedroom. LED stripe lights were arranged to define the ridges of the roof while providing illumination for the newly constructed north room.

Since the owner of the house is a lover of photography, pictures that record the construction of the new backyard are hung on the walls, decorating the new space and telling the story of the transformation.

01 / Southeast entrance allowing view of other houses in village
02 / Courtyard with view of dining area
03 / East elevation with mountain views

04 / Gable on west side of house seen from dining room
05 / Window showing courtyard
06 / Close-up view of courtyard

07 / Meandering path circling around site

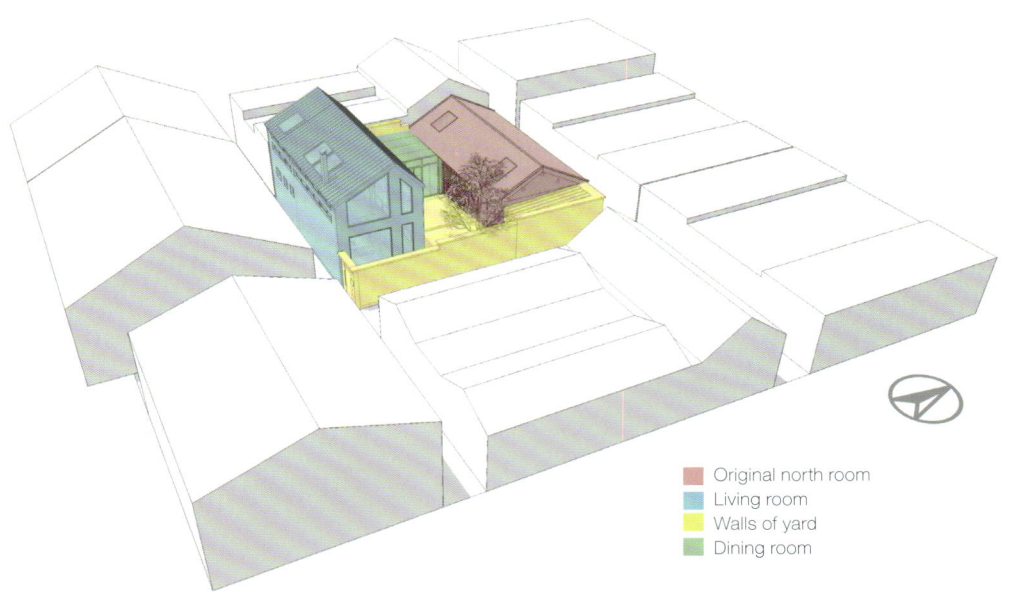

- Original north room
- Living room
- Walls of yard
- Dining room

08 / Top-down view of living room

154　Urban Guest House

09 / View of old north house through transparent windows
10 / Mezzanine of living room on second floor
11 / View of stairs from top floor

12 / Master bedroom
13 / Bedroom on west wing of old north house

14 / Entrance façade of old north house
15 / Bathroom
16 / Paintings on wall in dining room
17 / Wooden space in wine cellar

LIBERTINE LINDENBERG

Location /
Frankfurt, Germany

Area /
21,915 square feet
(2036 square meters)

Architecture and design /
Franken Architekten Gmbh

Photography /
Dieter Schwer

Franken Architekten was commissioned for the building and interior-design planning of the renovation and expansion of a Gründerzeit building in Frankfurt Alt-Sachsenhausen. The late-19th-century building was completely renovated and updated with a new elevator core in the courtyard. The gaps in the natural stone façade were restored and the remedial measures of recent years dismantled and adapted to the Wilhelminian façade.

There is a high-contrast, often eclectic, mix of rigorous, multi-functional devices and handmade unique pieces with 'history.'

The detailed presentation is characterized by tactile materials such as wall textiles, hand-blown lamps, and ornamental concrete tiles. The complementary artwork was developed in editions and one-offs from international designers and artists as a reflection on the interior context and the context of Alt-Sachsenhausen led by Dr. Steen Rothenberger and Kathi Käppel: textile installations, 'Brandritzungen' and limited art prints complete the storytelling.

The delicate and pastel playfulness of the house was considered in harmony with a native orchard. Birds, beetles, butterflies, grasses, and apples play on the surfaces throughout the house, whether in the forged entrance gate or the hand-embroidered internals of rooms.

A break with this lovely scenery takes place in the so-called 'black holes'—deep dark areas that lie consistently across all elements of the design. Functionally, they serve, for example, in the suites as monolithic blocks of closet and kitchenette.

Elsewhere they act as zoning between entrance, bathroom, and living area or mark a transition in the stairwell. The black holes are also used on the façade as soffits in steel garments of enclosed windows and the front door.

LIBERTINE LINDENBERG extends over seven floors. In the basement, there is a recording studio, which opens the door for joint jam sessions, concerts, and film screenings, as well as a gym. On the ground floor is a living-room café and an office space. In the attic, there is a cooking landscape, a pantry kitchen for events, a dining room with picturesque views on the winding roofs of Alt-Sachsenhausen and Lekker grocery store where the residents can purchase culinary delights. Spread over the floors there are 27 suites of one to three bedrooms, six of which extend in new buildings and maisonettes over two floors.

The LIBERTINE LINDENBERG reflects the societal need for communal living and working. The increase in one-person households is leading to increasing isolation and increased desire for community, which is offered with this flexibly designed living concept that adapts to the current life of its inhabitants.

LIBERTINE LINDENBERG realizes collaborative living and transmits the culture of swapping and sharing in real space. Thus, it creates a new quality of living with 'we-feeling,' but receives in parallel the possibility of individuality and, thus, masters the fine line between sociability and intimacy, which is participative and transparent exclusively.

01 / Old building
02 / Wohnzimmer Café

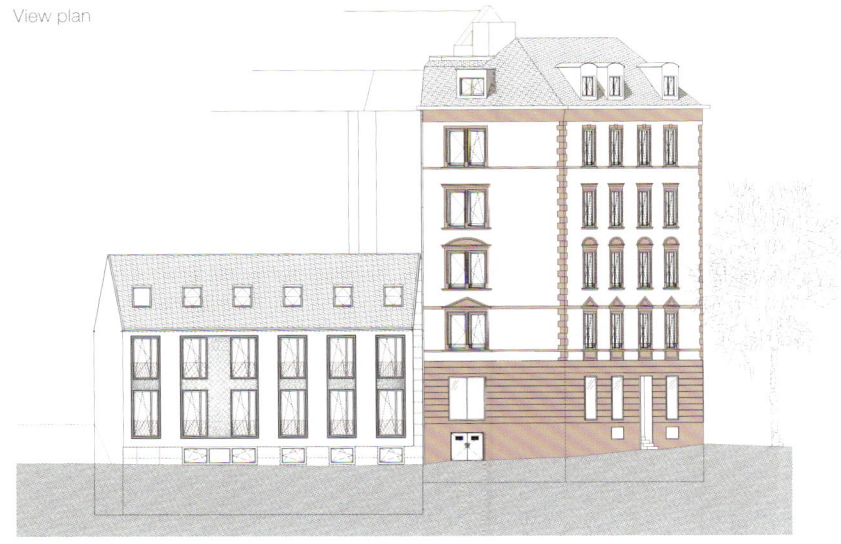

View plan

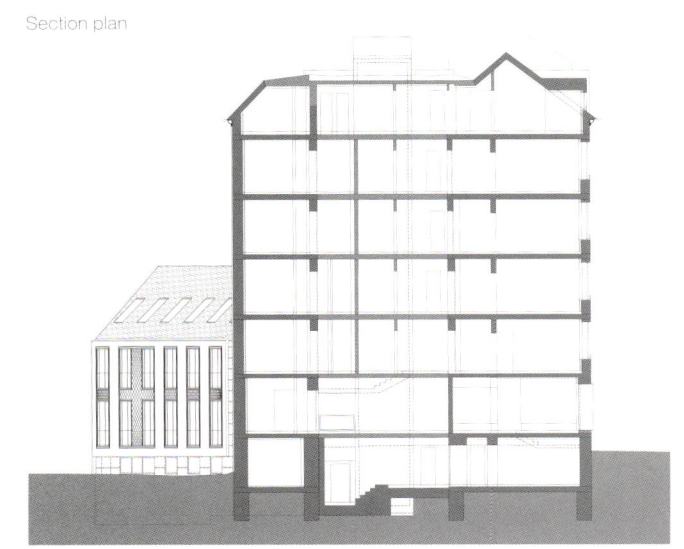

Section plan

03

04

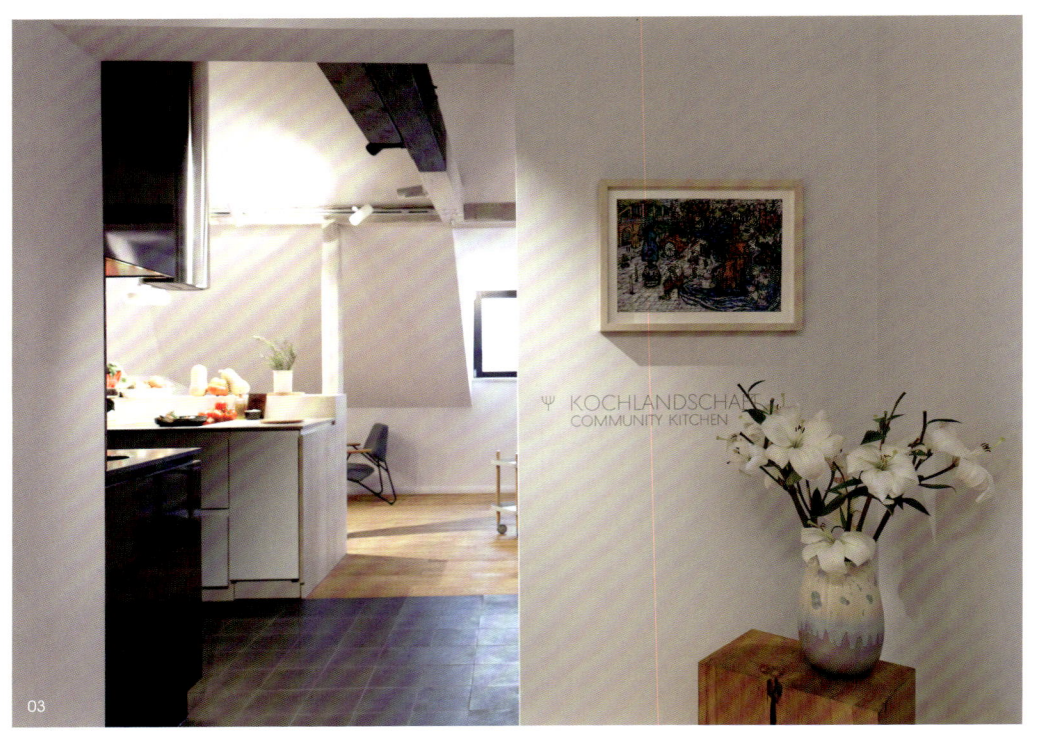

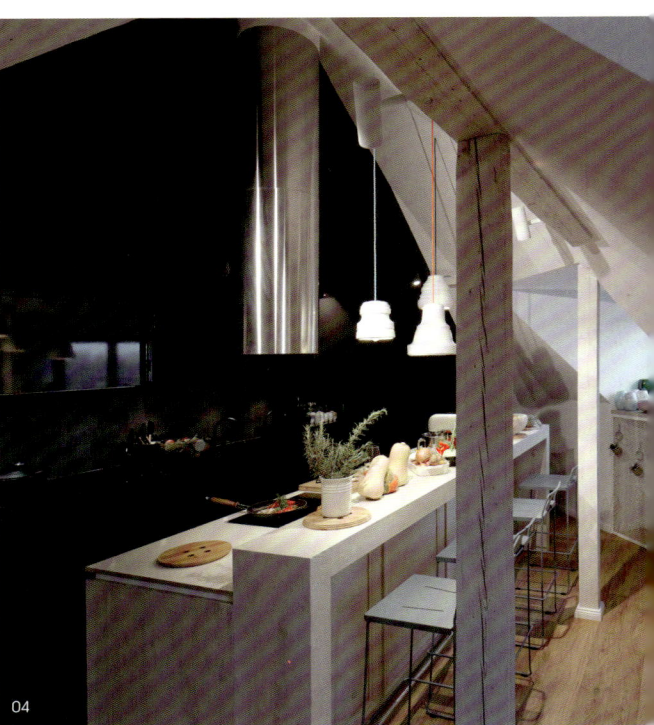

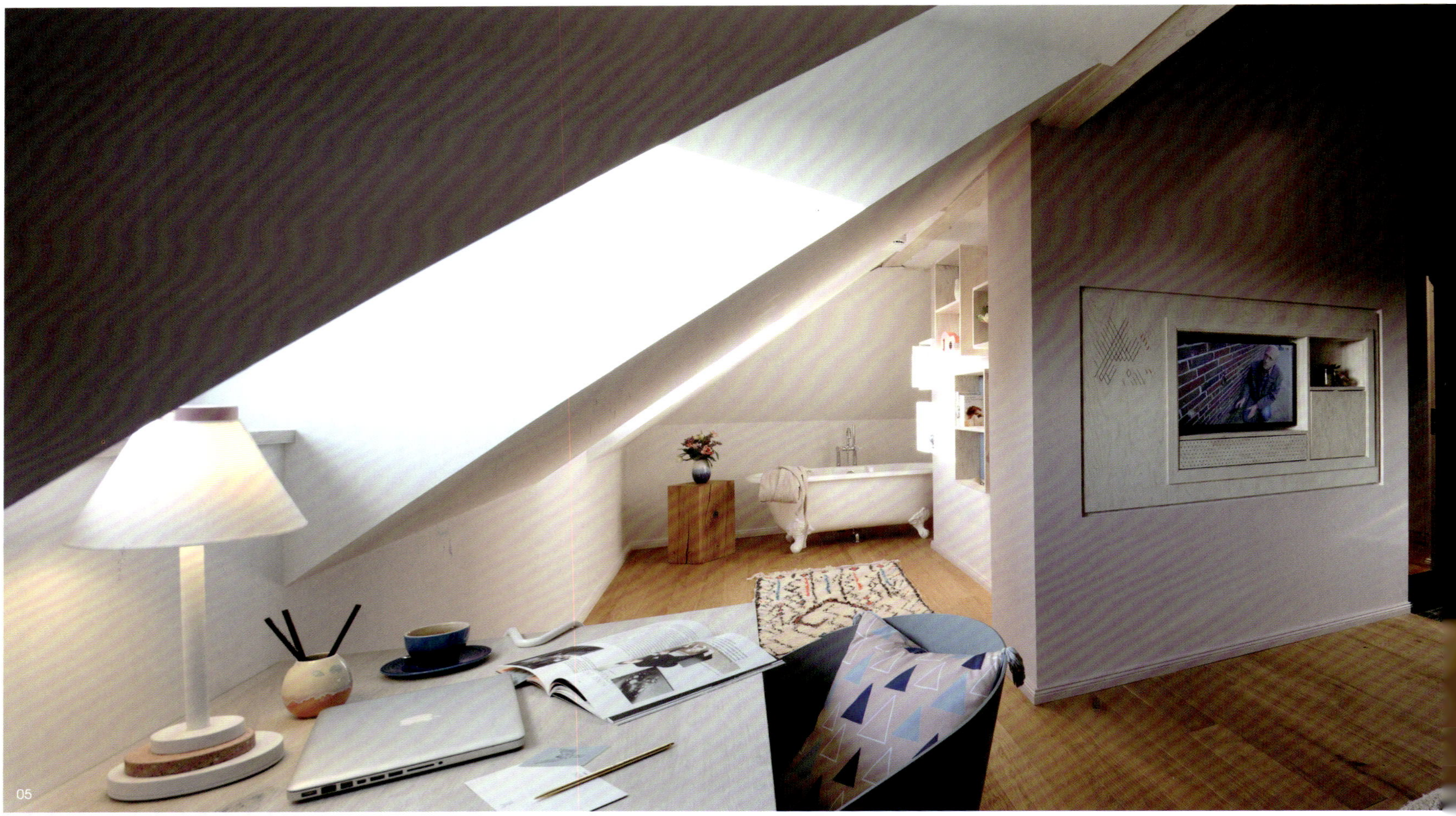

05

03–04 / Old building
05 / Suite
06 / Dining hall

Basement floor plan

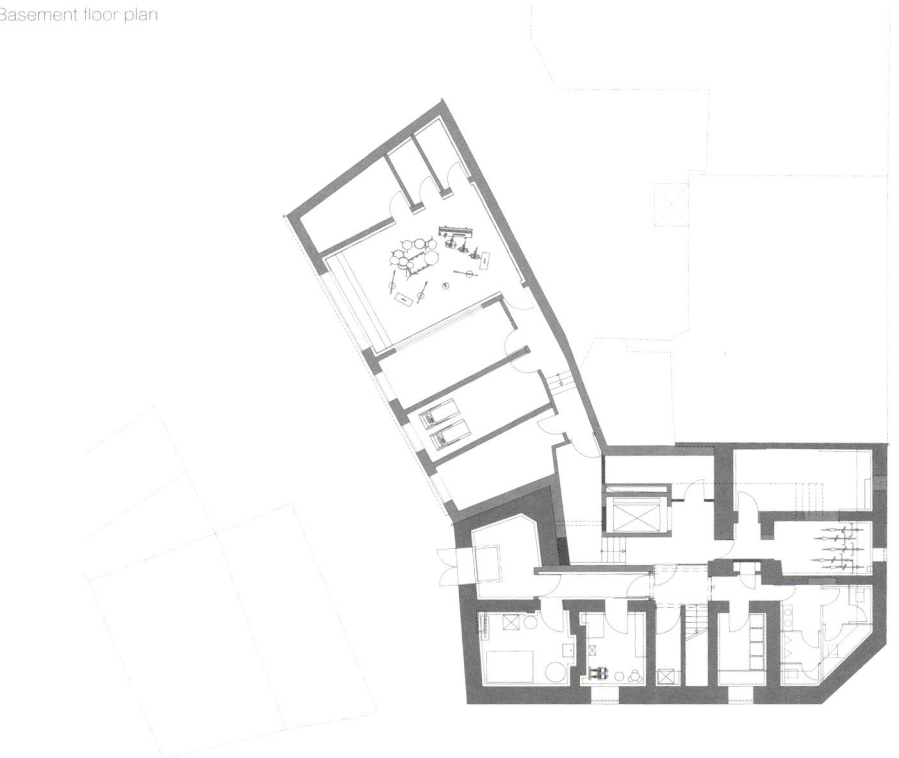

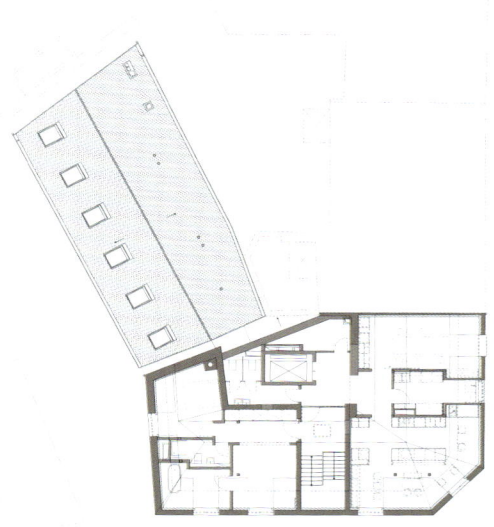
Fifth-floor plan

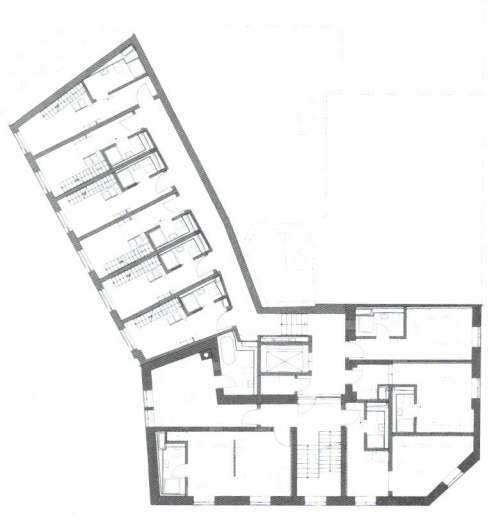
Second-floor plan

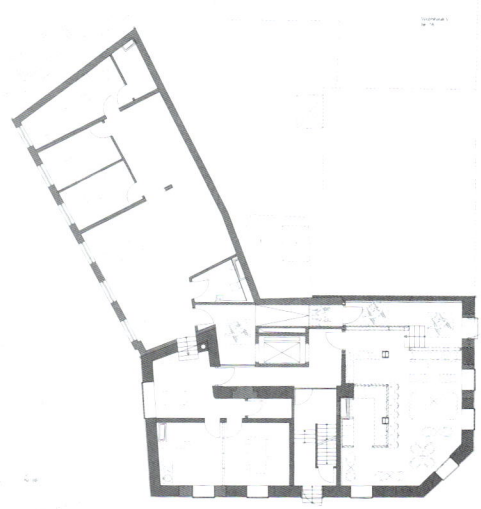
First-floor plan

07 / Community kitchen
08 / Maisonette
09 / Gym
10–11 / Zimmer Suite

Location /
Lishui, Shanghai, China

Area/
807 square feet
(75 square meters)

Architecture and design /
G&S Design

Photography /
Huang Miangui

One House

Situated in Zhujiajiao Ancient Town, Shanghai, One House was transformed from a former copper-pipe factory. This guest house is very interesting in that it has only one room. Everyone here is a tenant and householder. In fact, it is a self-service guest house and the owner encourages guests to experience the space actively.

Old objects, seemingly from childhood, are placed strategically to trigger memories in guests. They represent daily necessities and the ups and downs of growth. The objects aren't collected for their history or value, rather, to add warmth to the house for guests. They are small deposits of 'life' to strum the heartstrings.

In the design of the guest house, original features were preserved. The second floor above the former living room, however, was removed to open up the space and allow more light, while also revealing the original structure of the building.

The guest house is situated in the metropolis, yet is also close to nature, where people can feel the peace and vitality. Natural materials were used as much as possible, each of which is unique and full of natural beauty. The concept of environmental protection and repurposing items is also embraced, while contributing to the homely feeling of the old building.

Old objects are used to create atmosphere, new equipment is used to provide functionality and this fusion of new and old elements not only meet the needs of modern needs—particularly in the bathroom—but also tells the story of the guest house.

01 / Building façade
02 / Lounge in living room

03 / Lounge in living room
04 / Corner of living room

Elevations

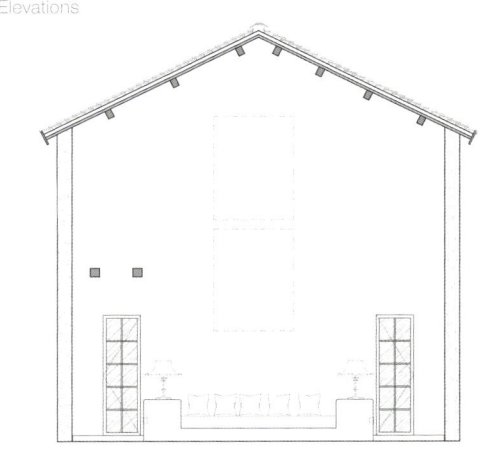
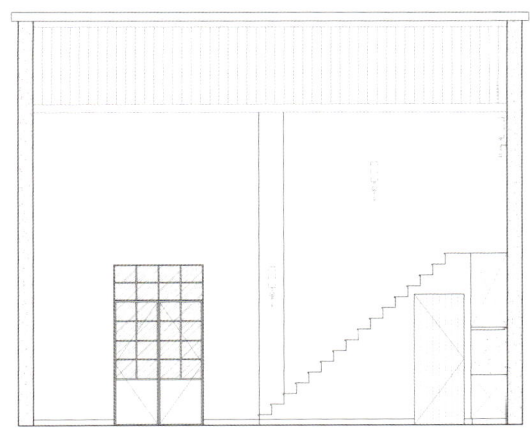
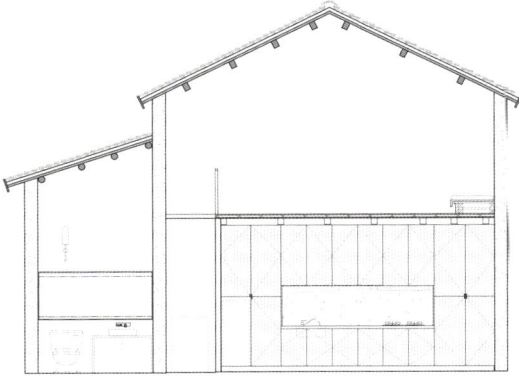
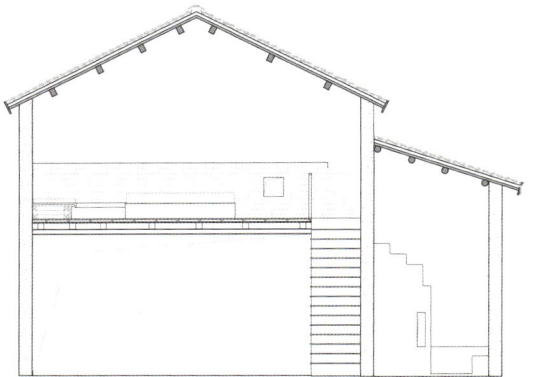

167

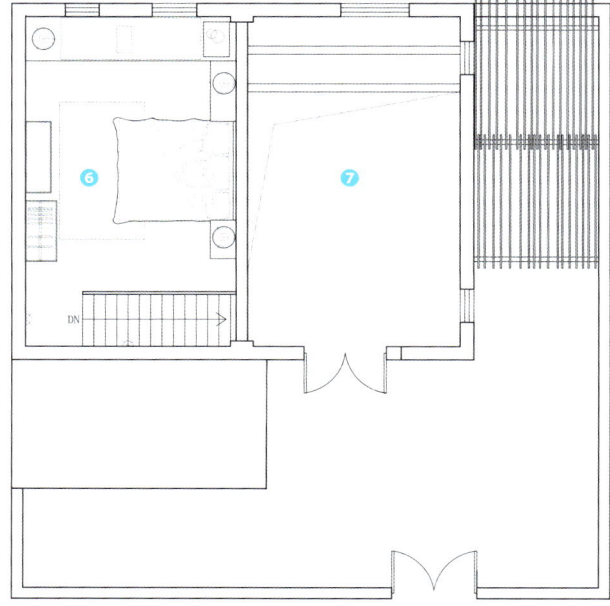

Second-floor plan

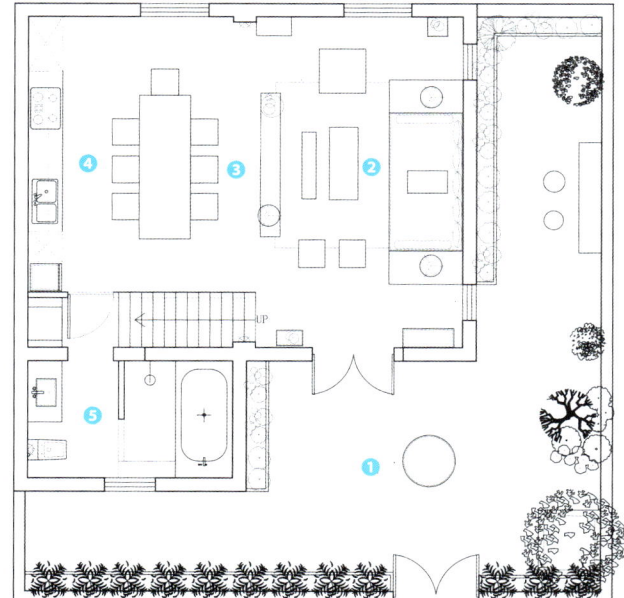

First-floor plan

1. Garden
2. Living room
3. Dining room
4. Kitchen
5. Bathroom
6. Bedroom
7. Void

05 / Entrance
06 / Bedroom
07 / Corner of living room
08 / Bathroom

iii_house

Location /
Xi'an, Shanxi, China

Area /
2906 square feet
(270 square meters)

Architecture and design /
Jieyufeibai Studio

Photography /
Jieyufeibai Studio

iii_house is located at No. 3 Chang'anxue Alley of Beilin District in Xi'an, which is the site of Jieyufeibai Studio that founded by four designers. It is an open living space embracing guest house, design, manual craft, exhibition and photography to provide diversified experiences of design life and unique experiences of living space.

Guests can travel during the day and lodge here at night. The studio hopes that everyone that meets iii_house can gain a unique space design experience, thus giving its present name. iii_house is an old dwelling at Chang'anxue Alley, whose owner is very thoughtful, reserving a small yard for the old scholar tree in front of the house specially so that it becomes the only dwelling with a yard at Chang'anxue Alley. When people enter the yard, mottled landscape walls jump into their sights, creating a quiet and mysterious atmosphere among lights and shadows under the old scholar tree. People can sit in the yard quietly and enjoy a good time alone.

Integrating nice elements into design: expounding interesting and wonderful things in daily life with the method of designers. iii_house is a practice of space design on home and life. The whole dwelling sites the east toward the west, retro and dignified. It is situated between the first door and the second door in Chang'anxue Alley, and is a quiet spot in a noisy neighborhood. Therefore, the design team decides to transform this dwelling of 30 years old with the design strategy of reserving the exterior space and renovating the interior space. After 60 days of Project design and 120 days of construction, a spatial dialogue between the new and the old is completed by the design team. The house uses concrete, logs and steel plates as main materials; black, white and gray as main colors; red as a decorative color. As people walk through the small yard into the living room with black, white and gray interweaved, they can see a long red oak table that can be used in handcrafting activities, lectures, parties and film events. In fact, this is also an ideal place for designing and talking. This place uses a concrete bar with traces of plants, focuses on the interest of space and fully respects the diversity of people and things in space to manifest the unique space character of each corner. Designers' basic attitudes toward life and hobbies are shown by design—they transform the existing space by themselves; they repair bamboo beds and broken clay pots; they design and make indoor furniture, window catches, lanterns and decorative ornaments with wild flowers and grasses. Designers add more natural traces to iii_house so that each room, corner and detail can convey the quality and temperature that are endowed by design.

Five rooms and design thoughts of soft furnishings:

Chimu (twilight)—An old tea table at sunset, storytelling at twilight; the sunset afterglow pours onto the tea table and floor through carved windows at 4 p.m.. The whole room is like an elderly man who is telling the history of Chang'an to people. At twilight, people may as well make a cup of tea by themselves and become one-day masters of Chang'an.

Huajian (among blossoms)—Waking up to sit among the flowers, sleeping to dream under the flowers; the rosy room uses the design style of air-curing barn, and its slope roof, big roof truss, barn door and the handmade sofa inside offer people a variety of spatial experiences. No matter who you are, you can begin a rosy journey there.

Suye (fields)—Defined with plain decorations, creating a sense of living in the fields; transparent wooden windows, plain soft surfaces, handmade garlands and custom furniture create a quiet and elegant atmosphere.

Cangji (heavens)—Tall windows borrow beautiful views in the distance, thin clouds drift across the sky; full height duplex room with a panoramic skylight…in the morning, people can lie in bed to see clouds drift across the sky and pigeons fly over the clouds ; at night, they can say good night to the moon and fall asleep with the starry sky.

Jingqian (changing with the time past)—The rubble and city wall wait quietly, people leave but the city wall and moat still exist; the room faces the Ming Dynasty City Wall in Chang'an and uses French windows. It uses show stands and bedside items made of bricks from the old city wall; old tickets are embedded in the photo frame. People will meet Chang'an in history in this room.

South elevation

01 / Main entrance

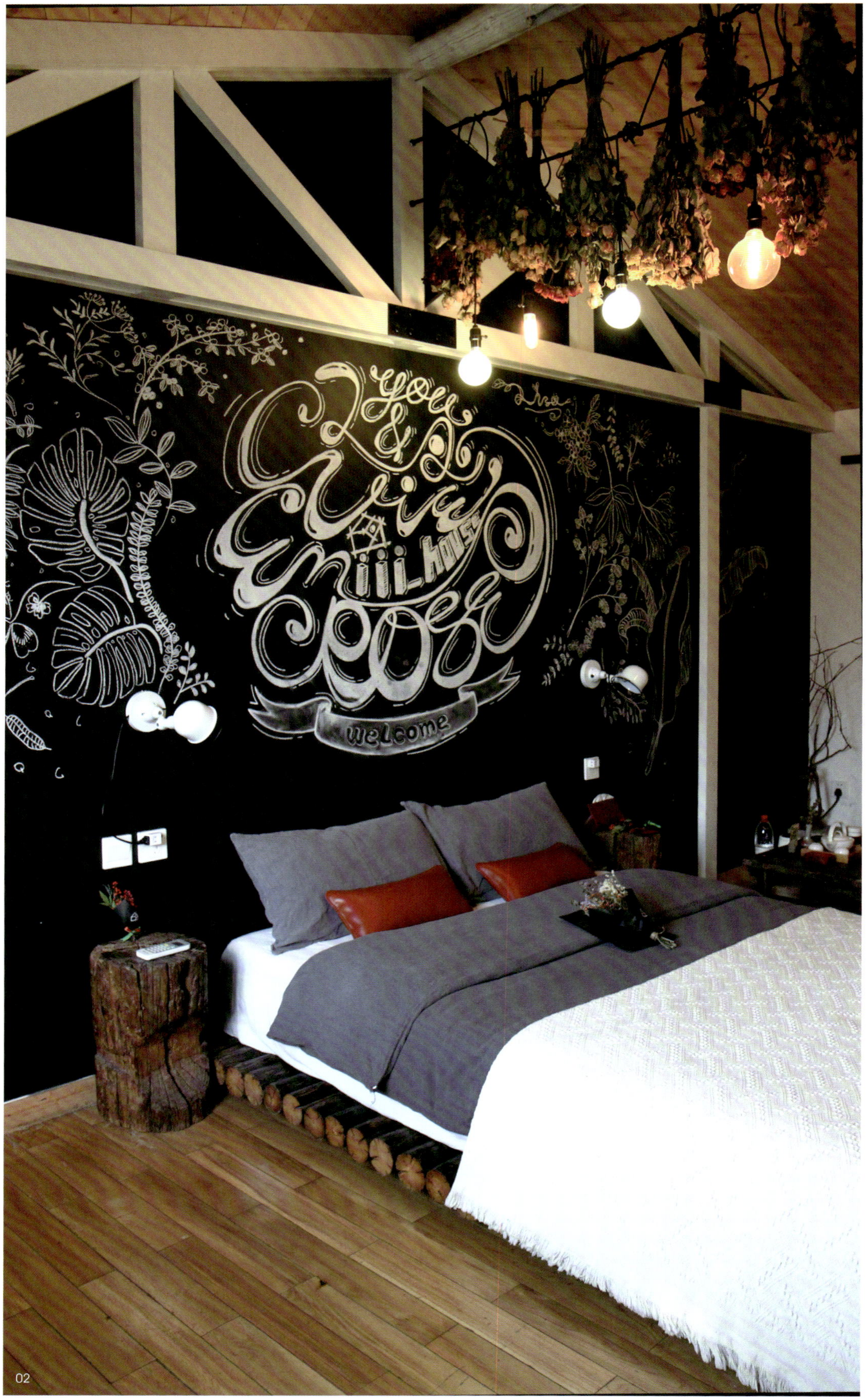

02

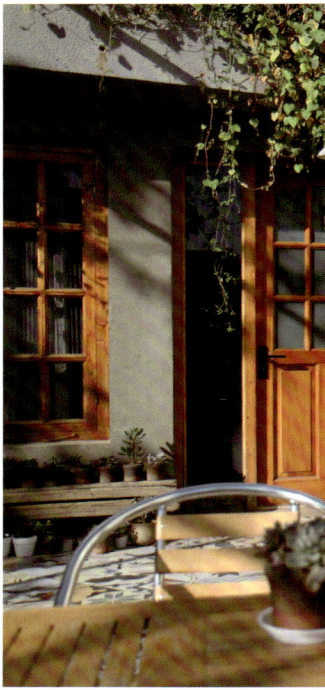

02 / Huajian Room
03 / Public terrace
04 / Cafe on first floor
05 / Public terrace

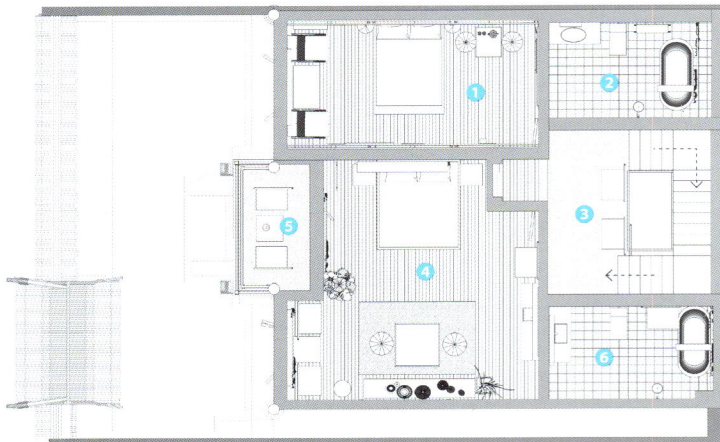

Second-floor plan

① Bedroom in Huajian
② Toilet in Huajian
③ Staircase
④ Bedroom in Chimu
⑤ Balcony in Chimu
⑥ Toilet in Chimu

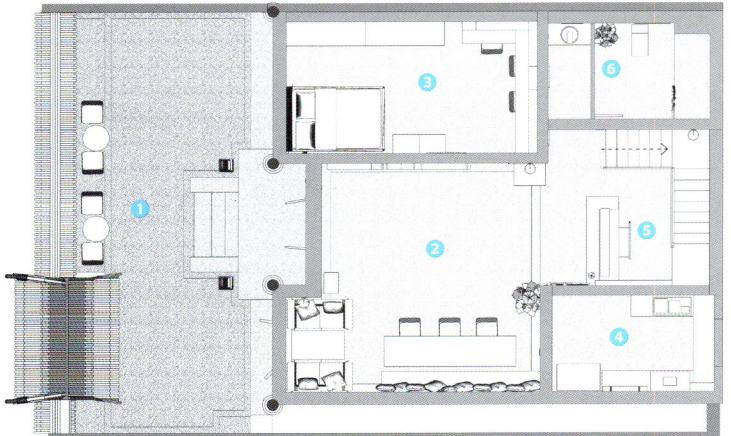

First-floor plan

① Small yard
② Living room
③ Duty room
④ Kitchen
⑤ Bar counter
⑥ Toilet

06 / Suye Room
07 / Jingqian Room
08 / Small terrace out of Jingqian Room
09 / Living room in Jingqian Room

① Staircase
② Terrace garden
③ Living room (Cangji)
④ Bedroom (Suye)
⑤ Toilet (Suye)
⑥ Stairs (Jingqian)
⑦ Terrace (Jingqian)
⑧ Bedroom (Jingqian)
⑨ Toilet (Jingqian)
⑩ Bedroom (Cangji)
⑪ Toilet (Cangji)

Third-floor plan

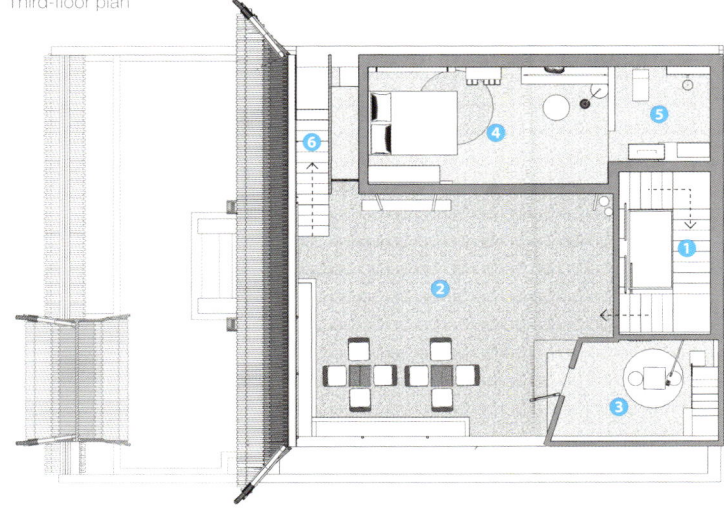

Fourth-floor plan

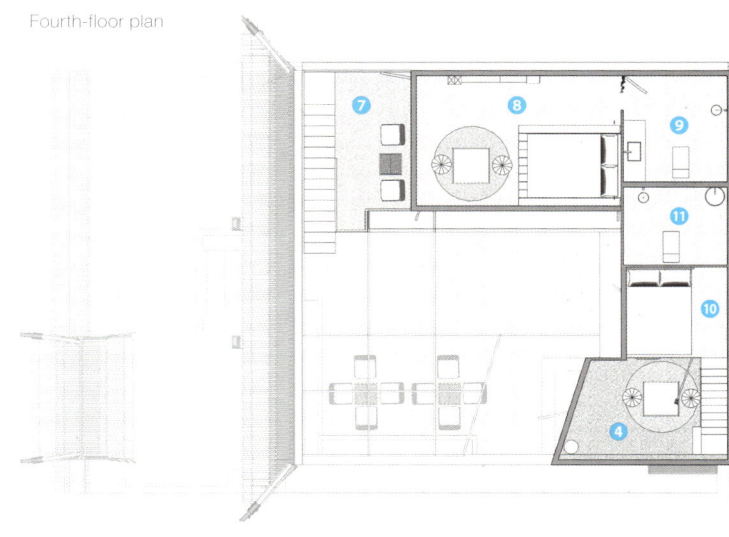

10 / Living room in Cangji Room
11 / Chimu Room
12 / Living room in Chimu Room

Location /
Florida, United States

Architecture and design /
TS Adams Studio, Architects, Inc., Tim Adams, Courtney Dickey

Photography /
Emily J. Followill

Written and produced /
Lisa Mowry

Florida home with relaxed patina

This is a vacation home for a family and their visitors and guests. The home's main level is wrapped around a courtyard that's key to the airy look and casual feel of the interiors. Retractable doors in the great-room open to the courtyard, which includes a sitting area, water feature, and summer house—the latter a multipurpose television-watching and dining area that can be screened off from insects.

The alfresco living area is complete with weather-resistant sofas, a bar/potting shed cove, and container trees, which serve as a room divider. Limestone tiles provide the main flooring for the space, but the water feature includes a small wooden bridge—a particular treat to play on for the Harrises' young visitors. For the courtyard water feature, the architect combined a small gunite pool with a recirculating pump and copper spouts, keeping the depth very shallow. As an added bonus, the gurgling sound drowns out any neighborhood noise, and provides a spa-like visual presence.

The exterior's hipped roof, shutters, and large columns take their architectural cues from French Low Country style. The interior pays homage to the style by calling on natural materials—such as reclaimed wood, Venetian plaster, and brick—to lend subtle yet rich texture to the walls. Heart-pine boards line the great-room's 14-foot (4.3 meters) tall ceilings, and reclaimed cypress cabinets in the kitchen add a layer of warmth.

01 / Front elevation
02 / View between carriage houses towards courtyard

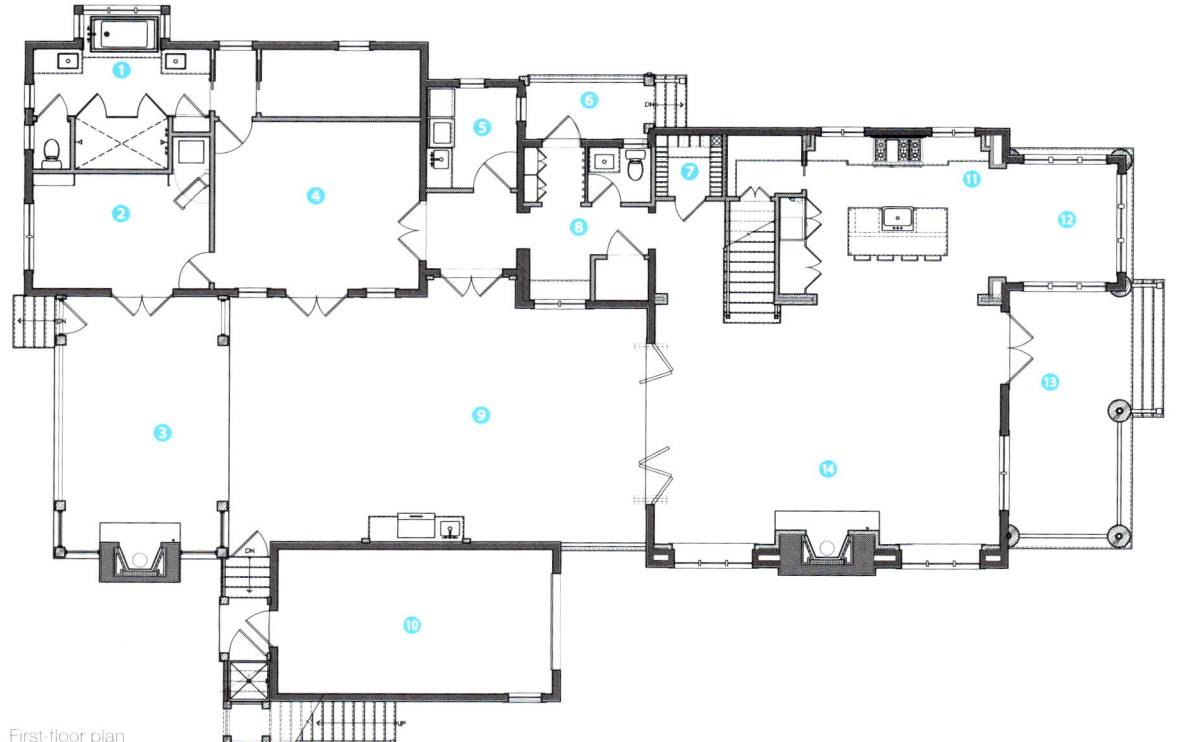

First-floor plan

1. Master bathroom
2. Study
3. Summer house
4. Master bedroom
5. Laundry
6. Side porch
7. Wine room
8. Sand room
9. Sitting terrace
10. Car garage
11. Kitchen
12. Breakfast room
13. Front porch
14. Great room

180 Urban Guest House

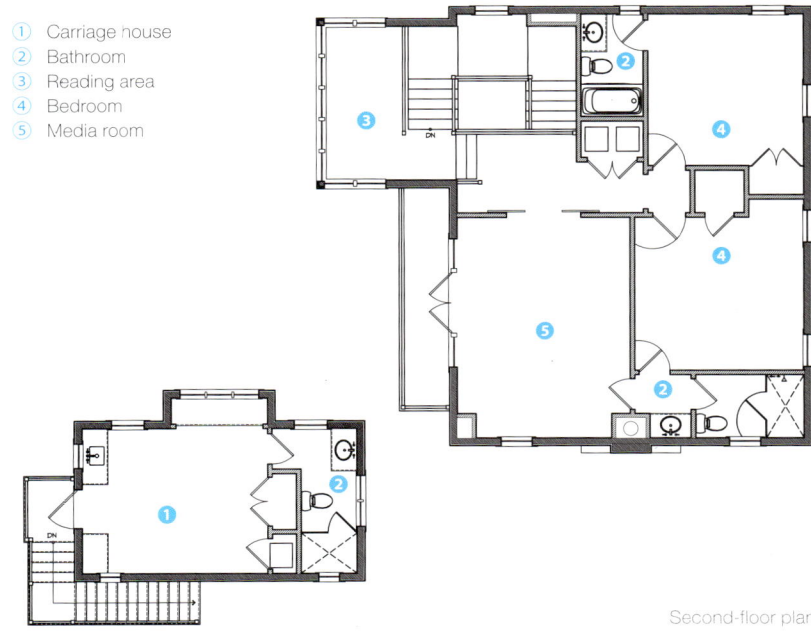

① Carriage house
② Bathroom
③ Reading area
④ Bedroom
⑤ Media room

Second-floor plan

03 / Courtyard
04 / Great Room towards kitchen
05 / Great Room towards fireplace

06 / Back hall towards bedroom
07 / Staircase
08 / Stair landing
09 / Sitting area
10 / Kitchen
11 / Master bathroom
12 / Master bedroom

Location /
Bruton, Somerset, United Kingdom

Area /
2583 square feet (240 square meters)

Architecture and design /
Emil Eve Architects

Photography /
Mariell Lind Hansen

Quaperlake Street

Quaperlake Street, located in Bruton, Somerset, was extensively reconfigured, refurbished, and extended to contain Caro Somerset, a new lifestyle store, café, and bed and breakfast, as well as a private family home for owners Natalie and Tom.

With its low ceilings and doors, uneven walls and floors, and original features, the shop and café were never going to be slick white designer spaces, neither did the designers want to over-reveal or strip back and expose surfaces in a shabby-chic style. Instead, they sought to place flexible furniture pieces into the rooms and to use original elements of the building, such as the fireplaces, niches, and deep window reveals for display. Materials and colors were chosen to complement the existing character of the rooms: shady, welcoming, and intimate.

The existing shop-front was restored, revealing beautiful green tiling. Through this doorway, visitors immediately enter the café where they can perch at the counter with a coffee and cake, or retreat to the calm salon. The historic arrangement of the rooms was retained and visitors pass from one cellular room to the next, each with a different character. The nature of the furniture allows these spaces to be rearranged so repeat customers may discover a different place to sit, and certainly new things to buy, on their return.

The rear extension provides a larger open-plan space for contemporary living. Externally, the mass of the extension has been broken down into three volumes to reflect the proportions and volumes of existing house, which has been added to many times over the years. Natalie and Tom were keen to avoid a glass-box type extension with large-sliding doors, and so forth. So, instead the designers created an articulated volume with large uninterrupted framed views of the garden.

Upstairs, alongside the family's three bedrooms, is the one B&B room with large en-suite bathroom. Guests enter through the family's street entrance and past their living and dining spaces. Once in their suite they find themselves in a quiet and cozy private world, with a free-standing bath and complimentary breakfast at The Chapel the next morning.

01 / Façade of 18th-century stonework
02–04 / Rear extension clad in larch boards

05–06 / Plants decorating interior
07 / Dark green living areas complementing outdoors

Floor plan

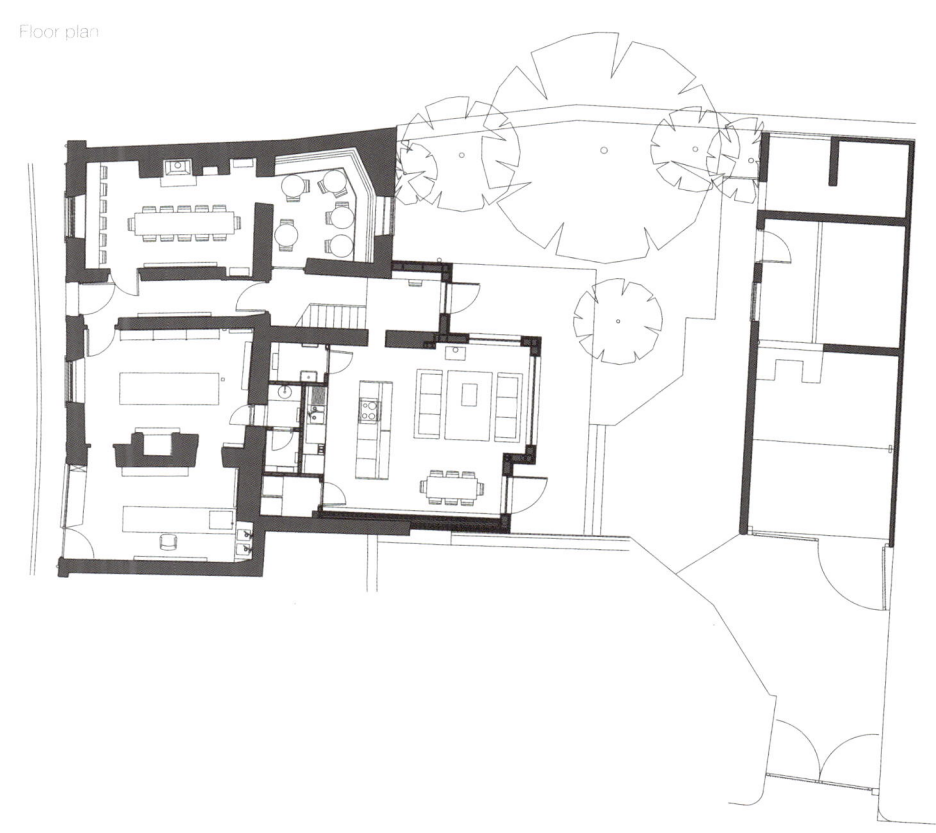

08–09 / Gift shop with custom furniture
10–11 / Public kitchen and dining area
12 / Smaller room in original house

13 / Original details accented with contemporary furniture
14–16 / View of different guest suites

Štajnhaus

Location /
Mikulov, Czech Republic

Area /
1302 square feet
(121 square meters)

Architecture and design /
ORA Atelier Znojmo
– architect Jan Hora,
architect Jan Veisser and
architect Barbara Hora

Photography /
Jakub Skokan, Martin
Tůma / BoysPlayNice

The Štajnhaus was not so much a project, rather it was a process. This house with a Renaissance core stands right at the foot of the chateau hill, in the former Jewish quarter of Mikulov. Throughout its existence it has suffered many scars, going through dozens of reconstructions and operations. All of these have altered the house beyond recognition. Yet it has maintained its almost medieval picturesqueness.

The more individual layers, spaces, and surprising circumstances the designers uncovered, the more revisions and alterations they had to make in this project; and this lasted until the end of realization. They wanted to preserve the house as an organic unit—there are no straight walls or rectangular openings—so they had to reinvent and remake to measure all the elements.

Originally, their job was just interior design. Gradually, however, they realized that the interior and exterior could not be solved separately, as the space and the shapes blended together and created an indivisible unit.

The house was reconstructed for the needs of a guest house, with part of it to be used as a private flat by the owner and the remaining rooms for guest houses. Each room is unique; each has its own specific atmosphere, while the wine cellars under the house have returned to their original use.

Section plan

01 / View of tower courtyard
02 / Alley in back of house

03 / Bike shed
04 / Entrance hall
05 / Clothes rack with seat
06 / Wine cellar

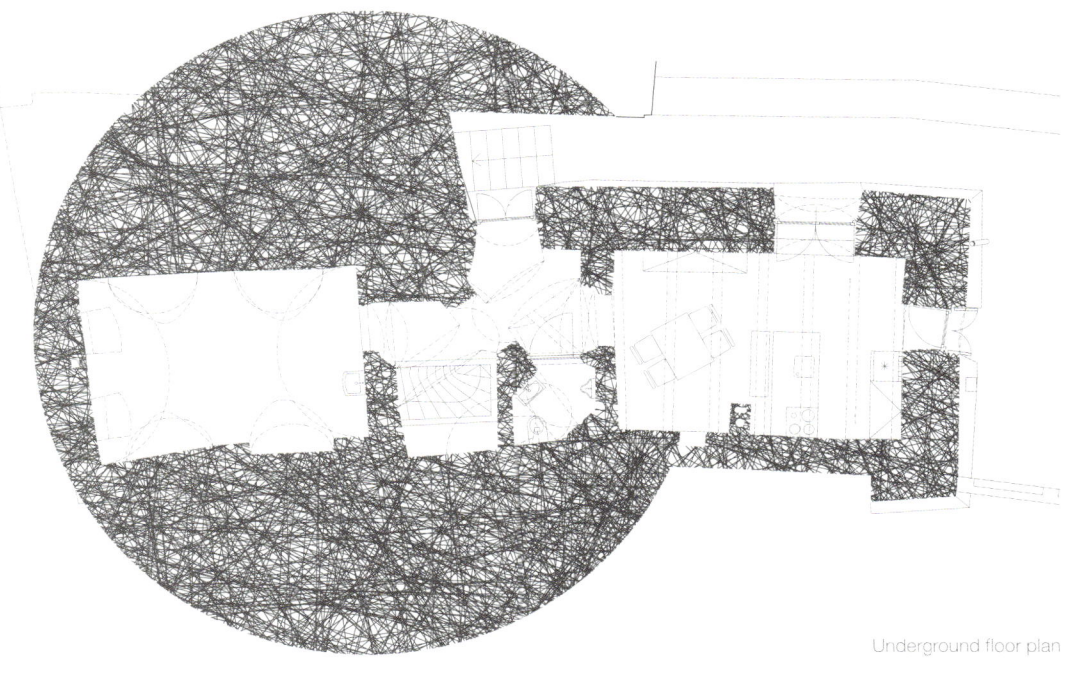

Underground floor plan

First-floor plan

07 / Shared kitchen
08 / Skylight
09 / Windows looking out towards stairs
10 / Staircase

196　Urban Guest House

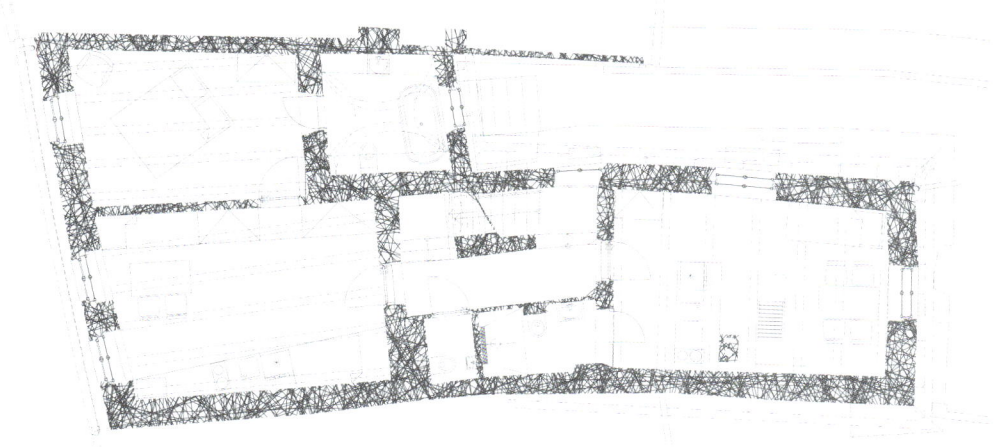

Third-floor plan

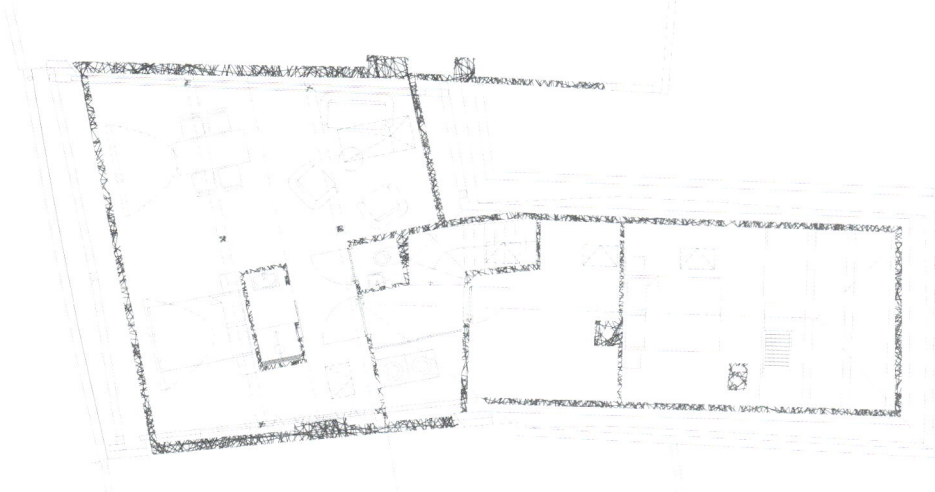

Second-floor plan

198   Urban Guest House

11 / Green loft room
12 / White room
13 / Bathroom of grey room
14 / Flooring of green room
15 / White room
16 / Blue room

Location /
London, United Kingdom

Area /
2851 square feet
(265 square meters)

Architecture and design /
Hostem Limited

Photography /
Courtesy of The New Road Residence

The New Road Residence

The New Road Residence—a project initiated by Hostem founder James Brown and artistic director Christie Fels—is a curated residence located in Whitechapel that is available for short to long stays.

The house is a showcase of fine linens, art, furniture, books, and objects. Set within the intimacy of a private home, it is an immersive environment in which the products and surroundings interweave seamlessly. This project was the living, breathing culmination of the designer's Hostem's ever-growing identity. Wisteria-clad and carefully refurbished, New Road is a 1797 Georgian townhouse that sprawls across approximately 2851 square feet (265 square meters) of open-plan living areas and accommodation for up to six guests.

Working fireplaces on every floor make it an ideal winter retreat, and a truly unique opportunity to experience one of the most historically preserved houses in East London. Once a linen drapers' store, its immaculate character has been retained in the detailing—cornices depict vines and hops, while views over a private walled garden are framed by a bay window across the lower, first, and second floors. Original stripped wide pine floorboards and paneling feature throughout. An open-plan kitchen and second dining area include their own fireplaces, an original Georgian pantry, larder, and wine cellar. A private, west-facing garden can be accessed either through a glass-roofed summerhouse or through the kitchen's dining area.

The original staircase leads to a gracious master bedroom and en-suite bathroom and dressing room with a freestanding copper bath and wrap-around wardrobes. A beautifully tiled shower room caters for the two large double bedrooms found on the third floor. Through minimal structural intervention, an aesthetic overhaul transformed New Road into a rustic and minimal haven, with an utmost attention to comfort and detail. A serene and earthen color palette extends from the original framework and stone flooring towards harmonious elemental tones, which in the bedrooms includes deep greens, warm reds, and pops of chocolate or chartreuse by way of Once Milano bed linen paired with luxurious Norvegr goose down duvets.

Elsewhere, the mid-century elegance of Pierre Jeanneret writing desks, chairs, and card tables is countered by the abstract, textural richness of artworks curated by Stuart Shave/Modern Art, from the likes of Tory Thornton, Mark Flood, Richard Tuttle, and Paul Lee. New industrial design pieces by Faye Toogood counteract the building's historical roots, while blending seamlessly with other organic décor elements.

Throughout New Road, functional homewares from Labor & Wait enhance the practical aspect of the living spaces, allowing guests to feel truly independent and at home.

01 / Exterior of building
02 / Living room

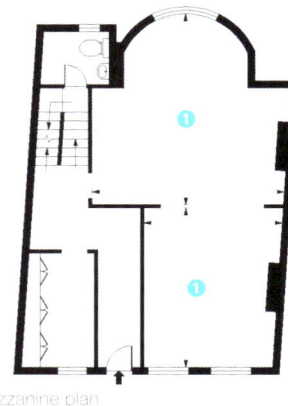

Mezzanine plan

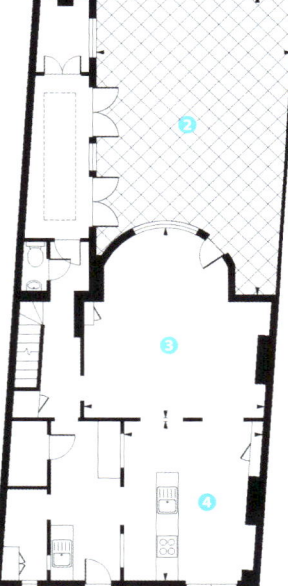

First-floor plan

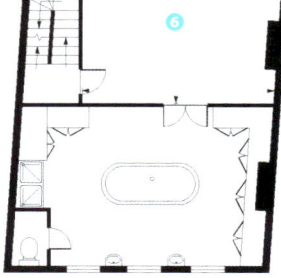

Third-floor plan

Second-floor plan

1. Reception
2. Garden
3. Dining room
4. Kitchen
5. Bedroom
6. Master bedroom

03 / View from courtyard
04 / Room with plenty of natural light
05 / Living room
06 / Dining table beside fireplace
07 / Shelf for displaying glass sculpture

08 / Chair beside entrance
09 / Table in corner
10 / Dinning area
11 / Old-fashioned fireplace
12 / Narrow staircase

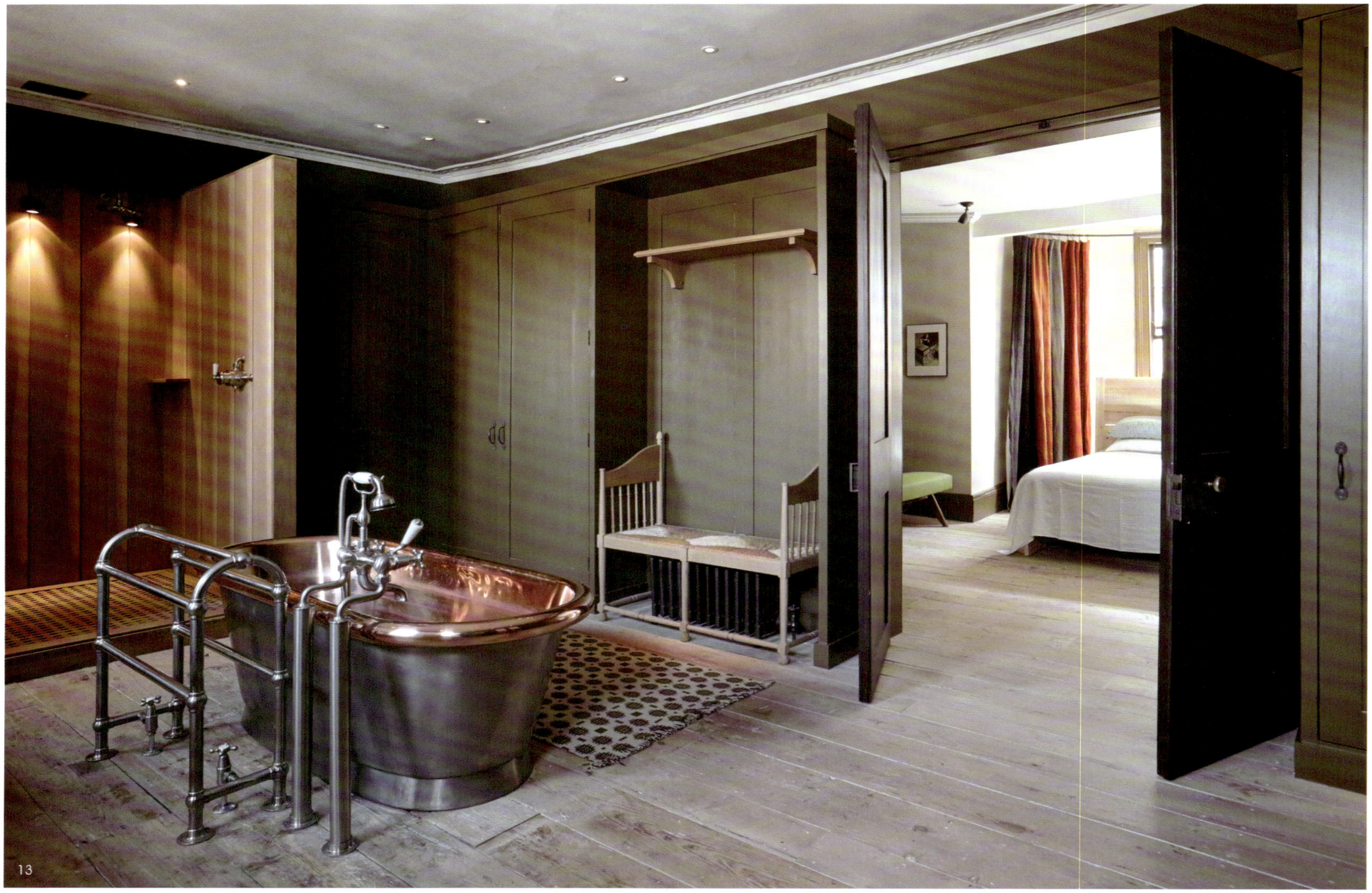

13

14

15

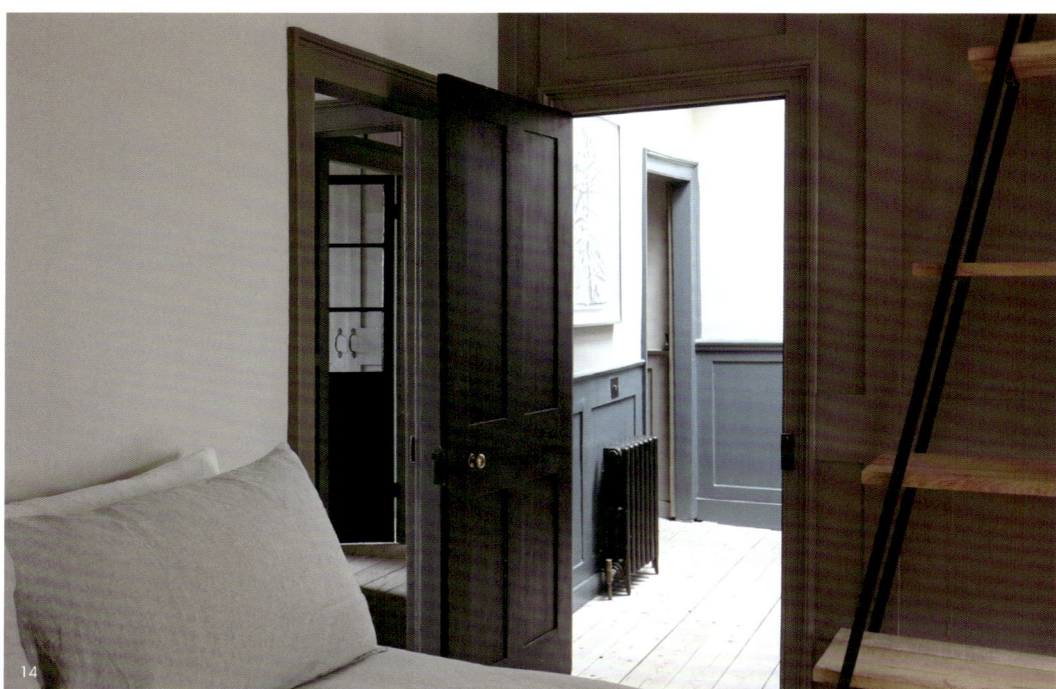

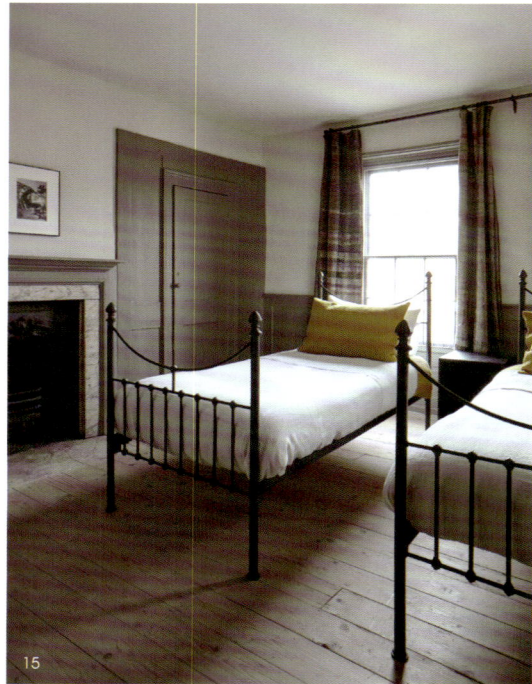

13 / Master bedroom and outside bath
14 / Door connecting inside and outside
15 / Double bedroom
16 / Partial view of bathroom

Location /
New Forest National Park, Hampshire, United Kingdom

Area /
2422 square feet (225 square meters)

Architecture and design /
PAD Studio Ltd.

Photography /
Nigel Ridgen

Warborne Farm – The Long Barn

Warborne Farm, located within a conservation area of the New Forest National Park, was built as a model farm in 1880. It is now a multi-award-winning organic farm, which has featured in several television documentaries.

The Georgian farm buildings were organized in a courtyard arrangement around the farmhouse and have for many years lain redundant. Farm diversification is now necessary and the owners decided to offer holiday accommodation on the farm where tenants could become involved with farm life and learn more about sustainable living.

The refurbishment provided five flexible farmstay units, which can accommodate up to 30 people per week. The alterations are sympathetic, highly sustainable, and retain the existing rural character of the barns. The double-height living spaces allow the buildings glorious proportions to be appreciated and add a sense of drama while helping to give the cottages a feeling of spaciousness.

Working closely with the client, on a very low budget, quirky features were introduced; including up-cycled furniture, recycled flooring, and family-made basins and kitchens, which fit with the ethos of the farm as a whole and the fun-loving nature of the client.

Mezzanine galleries and stair insertions form a contemporary counterpoint to the agricultural brick exterior and internally the walls are insulated using sheep's wool and recycled plastic bottles, a highly sustainable form of insulation. All the materials used were as natural and as locally sourced as possible. Biomass log burners within each unit provide a warm focal point and a carbon-neutral heating source.

Externally, the landscaping further increases the rich biodiversity that exists within the farm. A new gravel parking area is screened by fruit trees and a communal garden area was formed within a new natural meadow grass area. Raised beds are located close to the garden, allowing visitors to tend and pick their own vegetables.

01 / Full view of building
02 / Kitchen with comfortable living space
03 / Rest area
04 / Dining room

Sections

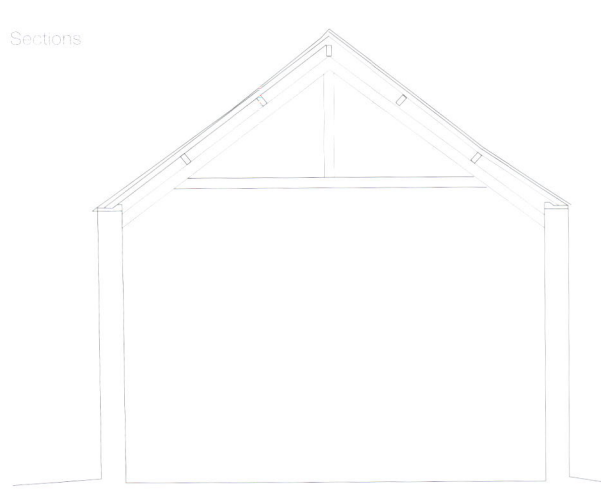

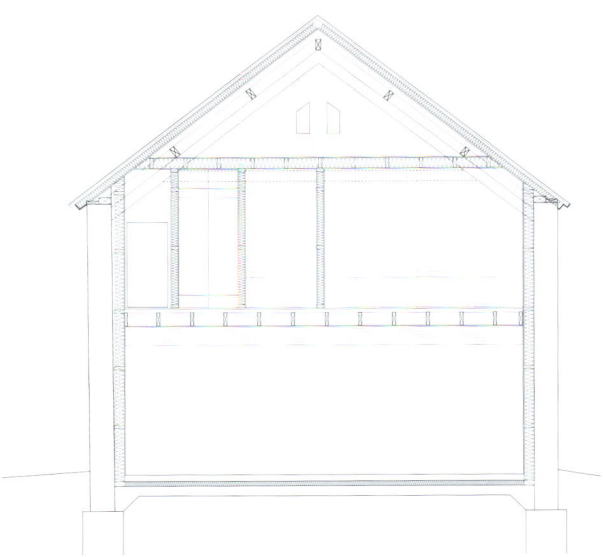

05 / Rest area
06 / Kitchen

07 / Kitchen
08 / Bedroom
09 / Bathroom with bathtub
10 / Attic seating area

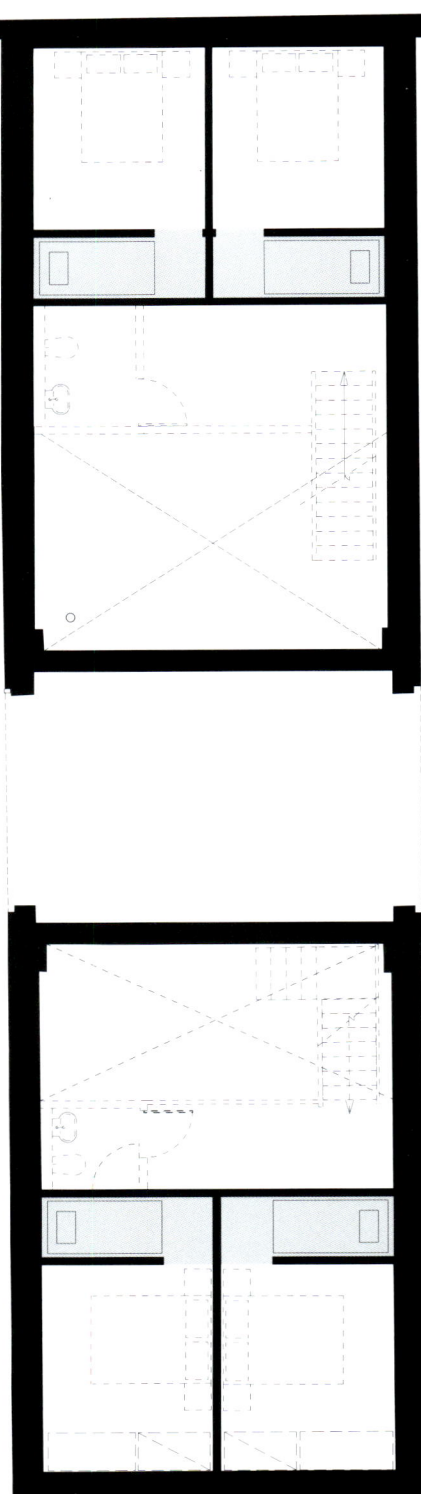

Loft plan

11 / Living room
12 / Stairs to attic
13 / Dining area

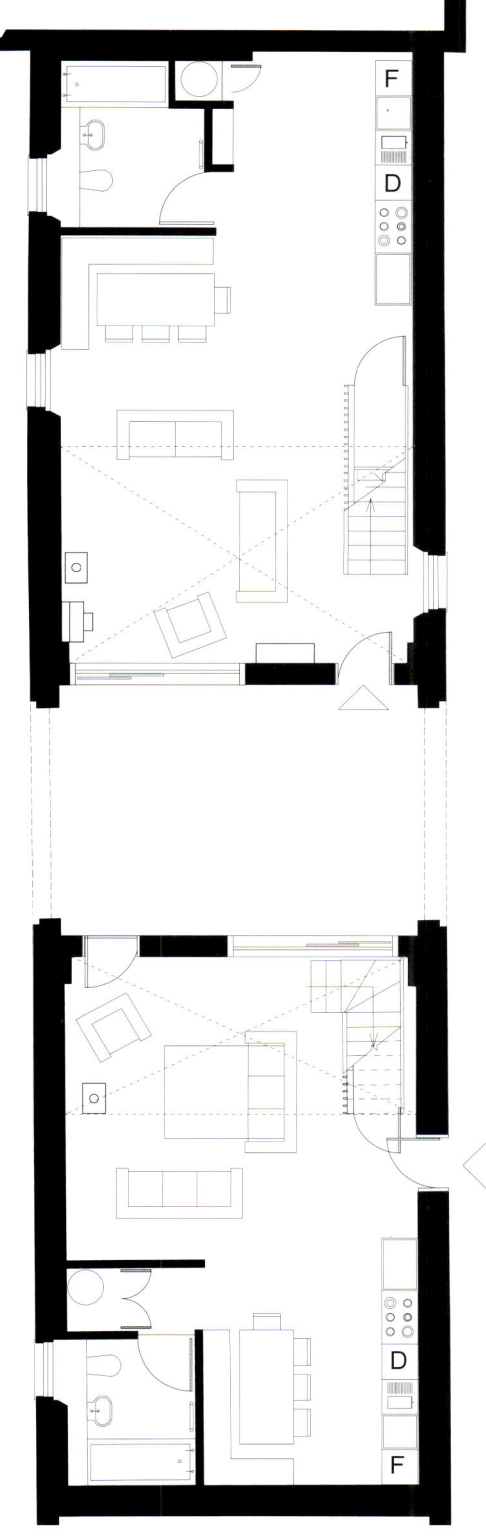

Ground floor plan

Mr. Yao's house #1

Location /
Wenzhou, Zhejiang, China

Area /
1119 square feet
(104 square meters)

Architecture and design /
Yaoliang Architecture and Space Design Office

Photography /
Xu Ninglong

Situated on Huagang Island in Dongtou County of Wenzhou, a coastal city of China, Mr. Yao's house#1 was transformed from a stone house. Based on the design concept of dual roles, the design of this single-family residential holiday accommodation sought to borrow elements from the surrounding natural environment.

In front of the house is a road of a fishing village. The designer used the space on both sides of the house to create a small courtyard enclosed with local stones. The stone enclosure and the stone wall of building extend in the same direction, which makes the building itself integrate into the local environment better. The existing small windows along the road of fishing village were reserved. This would not only retain the quality of stone house, but also make the indoor living space more private.

As for the stone wall in front and the steel glass under roof tiles, the designer made a ribbon-like lighting to reduce the sense of closeness indoor caused by a large area of stone wall. The back of the building against the mountain used large transparent glass walls, which is barely noticeable from the outside, but produces a strong contrast on visually and allows the people living inside the house to get closer to nature in all weather conditions.

The interior designer features a striped void structure throughout the upper and lower floors in an area of 538 square feet (50 square meters) on each floor to make the form of the indoor space look free and easy. A fully open kitchen was placed on the lower layer and the intermediate area can be used as a pastry-making table, as well as a dining bar.

More interestingly, an open tub and shower can be seen from the kitchen. The kitchen and dining space, the open shower space, and the real flame fireplace are arranged in 538 square feet (50 square meters) of space.

The stair extending through the hollow structure to the bedroom space on the upper floor is also fully open. The sofa at the corner of the upper floor and the couch in front of the bed make sleeping, living, and relaxing fully integrated.

There was no additional landscape design—the housing relationships interweave with the natural environment against the mountain outside the glass curtain wall of the building.

01 / Façade of Mr Yao's house#1 at noon
02 / Courtyard and building

Building elevation A

Building elevation B

Building elevation C

03–04 / Wooden door of courtyard and landscape at entrance
05 / Bathroom with skylight on top

Sections

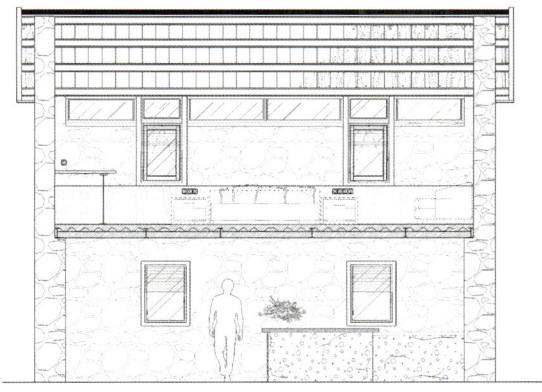
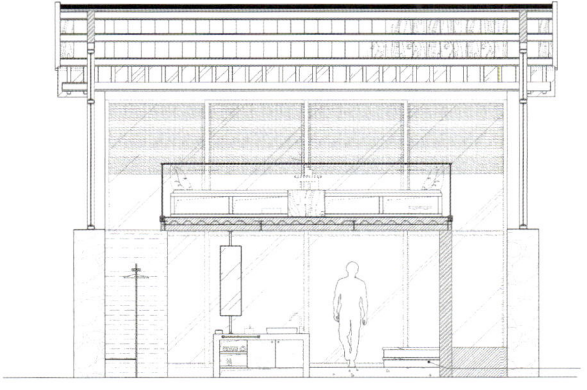

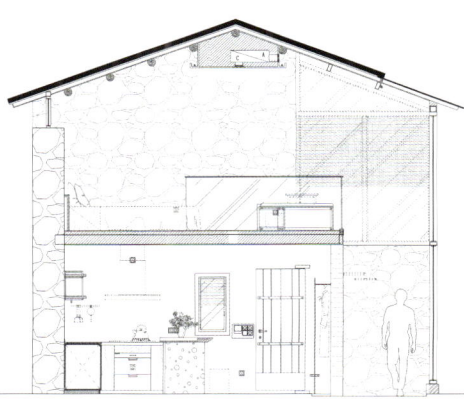
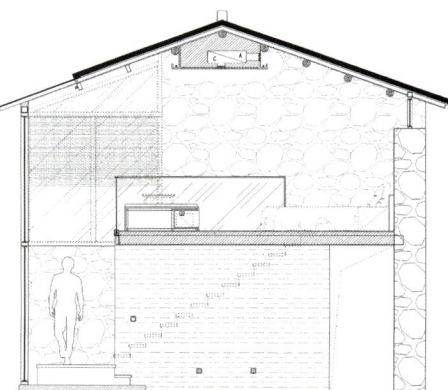

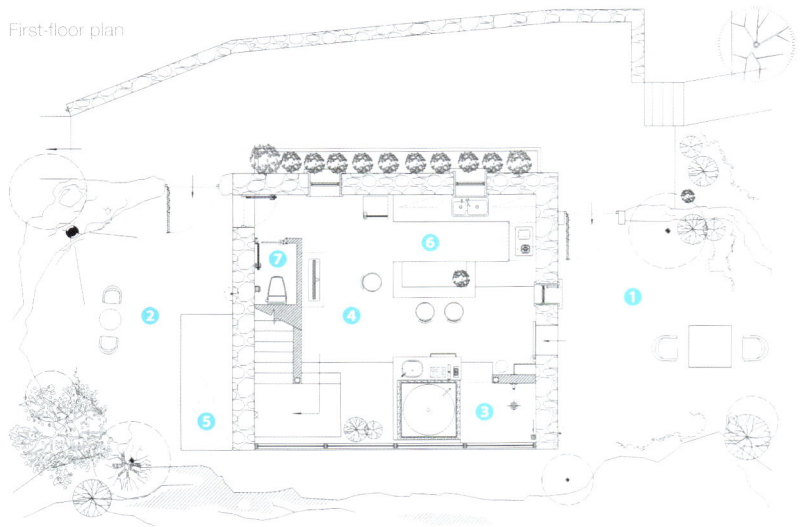

First-floor plan

Second-floor plan

1) Front yard
2) Back yard
3) Bathroom
4) Leisure area
5) Equipment room
6) Kitchen
7) Toilet

1) Bedroom
2) Leisure couch
3) Tea counter
4) Lounge

09

10

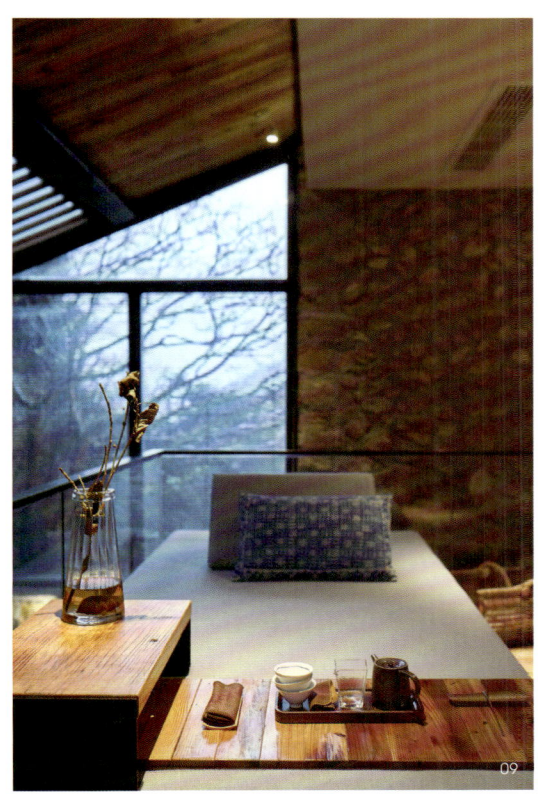

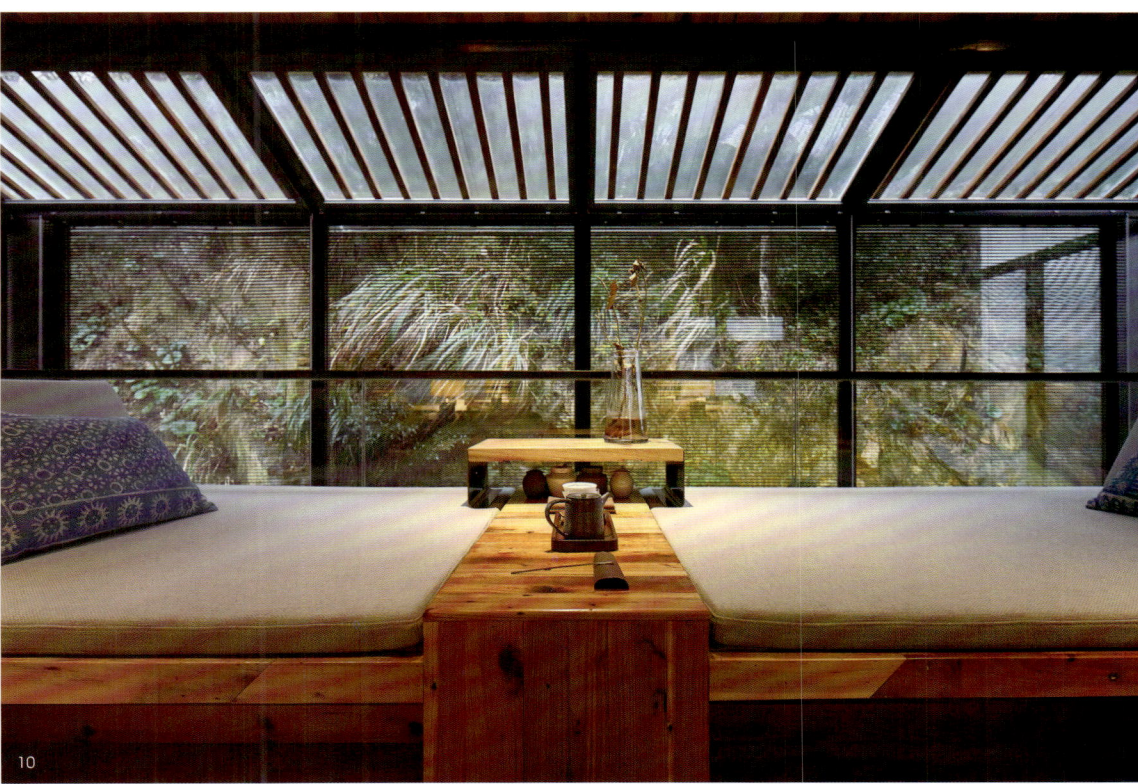

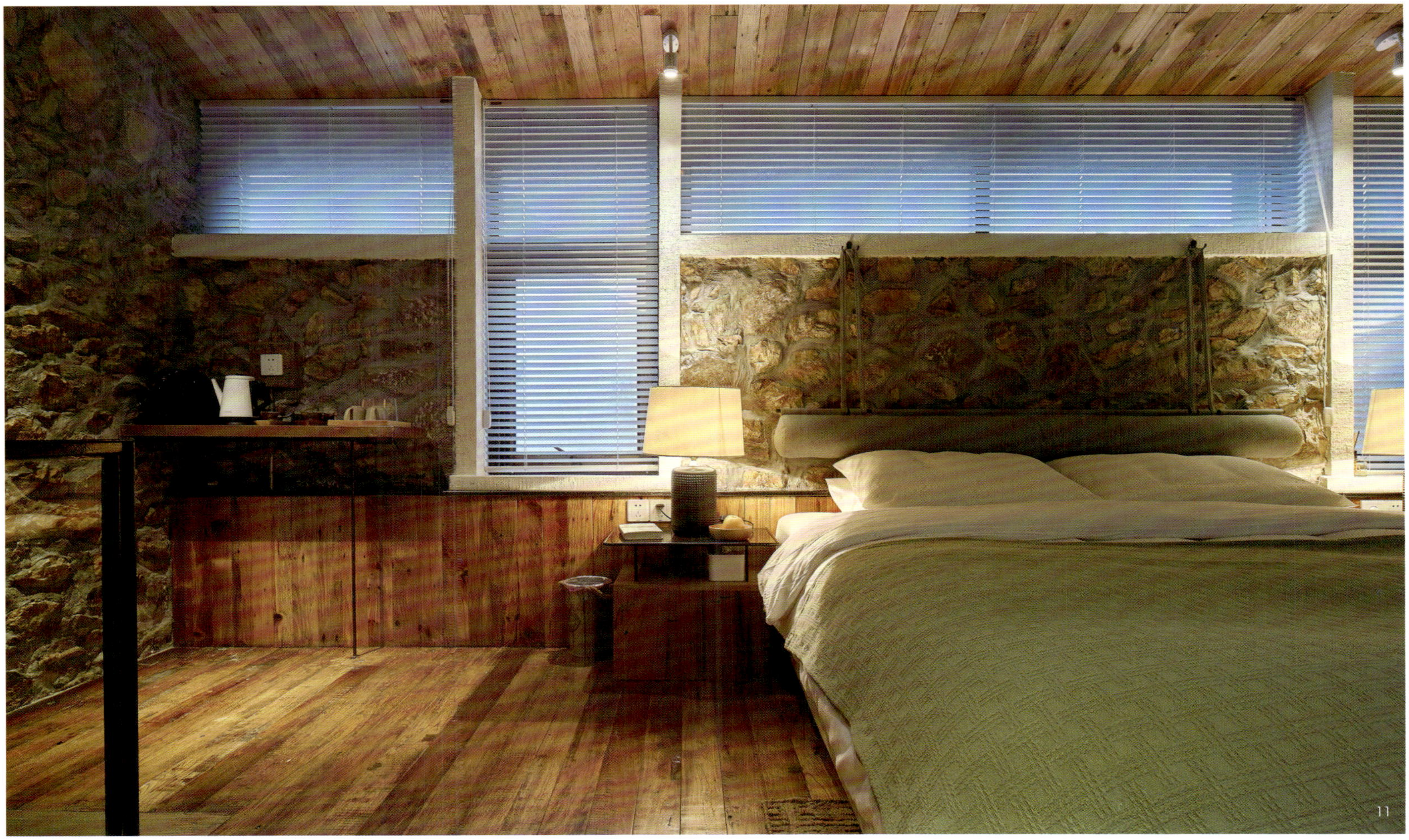

11

06 / Kitchen and dining area on first floor
07 / View of outdoors from dining area
08 / Indoor lounge
09–11 / Bedrooms on second floor with tatami mats for drinking or sleeping on

Location /
Acanceh, Yucatán, México

Area /
166,841 square feet
(15,500 square meters)

Architecture and design /
Salvador Reyes Ríos
and Josefina Larraín
Lagos, reyes ríos + larraín
arquitectos

Photography /
Pim Schalkwijk,
Rafael Lizárraga

Hacienda Sac Chich, Casa de Maquinas – Casa Sisal

The hacienda was built between 1890-1910 for the production of henequen fiber. The eclectic style and construction period correspond to the late 19th century, the peak of Yucatan's henequen haciendas. Similar to the fate of many other hacienda ensembles, after falling from its original use, the hacienda was divided among several proprietors. The main house remained as a living place, part of the lands was adapted as a nursery, while the Machine House was dismantled and left unused.

By 1990, it had lost more than half its roof structures and several rooms were misused as dumpsters. That same year, a couple of foreign artists acquired the property. They partially restored it and adapted it as their country house. Later in 2002, Howard and Cyndy Berger bought the property from them and began working on a full-scale restoration project, divided into two phases with the help of architect Salvador Reyes Ríos and designer Josefina Larrain.

The first phase (2003-04) comprised the conversion of old storage rooms of henequen bales into three new rooms with their own bathroom each. The master bedroom encompasses the complete section of the storage room, measuring 20 by 40 feet (6 by 12 meters) with an interior height of 23 feet (8 meters height).

In order to conserve the perception of the original continuous space, the division from the bathroom was achieved with the use of screens and curtains. A noticeable element of this area was the conversion of the former melting pit into a down-level living room. The creation of a frieze that frames the original wall's patina and follows the space perimeter is also a significant element of design as well as a witness of the previous condition of the space.

The second phase (2008–09) covered the upgrade of the ancient space occupied by the henequen's shredding machine into a terrace, as well as the construction of a sculptural stairway to access an open terrace on the roof. The water collection tanks were adapted as water gardens all along the complex. Additionally, a new guest house was built in the area of the old drying field where traditionally henequen was hung to dry.

The floor, ceilings, and walls of the new house were completely covered with masilla de chukum, a mix of white cement with the resin extracted from the local tree of chukum. Two large glass panels and two mosquito nets glide and hide completely to open or close the space towards the terrace. All of the interior design and furniture for both phases were designed accordingly.

01 / Southwest view of Casa Sisal

Master plan

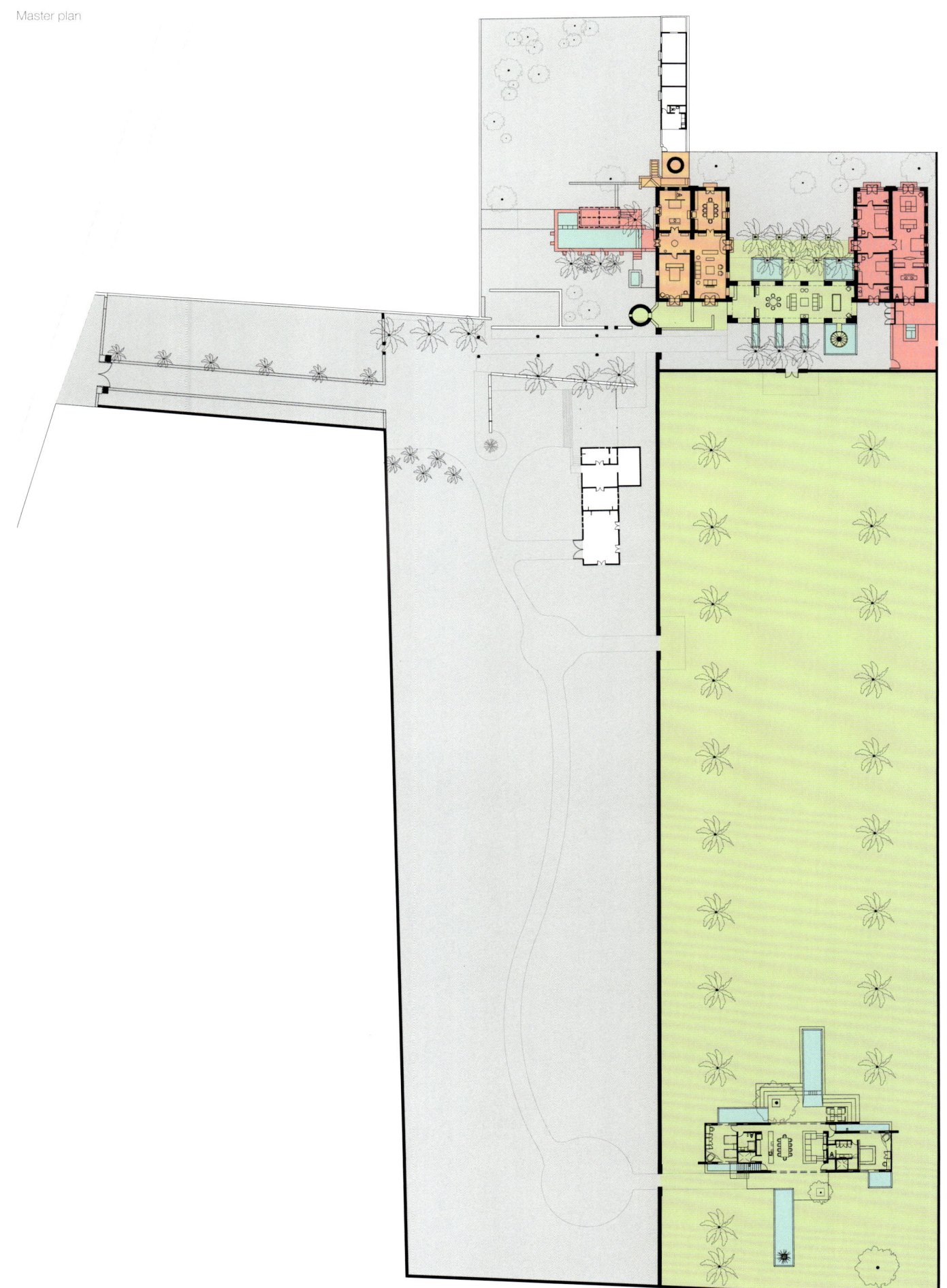

02 / Water gardens
03 / North façade
04 / Hacienda pool with old chimney behind
05 / Interior of Casa Sisal

06 / Master bedroom
07 / Common area
08 / Master bedroom
09 / Hacienda kitchen

East elevation

Cross sections of Casa Sisal

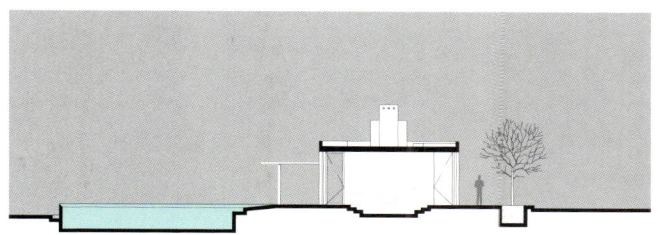

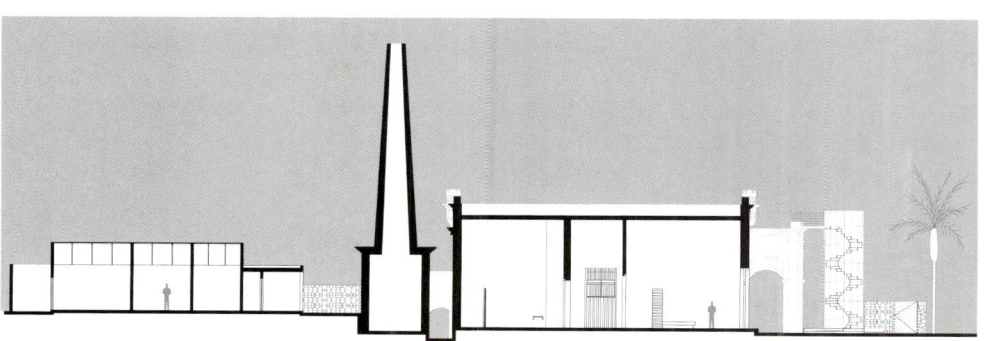

Location /
Wenzhou, Zhejiang, China

Area /
3197 square feet
(297 square meters)

Architecture and design /
Yaoliang Architecture and Space Design Office

Photography /
Xu Ninglong

Mr. Yao's house #30

MR Yao's house #30 is located in the Dongtou district of Wenzhou, Zhejiang Province. This building is 19.7 feet (6 meters) long and 22 feet (6.7 meters) deep. In the past, supplies were so scarce that the entire village was built with local materials.

The original building, constructed with local 24-inch (60-centimeter) thick stone, is a common dwelling of this fishing village. This building faces the sea with the hills for a background and is situated at the highest point of the fish village; as such, it has a very broad view. Due to its high ground, people can see dense stone houses here. These houses are built on mountains, and the path among houses as well as the wind-resistant tiles under stone form a unique scene of human life.

The fishing village is located on the edge of the island where the sea breeze is strong. Affected by the monsoon, the precipitation is intense, so the scale of doors and windows is narrow to keep out wind and rain. The designer retained the unique style of the stone houses on the island and put tables and chairs by the window. Guests can read books, drinking tea, chat, or think by the window to experience the poetry of life in this fishing village.

Since MR Yao's house #30 occupies a large area, taking more possibilities of business operations into account, the design team made a special design on the circulation and designed this guest house into a townhouse that can be split. The circulation of one duplex starts from the front yard, the outdoor terrace to the dining room and then to the bedroom on the second floor, while the circulation of another suite starts from the backyard, the living room on the second floor to the dining room on the first floor and then to the front yard. The front yard was divided into two parts, separated by a yard gate. If there are several families holidaying at the same time, the yard gate can be opened to convert the guest house into two living rooms, two dining rooms and four separate bedrooms.

The natural landscape around the guest house is relatively weak, so the designers hoped that the transformation of stone houses of this fishing village could bring a new form of business and attract more types of people to live there in order to create a new human landscape that reflects the spirit of the times on the basis of protecting the original dwellings.

01 / Building exterior and surrounding landscape
02 / Building façade and courtyard in dusk

03

Building façades

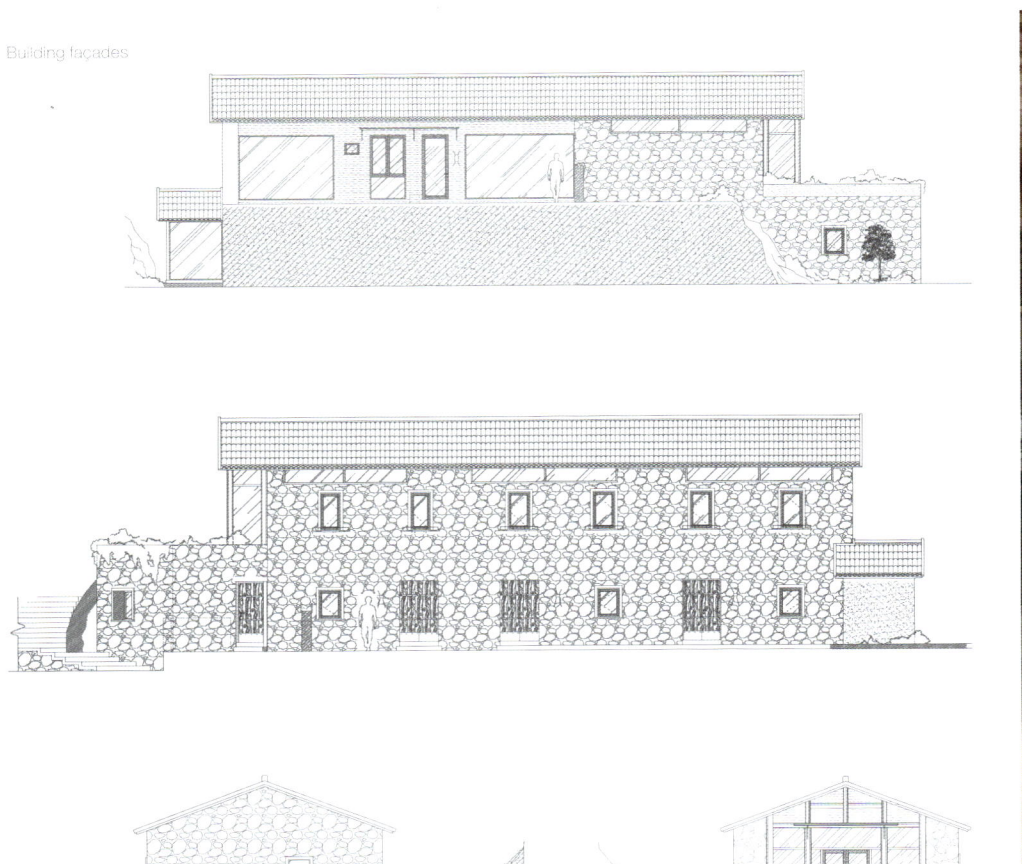

04

228   Rural Guest House

03 / Public lounge on first floor
04 / Kitchen and dining area on first floor
05 / Lounge in suite
06 / Lounge on second floor

07 / King-sized room on first floor
08 / Guest room on second floor
09 / Sightseeing terrace on second floor of suite
10 / Bathroom on first floor of suite

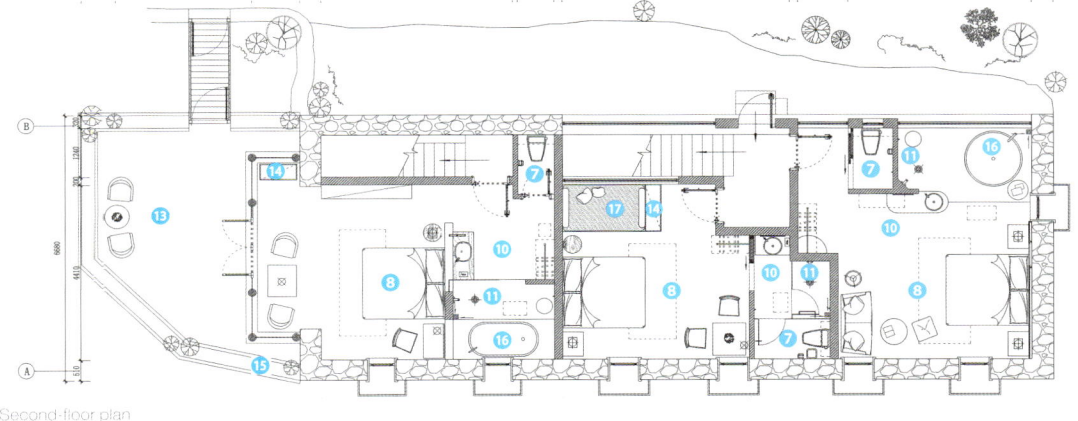

Second-floor plan

1. Kitchen
2. Dining room
3. Living room
4. Outdoor leisure area
5. Storeroom
6. Dressing room
7. Toilet
8. Guest room
9. Leisure area
10. Drying area
11. Shower room
12. Garden
13. Terrace
14. Water bar
15. Green area
16. Bathtub
17. Couch for relaxing

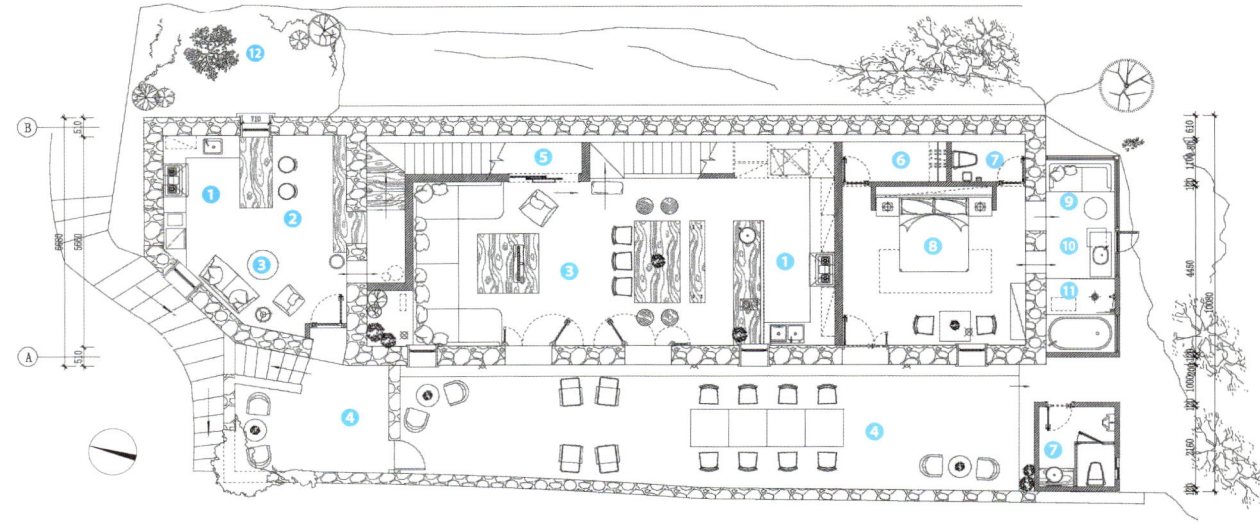

First-floor plan

Location /
Andratx, Mallorca, Spain

Area /
4392 square feet
(408 square meters)

Architecture and design /
APM, Mallorca

Photography /
APM

Can Guix

Can Guix is a historic Porta Mallorquin estate surrounded by the idyllic scenery of the Sierra Tramuntana Mountains overlooking the town of Andratx with views to Puerto de Andratx and the open sea. The aim of this ambitious restoration project was to renovate and rejuvenate this expansive Mallorquin finca and two other out buildings.

The result was a dramatic change from small, dark rooms to light-filled large open spaces retaining the property's best traditional features and enhancing these with a modern slant to create something quite unique. The façade was entirely restored and the stone facing replaced. All the windows and glass paneled doors were made a uniform size and extend from floor to ceiling to let more light into the rooms. The traditional 'persianas' (wooden shutters) were also replaced and painted in an elegant dark-green color.

The separate guest house—located 1312 feet (400 meters) away from the main house and featuring three bedrooms, a living room, kitchen, and a separate garage—also underwent a complete refurbishment. Additionally, a fitness/spa area located between the main house and the guest house was added as a new feature. All the dry-stone walls were restored, creating an attractive area leading down to the swimming pool and sunbathing terrace, which were also completely remodeled. The large, private grounds surrounding the property were fully landscaped and other areas of the estate where almond and fruit trees were planted have also been cleared and tidied up.

The Can Guix restoration project successfully managed to retain the look of a traditional finca while updating the living and exterior areas and bringing them up to date using high quality.

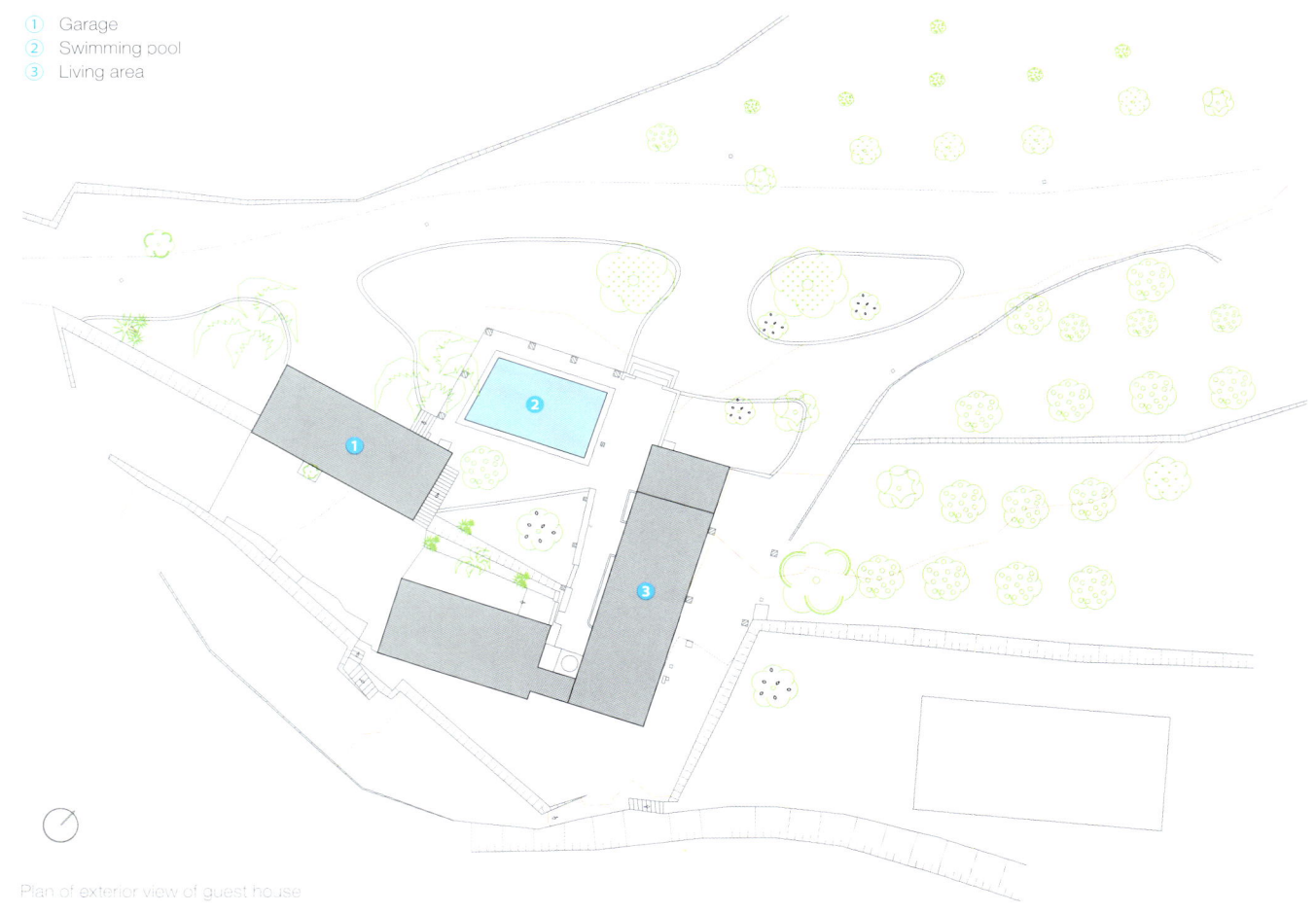

① Garage
② Swimming pool
③ Living area

Plan of exterior view of guest house

01 / Greenery with olive and almond trees
02 / Swimming pool in front of stone wall

① Garage
② Laundry room
③ Living area
④ Engine room
⑤ Swimming pool

Plan of main buildings

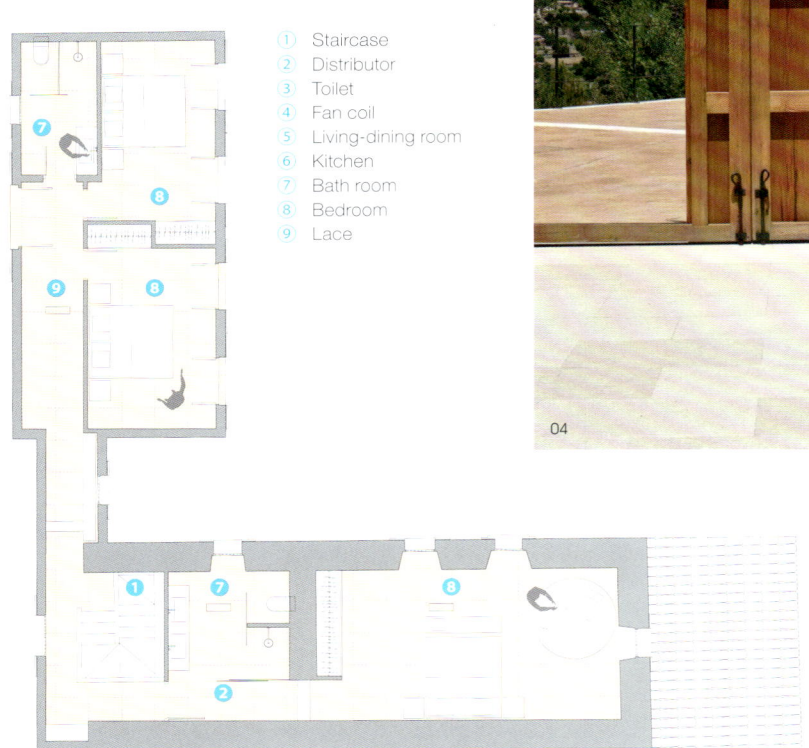

1. Staircase
2. Distributor
3. Toilet
4. Fan coil
5. Living-dining room
6. Kitchen
7. Bath room
8. Bedroom
9. Lace

First-floor plan of guest house

Second-floor plan of guest house

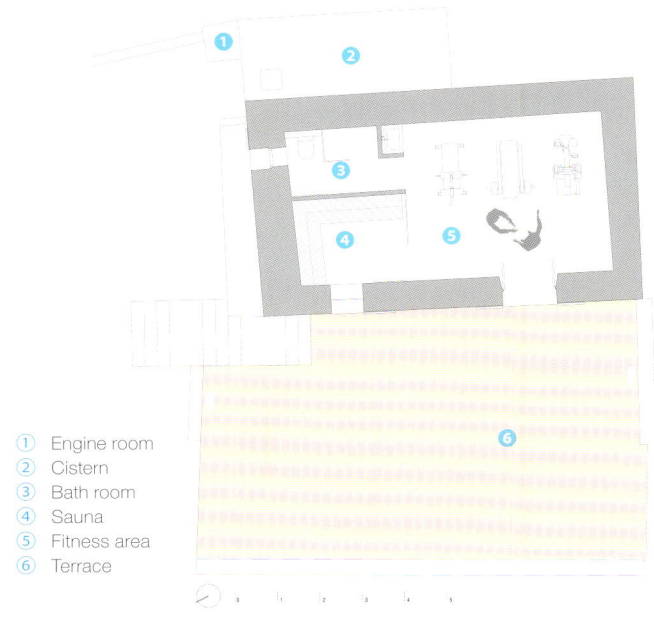

① Engine room
② Cistern
③ Bath room
④ Sauna
⑤ Fitness area
⑥ Terrace

Gym plan

03–04 / Design mixing Mediterranean and contemporary styles
05 / Rest area
06 / Windows looking out to courtyard

① Yard
② Kitchen
③ Kitchen smoke
④ Mechanical ventilation
⑤ Storage space
⑥ Fan coil
⑦ Hallway
⑧ Dining room
⑨ Toilet
⑩ Spare storage area
⑪ TV room

First floor plan of main building

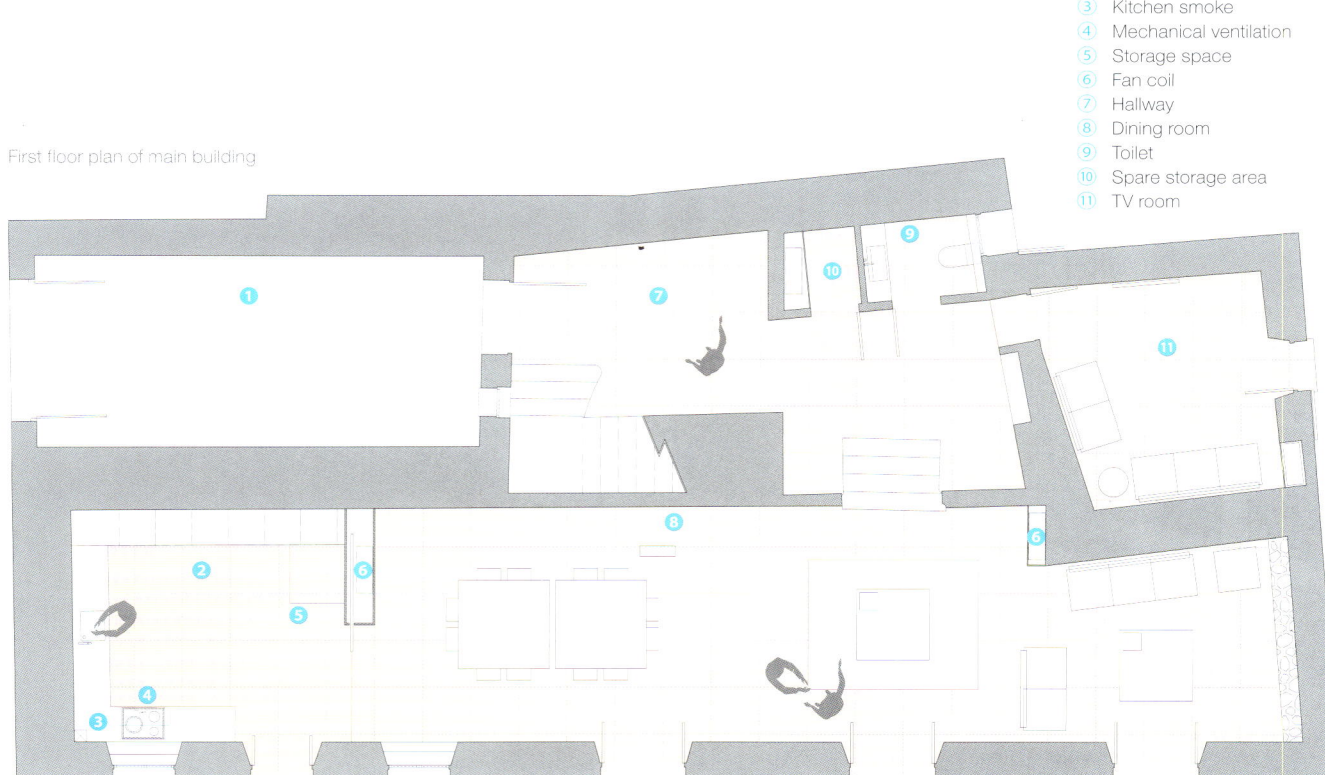

Rural Guest House

Second-floor plan of main building

1. Technical room
2. Bathroom
3. Bedroom
4. Office room
5. Dressing room
6. Fan coil

07 / Master bedroom
08 / Custom-designed kitchen
09 / Bathroom

Location /
Siena, Italy

Area /
43,056 square feet
(4000 square meters)

Architecture and design /
Studio FARSETTI &
BOSCHERINI associati

Photography /
Dario Redaelli

The Relais La Leopoldina

The Relais La Leopoldina, stands on a hill dominating the Valdichiana, a florid valley full of history south of Siena, Tuscany. The name of Leopoldina was given in honor of the Grand Duke of Tuscany Pietro Leopoldo d'Asburgo Lorena. He ordered these typical houses of the valley to be built, during the Reclaim of the Valdichiana to improve his peasants' way of life.

The Relais La Leopoldina was built at the end of the 18th century. It was part of the big property of the Passerini noble family of Cortona, members of the religious order of Santo Stefano knighthood. The original name was Podere il Vallone but for commercial purpose the name was changed.

The house was in a state of abandon since 1950. The current hall was the living room and the kitchen of the house. Families were larger than today and this room was the heart of the house. A big fireplace was located where now is the wooden staircase that leads to the tower. The tower was named Colombaio (dovecote) and was only reachable with a ladder.

The restoration works, taking place from 2007 to 2009, left unchanged the original structure: the quadrangular plan, the tower, the Tabaccaia (the house where the peasants let the tobacco leaves dry) and the other typical buildings of the old farmhouse.

Today, it is a pleasant B&B with a restaurant. The six rooms are on the first floor of the building and have been restored in a very authentic way, still preserving the original brick floors and wooden beams. The furniture was realized by skilful Florentine artisans. The ground floor of the building was once the stable of the old manor house. It has Tuscan red brick cross vaults and large windows that overlook the garden.

01 / Front building
02 / Swimming pool

02

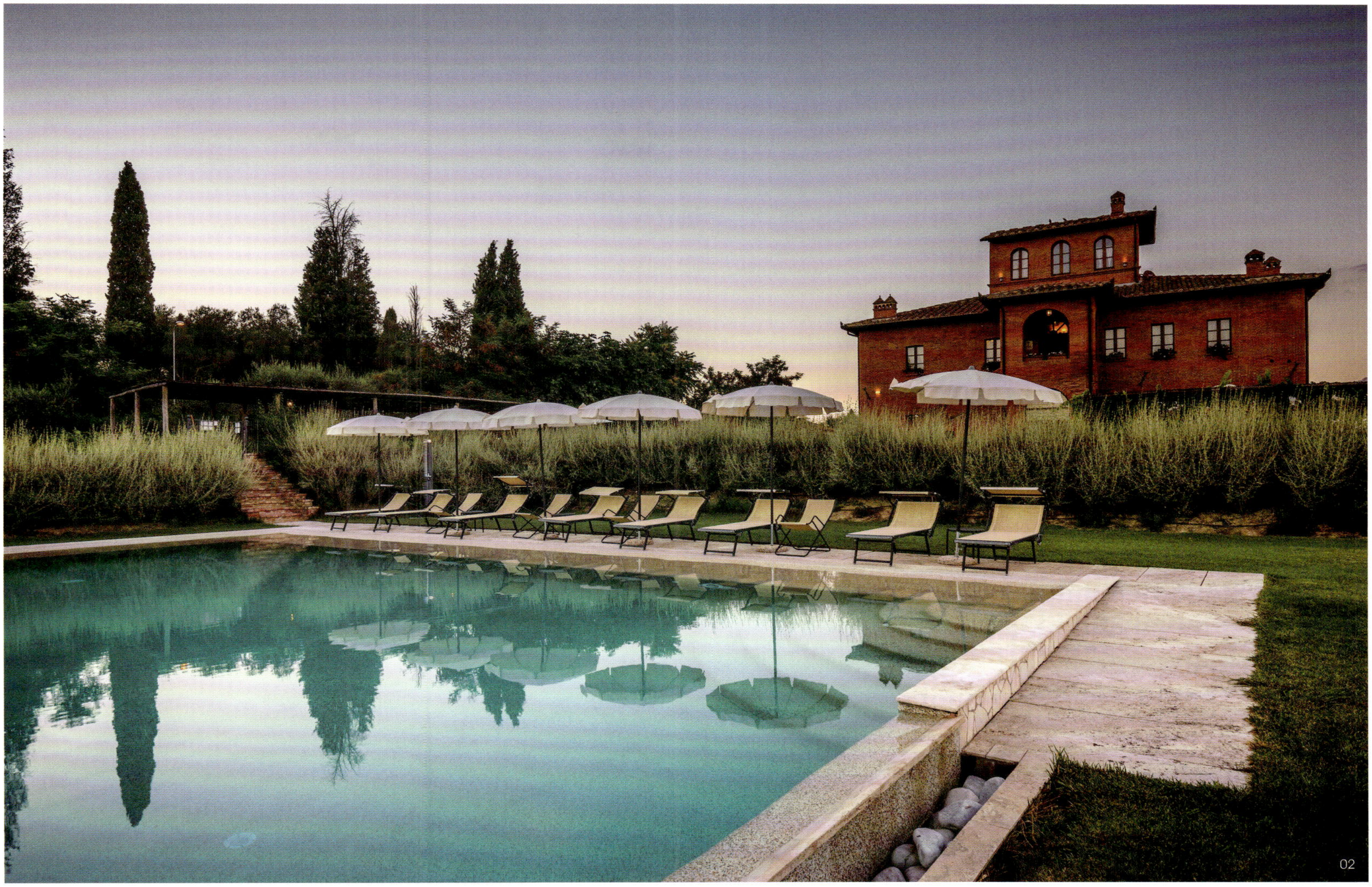

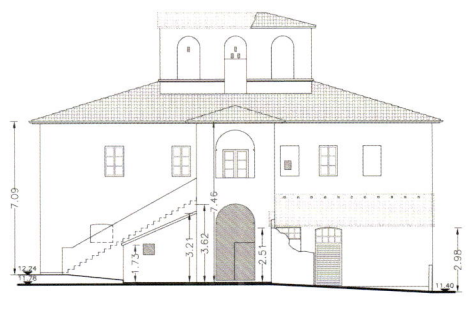

South elevation

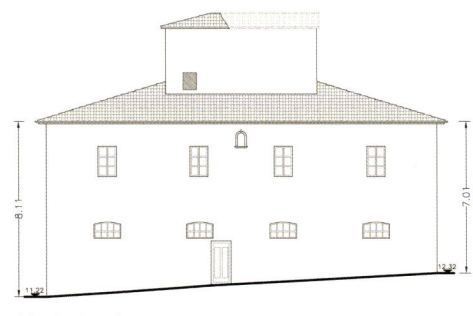

North elevation

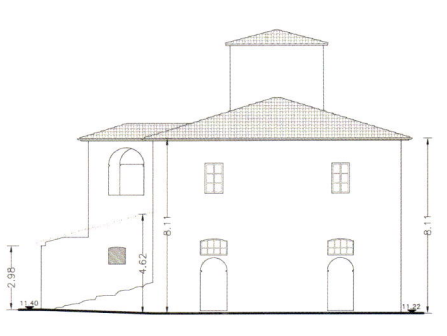

East elevation

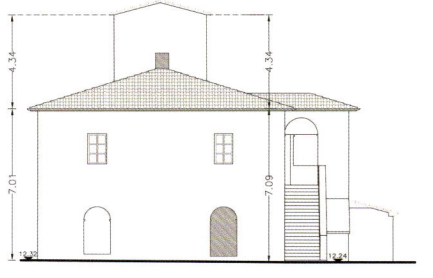

West elevation

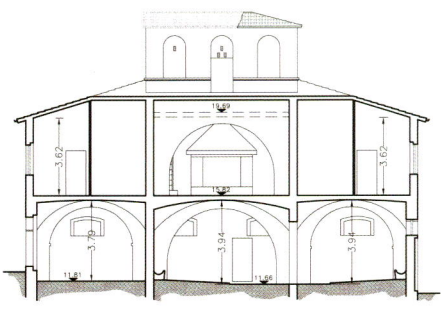
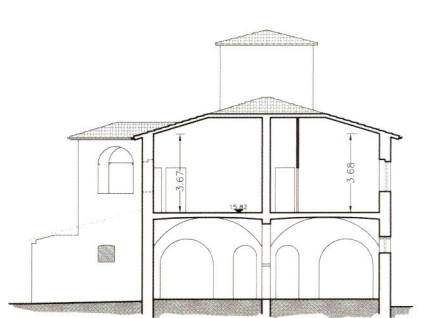

Sections

03 / View from parking area
04 / Corner of terrace
05 / Staircase to rooms
06 / Balcony with scenic view

07 / Entrance hall
08 / Dining area
09 / Wooden staircase to Tower Room
10 / Bedroom with fireplace
11 / Superior double bedroom
12 / Loft of superior bedroom with single bed

Location /
Sofia, Bulgaria

Area /
12,981 square feet
(1206 square meters)

Architecture and design /
bureau XII Ltd.

Photography /
Tsvetomir Dzhermanov,
George Palov

Cherry Orchard Residence

The restoration and extension of the existing pre-1945 era building aimed to provide a guest house with restaurant and recreation zone as a supplement of the property's natural setting and future sport facilities.

The site for the project was located on 11 acres of orchard land nestled between the Iskar River and Vitosha Mountain, 7.5 miles (12 kilometers) from the city center of Sofia. The owners purchased the plot with the old building, which was used as military quarters by the German and Russian armies due to its strategic location. The project requirements were to extend the existing building with a new built structure providing space for guest rooms, a kitchen with restaurant saloon, lounge, recreation zone, gym, and small spa unit.

The project envisaged the uniqueness of the location, the relation to nature and the planned future sport facilities. The old house with its simple look and façades, tiled alpine roof and deep eaves expressed the familiar image of a mountain home. The monolithic building with its strong presence in the property, surrounded by age-old trees demanded a sensitive design approach.

The newly created volume was connected through new openings in the existing façade, merging the interior spaces between old and new. A two-story atrium with glazed roof provides daylight to the central part of the ground floor, with a panoramic elevator going to the top terrace. The façades of the old and new buildings have the same plaster structure and white color, therefore, the disposition between old and new is displayed by the volume composition.

On its north side, the new building has two levels. The second one accommodates the guest rooms and, partly cantilevered, it extends towards the green surrounding. On the south side is the salon—a large, bright room, wide open with sliding façade glazing, which provides views towards the adjacent garden. This multifunctional area was foreseen for different scenarios such as restaurant, event place, conference room, and so forth.

On the second floor over the atrium is a small gym with spa facilities and a large terrace on two levels. On top of the building is a small belvedere open-air bar and swimming pool with amazing view to Vitosha mountain. In the basement, the wine cellar and the kitchen are located.

The interior of the old building leans on historical materials—wooden floorings, brick walls, terrazzo stairs and corridors, the attic is refurbished and the old roof's wooden structure is fully restored. In the new extension, natural materials like wood, exposed concrete and steel suggest continuity and provide environment for different scenarios.

01 / Existing building with new extension
02 / Salon with glazing toward garden

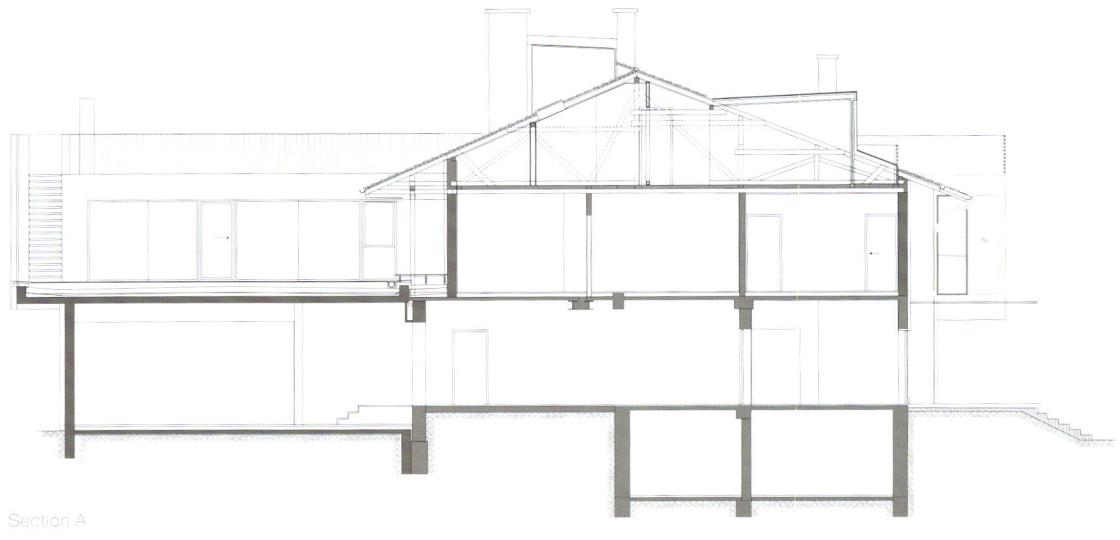
Section A

03 / View of skylight from second floor
04 / Salon with glass elevator
05 / Wide view of salon
06 / Second-floor guest room
07 / Stairs in existing building with new links to extension

Section B

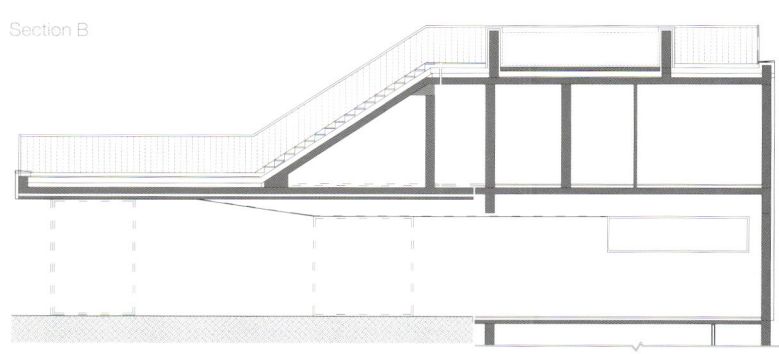

Second-floor plan

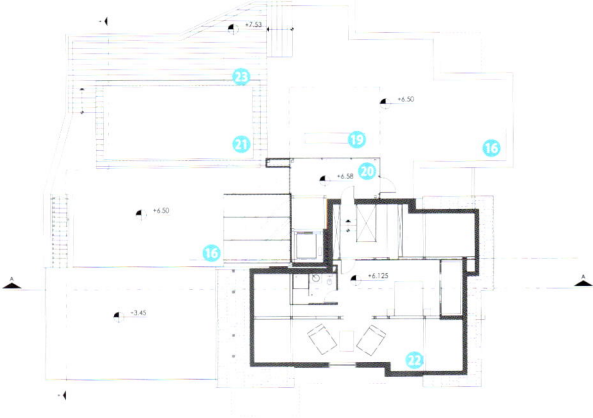

Rooftop plan

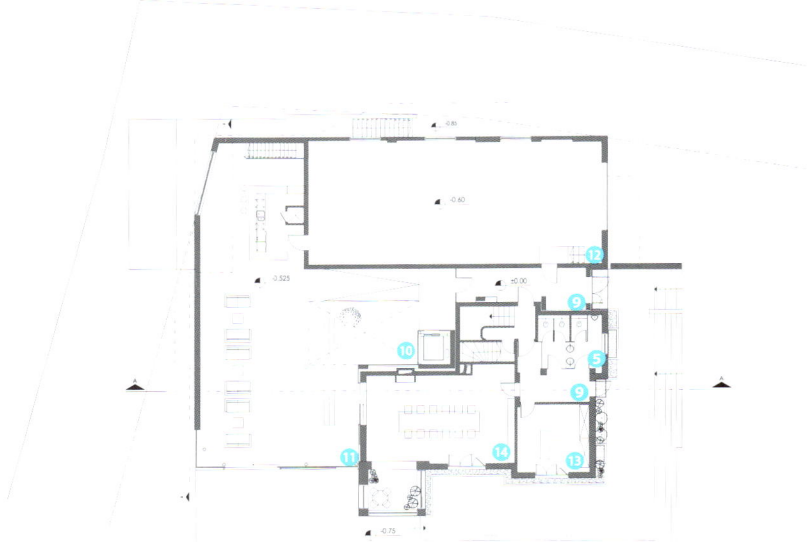

First-floor plan

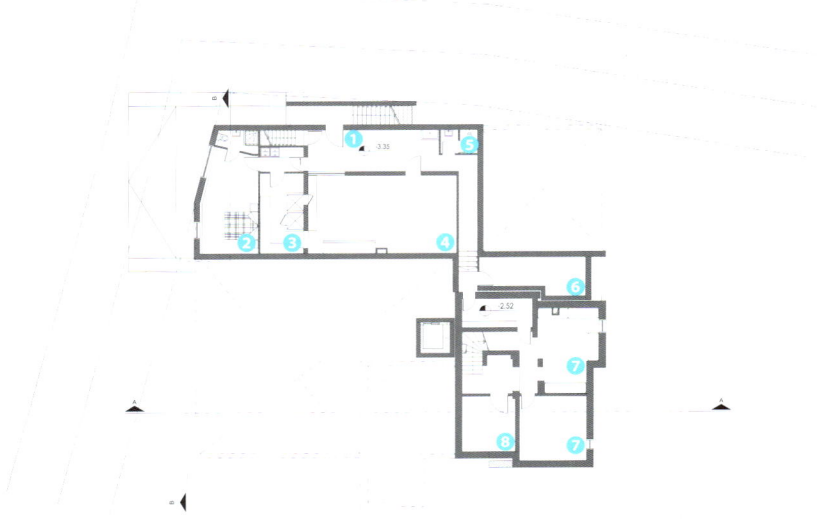

Basement plan

1. Corridor
2. Staff room
3. Washroom
4. Kitchen
5. Bathroom
6. Enclosure
7. Winery
8. Technical room
9. Entrance
10. Atrium
11. Salon
12. Multifunctional hall
13. Manager's office
14. Hall
15. Spa
16. Terrace
17. Bedroom
18. Living room
19. Open-air bar
20. Vestibule
21. Pool
22. Rooftop studio
23. Platform

08 / Rooftop studio

Location /
Moganshan, Deqing, Zhejiang, China

Area /
1291 square feet
(120 square meters)

Architecture and design /
QPdesign research office

Photography /
Wang Fei Imaging Studio

MOOYARD-II

MOOYARD-II Country House Hotel is located at Moganshan, Deqing. Since the size and function of the original architecture no longer met demands, the design team needed to create a new building on the original block of 1292 square feet (120 square meters), as well as complementary courtyard landscapes.

There was a little house with a rammed earth wall on the original site, with one side close to the mountain to the south and the other stretching to the road to the north. The applicable area of the construction site was a long and narrow form.

A higher terrain, together with the height of surrounding bamboo, resulted in relatively weak southbound lighting for the first floor on the south side. The privacy for the room was also a key issue since the northbound road is narrow and the distance to the opposite buildings is rather short. Moreover, the distance between the building and the mountain could not be kept too close due to seasonal humidity; it was more beneficial to indoor air ventilation and lighting if the space could remain open between the building and bamboo mountain.

Under limited spatial distances, issues need to be solved in regard to the distance between the building and road, and how to deal with the indoor lighting of the building and the façade. Gaining effective information onsite played a significant role for the entire layout and spatial design.

The design team divided the project into three components: the building; the landscape courtyards and two-floor public terrace between the building; and the bamboo mountain. Consequently, the team created a room in the southeastern façade in which the first beam of sunlight could be seen throughout a day. In regard to the fenestration, the natural ventilation of the room was also thoroughly taken into consideration.

They designed a terrace where the last beam of sunlight can be seen in the western façade, and people can lie in the bathtub and see the light slowly shifting. The first and second floors in the western façade have become duplex rooms connected by an independent inner stair, where people can enjoy the small space, which can be open and private at the same time. A sunken bathtub and a bed with three enclosed sides seem to play hide-and-seek between your imagination and the space.

The whole architecture scheme never over-addressed design languages. During the process, the designers often redefined their identification as interior designers. In regard to the ongoing conflict between the unification of the building outlook and the independent interior functions, they could always generate more profound understandings in regard to the space after fierce mental struggles.

01 / Building façade and main entrance
02 / North elevation and leisure area of swimming pool

Landscape plan

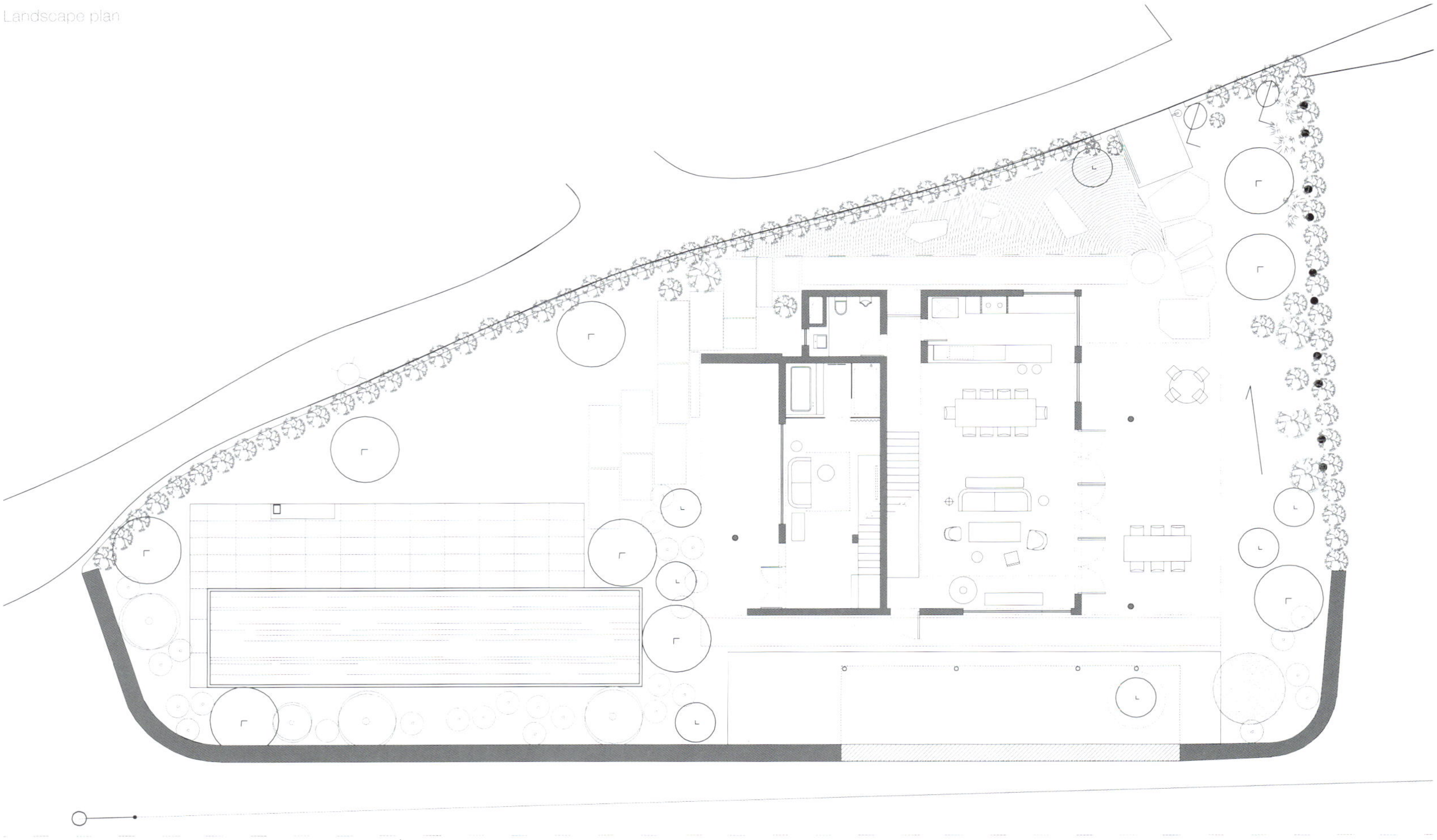

03 / Observation platform
04 / South façade
05 / Living room
06 / Outdoor rest platform
07 / Dining room

08 / King-size room
09 / Living room
10 / Corner of the room
11 / Sleeping area
12 / King-size room 5

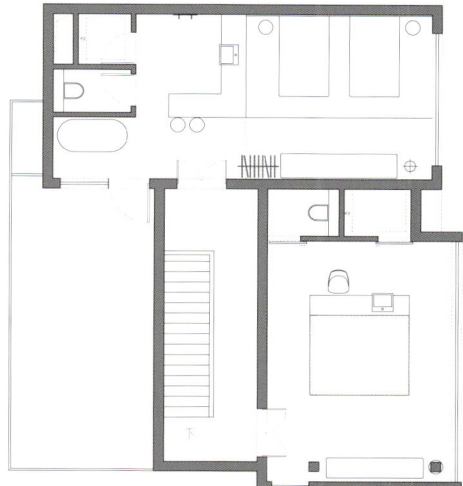
Third-floor plan

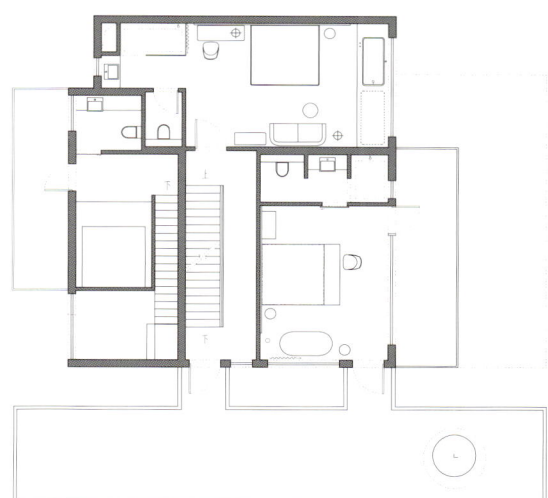
Second-floor plan

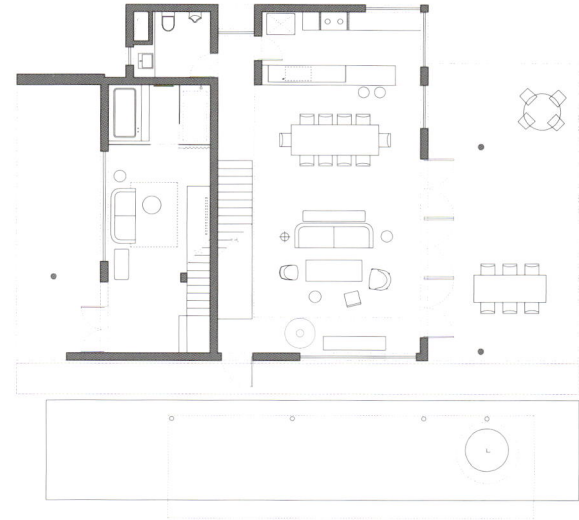
First-floor plan

Location /
California, United States

Area /
1023 square feet
(95 square meters)

Architecture and design /
Chuck Peterson Architect

Photography /
Technical Imagery Studios

Spanish Mission-Style Guest House

Meandering through this guest house is a journey coupling past Spanish inspirations with modern sophistications. From the outside, the building has an arched stucco centerpiece, which connects the guest house to a mirror-image pool house. The Spanish terracotta clay roofing tiles rest upon the exterior stucco walls. All the steel framed windows flood light and warmth into the inner space. One can enter this guest house through a small tower with arched column openings. Underneath is the knotty alder, distressed door underscoring the sense of history before entering.

Inside, a great room adjoins the living, kitchen, and dining areas. Keeping true to the mission inspiration, the ceiling is plaster with natural distressed stained-wood beams. The entire space is lit with four handmade wrought-iron chandeliers blending the delicate sophistication. The natural stone fireplace establishes the comfort at one end. While, at the other end of the room, there are two arched windows welcoming an outside gaze. Entering the warmth of the kitchen are stained mahogany cabinetry with a dark stained concrete top. The island gently separates the kitchen from the main space, allowing for informal dining.

The two bedrooms in the structure invite the outside in. They bring a feeling of sleeping outside, minus the cold and bugs. One serves as the master bedroom with a larger bed and the other has two twin beds. Each bedroom has its own bathroom, which have Spanish mission-style brightly painted tiles. The floor for the entire building is natural limestone tiles.

The guest house and mirror-image pool house wrap around a central pool. The main house is at the opposite end of the pool, creating a central courtyard for the compound. The wrought-iron fencing with stucco arched entry openings creates an enclosed comfort from the wild countryside in this rural central Californian region.

01 / Wrought iron gate framing entrance to courtyard
02 / Arched colonnade with towers
03 / Evening view of pool

02

03

Floor plan

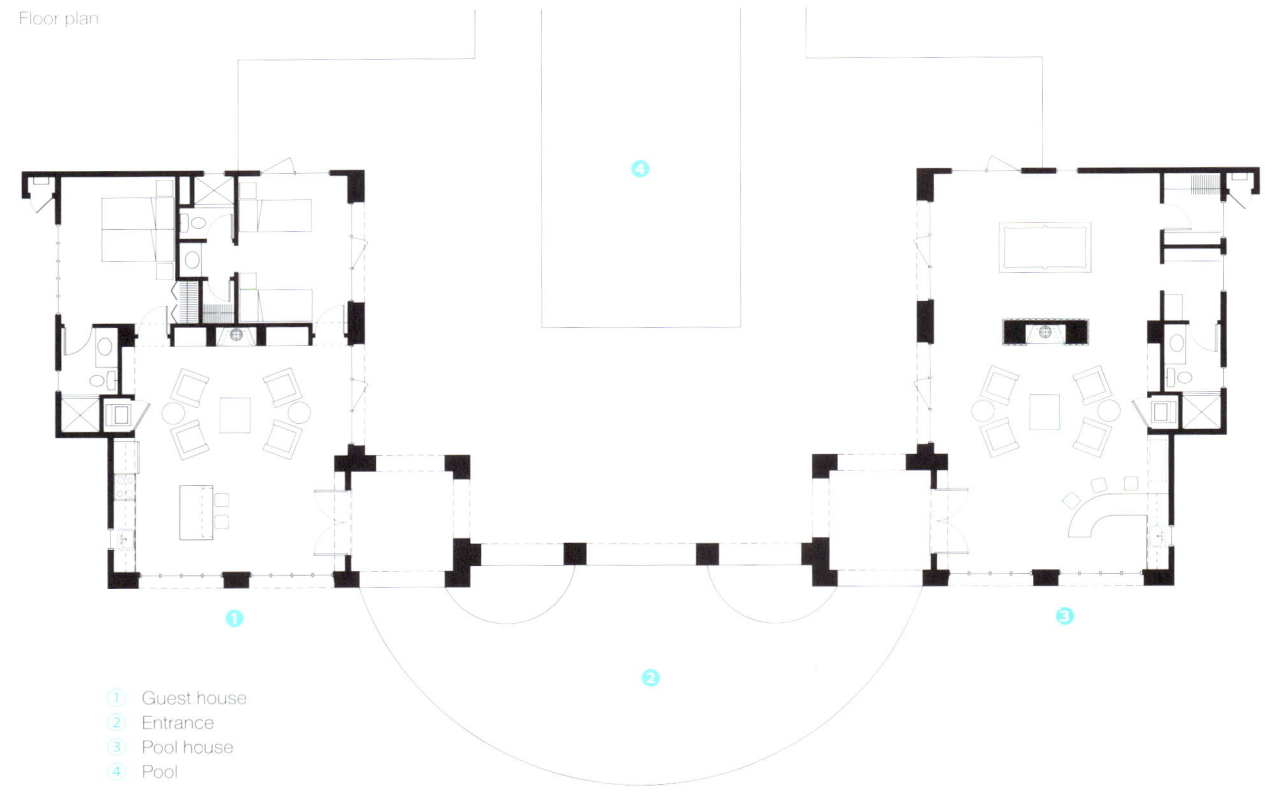

1. Guest house
2. Entrance
3. Pool house
4. Pool

258 Rural Guest House

04 / Bedroom with French doors to courtyard
05 / Bathroom with Spanish tiles
06 / Common area opening up to courtyard
07 / Common area

Location /
Ibiza, Spain

Area /
484 square feet
(45 square meters)

Architecture and design /
Ibiza Interiors

Photography /
Youri Claessens

The Ibiza Campo House

On a mountain in the rugged north of Ibiza lies this beautiful cabin. What formerly served as stables and storage is now transformed into a contemporary dream house. The owners of Ibiza Interiors developed this 200-year-old ranch into their company showroom and a guest house.

To keep the character of the original building, basic materials are used. The beautiful authentic beams were preserved, just like the original ancient stone walls in the kitchen and bathroom. The architects only used materials that were used traditionally on the island, like the iroko window frames, concrete, and white-chalk plastered stone walls.

The building had been unused for years, and was in very poor condition. Therefore, only the walls and parts of the roof could remain. Electricity, water, and sewage were not present, so the architects had to add these connections to make it work as a contemporary home. Water comes from a private well and there are solar panels installed for hot water, floor heating, and electricity. The cottage is consequently completely independent of the grid operation and is thus self-sustainable.

For the interior, the designers used a number of brands and partners, which they often worked with in their hometown of Amsterdam. So, there are coco-mat beds, made from natural materials, and there's art from the gallery Vroom & Varossieau. The upholstery is Etoffe Unique and all the other furniture, lighting, and carpets are from their partner shop, Modern Vintage.

The beautiful steel designer kitchen with marble top is from Eginstill. The married owners, Jurjen and Selina, represent these brands and the architectural firm Standard on the island through their new company, Ibiza Interiors.

01 / Building façade
02 / Building entrance
03 / Outdoor lounge
04 / Swimming pool

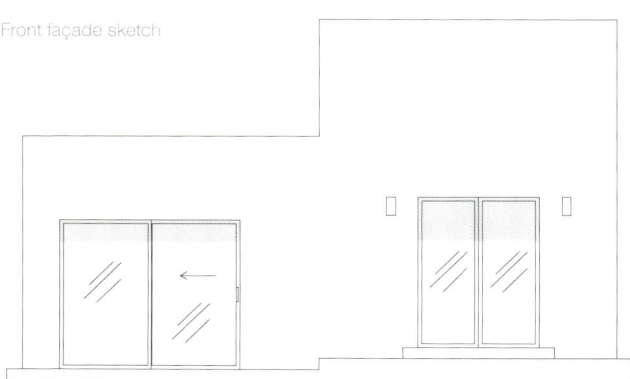

Front façade sketch

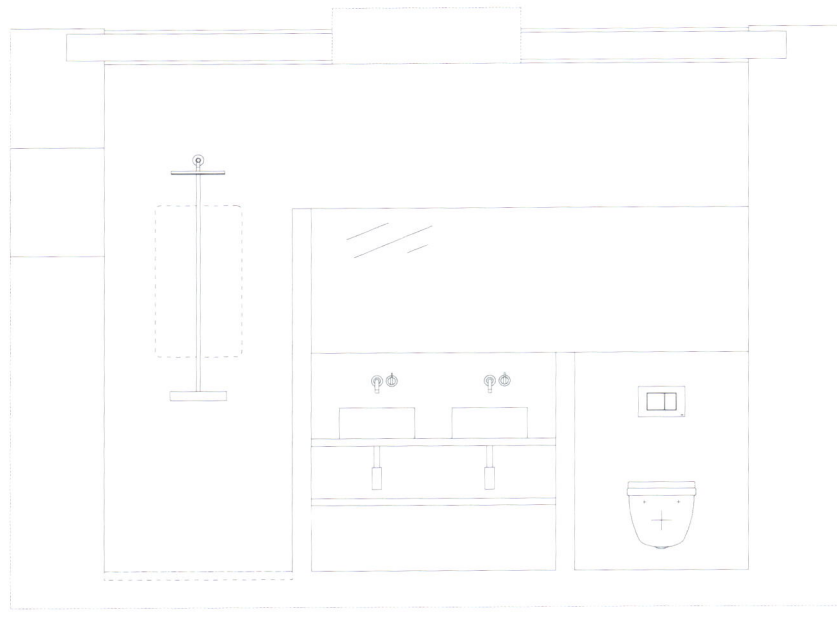

Bathroom sketch

05–06 / Small decorative items in room
07 / Living room on first floor

Floor plan

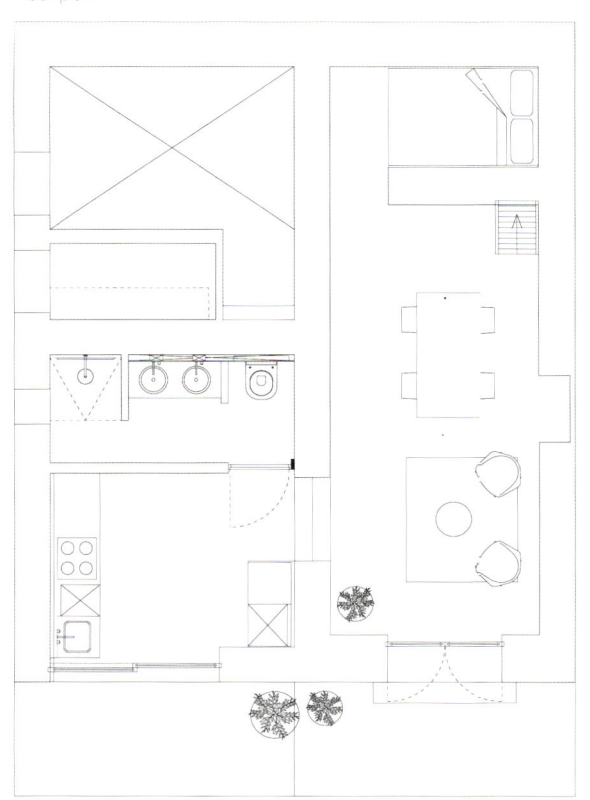

08 / Living room on second floor
09 / Sink
10 / Hearth

Location /
Porto Heli, Greece

Area /
4844 square feet
(450 square meters)

Architecture and design /
GEM Architects

Photography /
Costas Vergas

Vacation House in South Peloponnese

The guest house is placed in the peak of a natural hill with a magnificent view towards the island of Spetses. The aim of GEM Architects was to create a modern language based on the vernacular. The rectangular volumes refer to the tradition while at the same time, the spans of openings, the beams as well as the choice of materials refer to modern constructions. Glass rails and wood structure follow this logic.

Colors and materials where inspired from the surrounding landscape. The olive-tree palette dominates. This approach was completed with the overall design of the interiors and custom-made furniture in an attempt to achieve a holistic statement.

The house unfolds in three levels. In the ground floor, the main living room, dining room, and kitchen are situated. The wide folding French windows create a unity between the interior and the exterior courtyard, all facing the sea. In this courtyard, southwest orientated, unfolds a swimming pool with its long axis vertical to the view plane. Areas well protected from the sun are created under the pergolas, a lounge sitting area, as well as a barbecue with dining table.

In the mezzanine, three kid's bedrooms were created, with sleeping areas placed in attics. On the first floor, the master bedroom creates the main volume of the synthesis. The central position of the bed overlooking the view dominates the interior under the wooden roof. At the lowest level of the site, a stone wall formation is the only sign of the otherwise underground guest house.

The house's garden, which is about 4 acres (1.6 hectare), was created in different levels with landscape formations following the natural site inclination. An alternation of herbs and indigenous plants, citrus, fruit, and olive trees, along with a miniature vineyard, participate in an orchestration of nature, using curved stone mantels as paintbrushes, borders in the whole synthesis.

01 / Building façade
02 / Entrance with steps

Elevation A

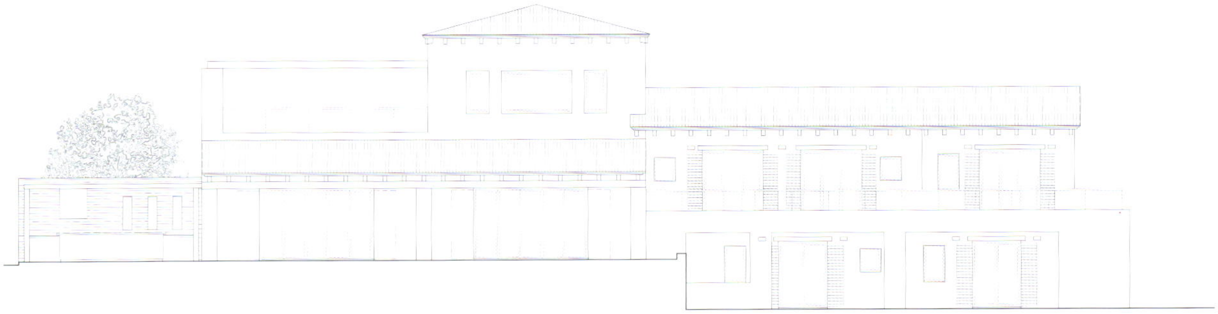

Elevation B

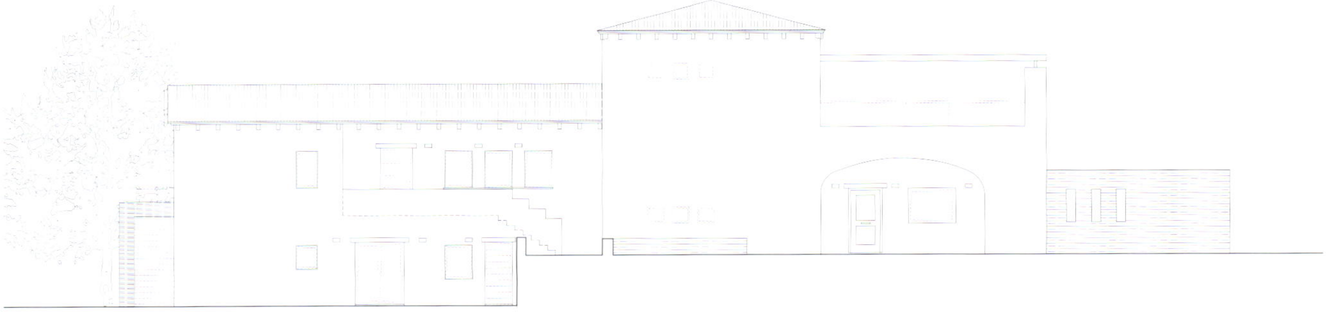

Elevation C

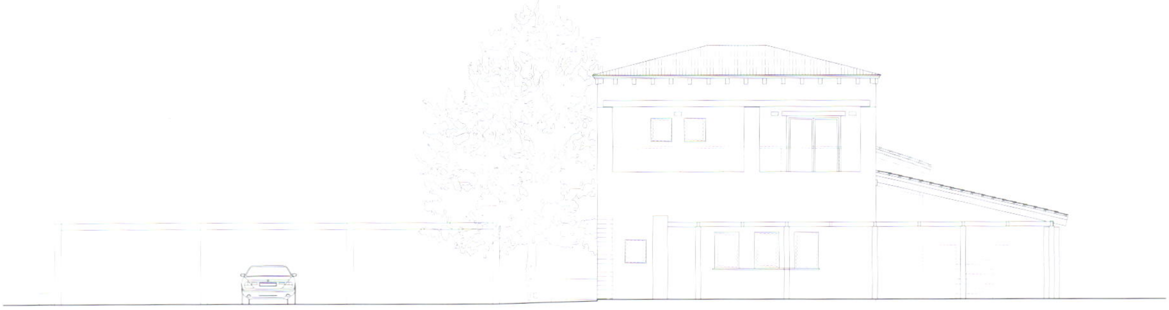

03

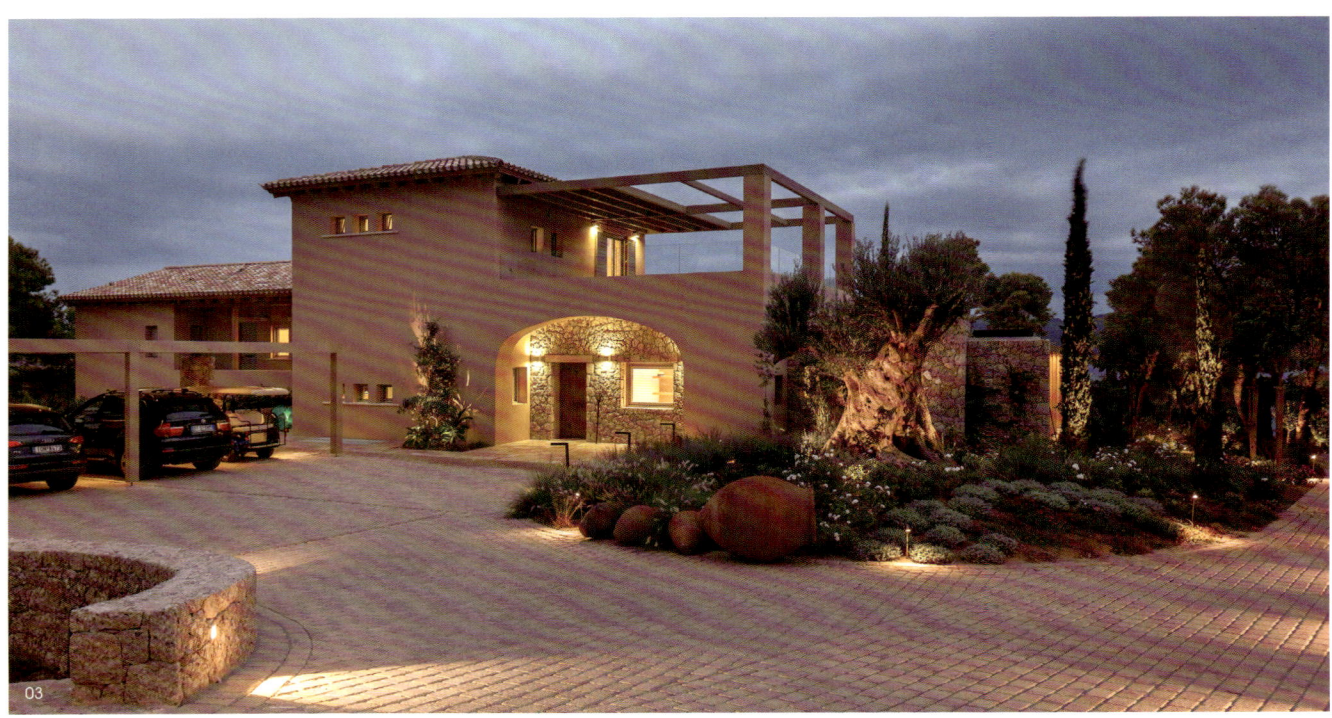

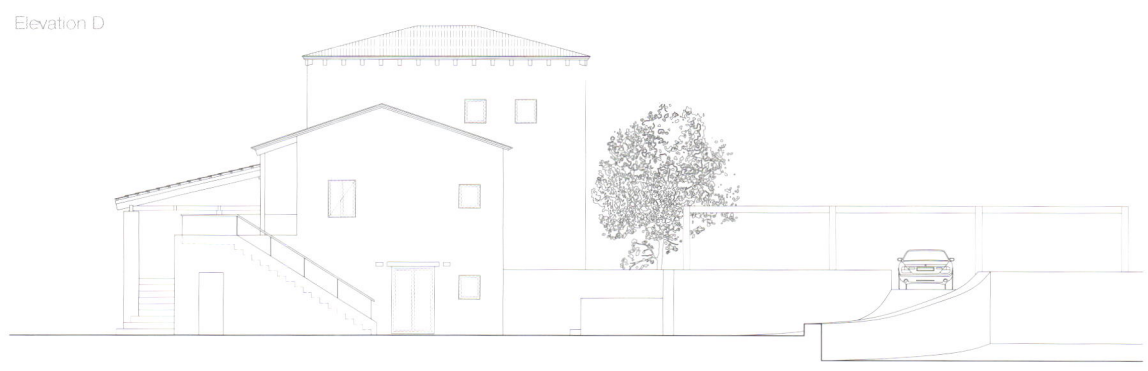

Elevation D

03–04 / Guest house at night
05 / Swimming pool
06 / Semi-open lounge

07–08 / Living room on first floor
05 / Indoor space

Topography

10

11

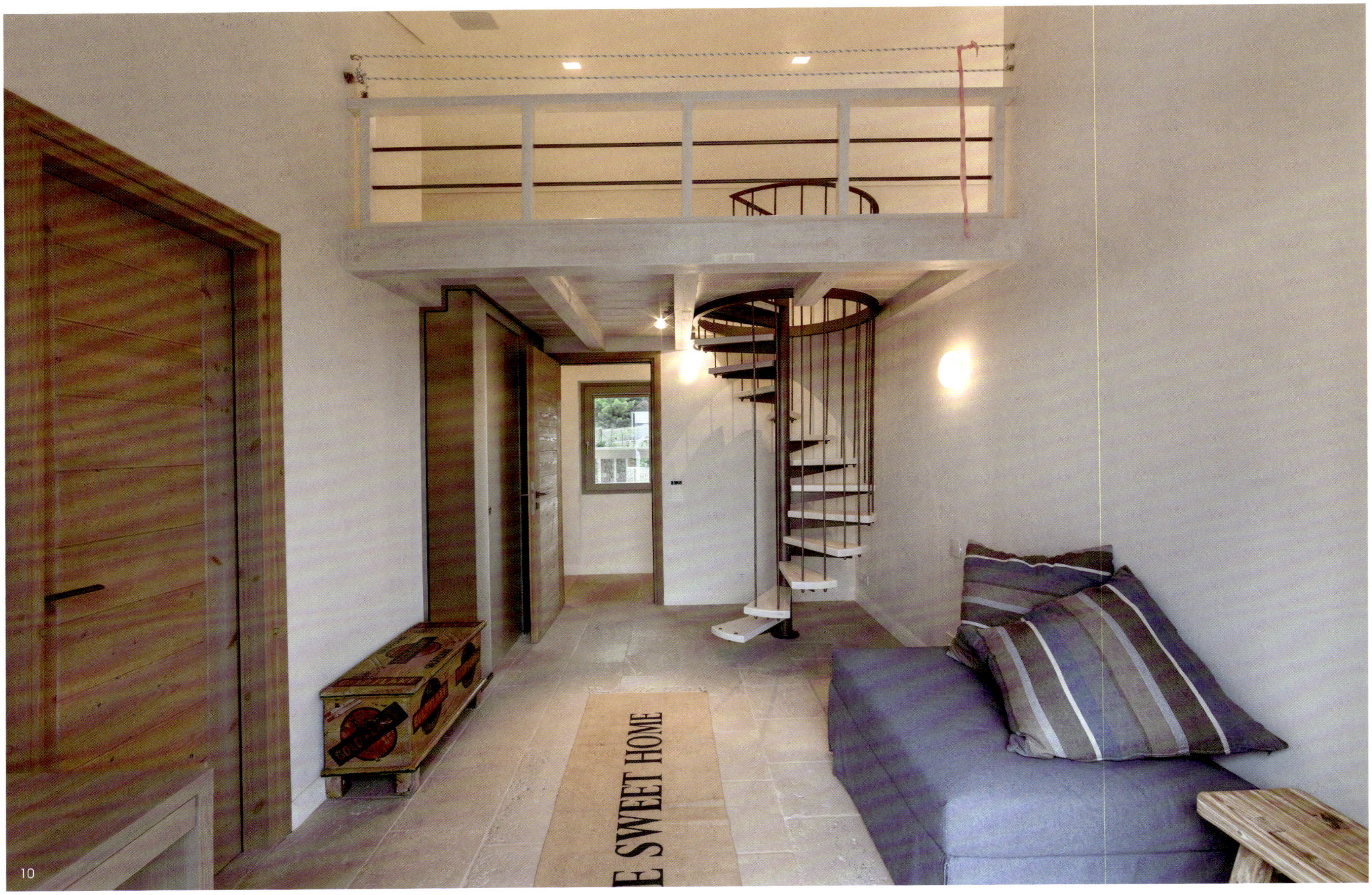

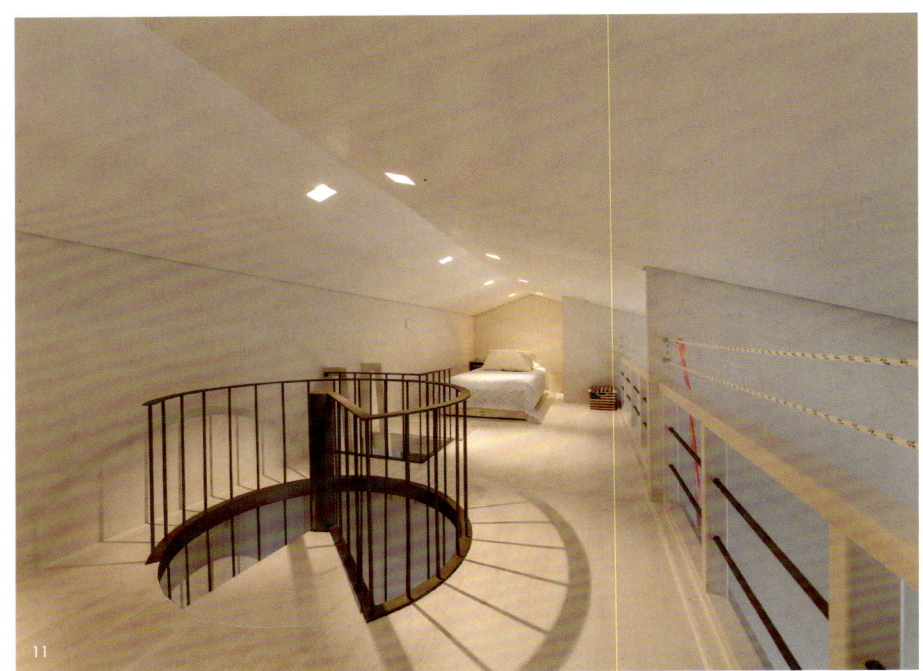

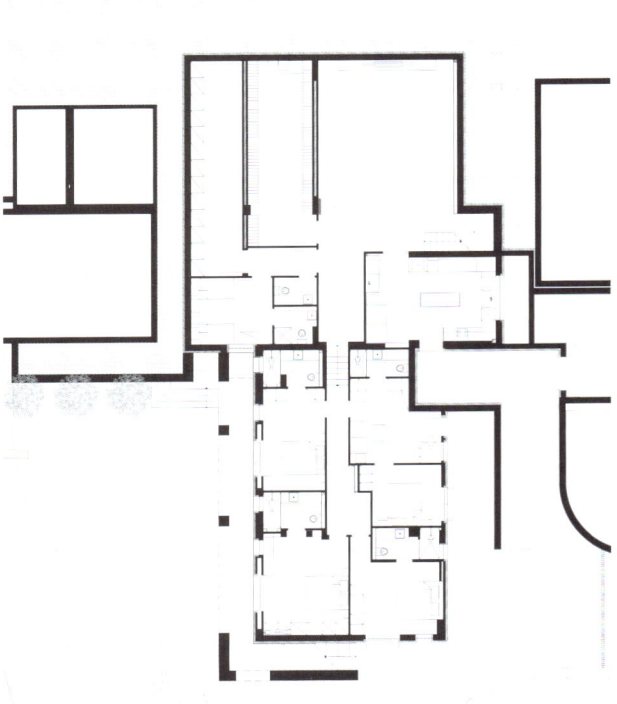

Underground floor plan

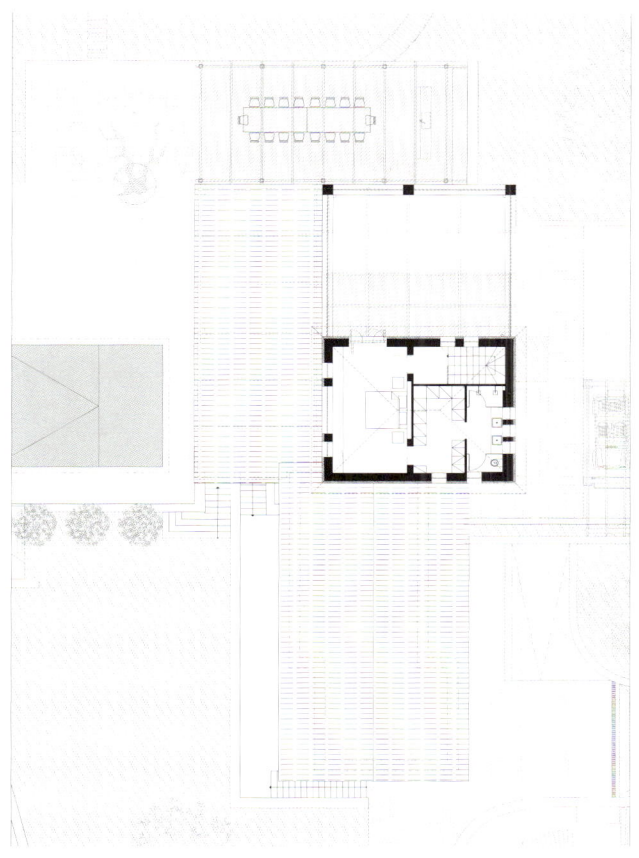

Second-floor plan

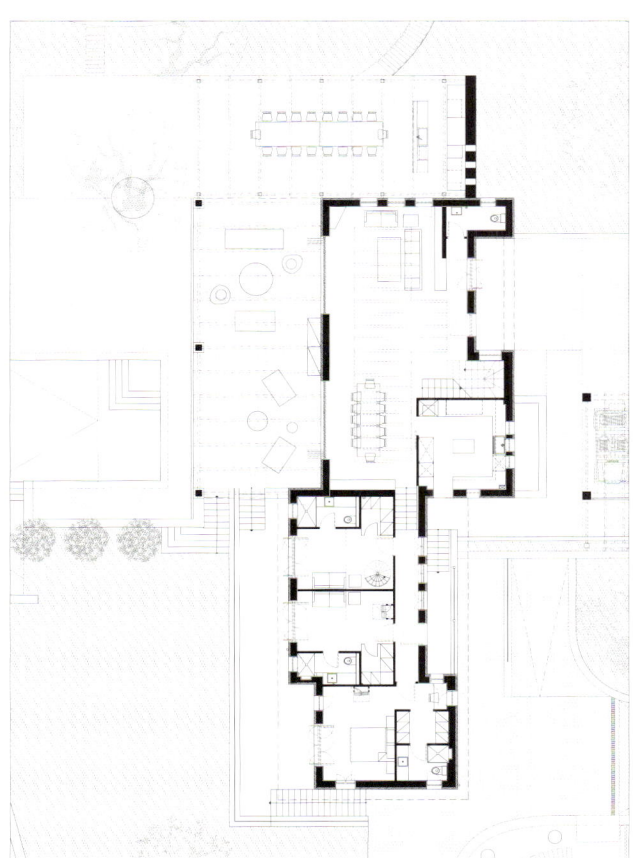

First-floor plan

10 / Lounge on first floor
11–12 / Bedroom upstairs
13 / Cloakroom
14 / Bathroom

Location /
Thorpeness, Suffolk, United Kingdom

Area /
2691 square feet
(250 square meters)

Architecture and design /
Jarmund Vigsnaes Architects and Mole Architects

Photography /
Nils Petter Dale, Ivar Kvaal, Chris Wright

Dune House

Mole Architects collaborated with Norwegian practice Jarmund Vigsnaes Architects on this holiday home commissioned by Alain de Botton's Living Architecture. The Dune House is situated on the edge of an area of outstanding natural beauty, overlooking the sea on the Suffolk coast.

A complicated roof geometry draws inspiration from the seaside strip of houses with an eclectic range of gables and dormer windows. It's a romantic house, designed to be both a refuge against the expanse of the North Sea, and a beachside house open to the sandy dunes. Downstairs all the 'kit' is contained in the centre of the house, allowing the rest to be open plan, with areas defined for cooking, eating, and living. Accessed from a secret staircase, the all-wooden bedroom floor has four bedrooms, each under its own pitched roof.

The design and construction of such a striking house took perseverance. The design itself needed a great deal of work to ensure that all the geometries would work, and that the various spaces would feel right. Once designed, obtaining planning wasn't as easy as a more conventional house, and much work was put into the planning documentation to demonstrate that the house wouldn't detract from the area, and that the scale and material were appropriate. Structurally the house isn't normal either, with a reinforced cantilevered concrete slab supporting most of the upper floor loads.

The ground floor is contrasting this by its lack of relationship to the architecture on the top floor. This architectural ambiguity of the house also addresses the programmatic difference between the private upper floor and the social ground floor. The living area and the terraces were set into the dunes in order to protect it from the strong winds, and opens equally in all directions to allow for wide views. The corners can be opened by sliding doors, which emphasizes the floating appearance of the top floor.

While the materiality of the ground floor—concrete, glass, aluminum—relates to the masses of the ground, the upper floor is a construction made of solid wood, cladding stained dark as the existing gables and sheds found in the area.

01 / House and building for utilities
02–03 / Open area on first floor

Site plan

04 / Kitchen
05 / Library and terrace with sea view
06 / Bedroom in attic
07 / Dining area

276 Rural Guest House

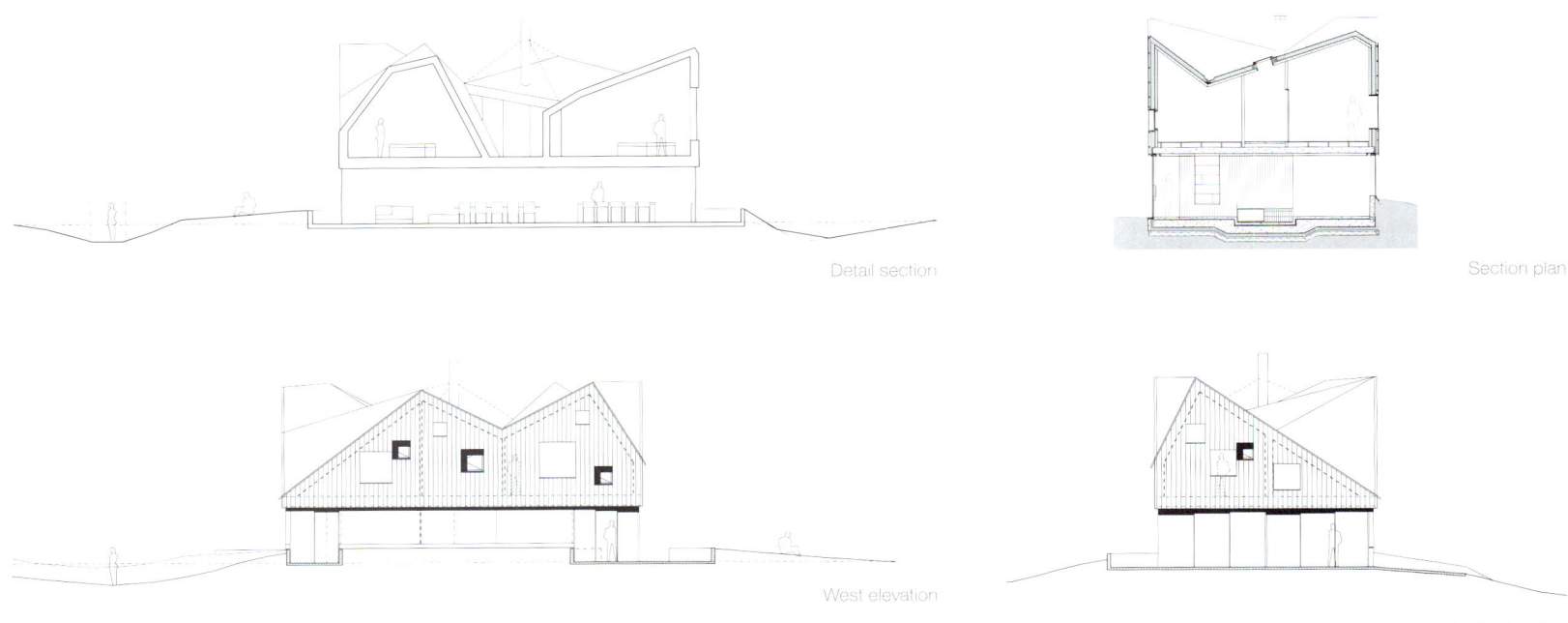

Detail section

Section plan

West elevation

South elevation

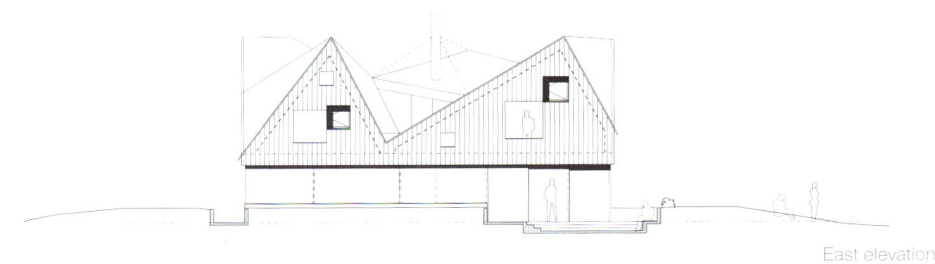

East elevation

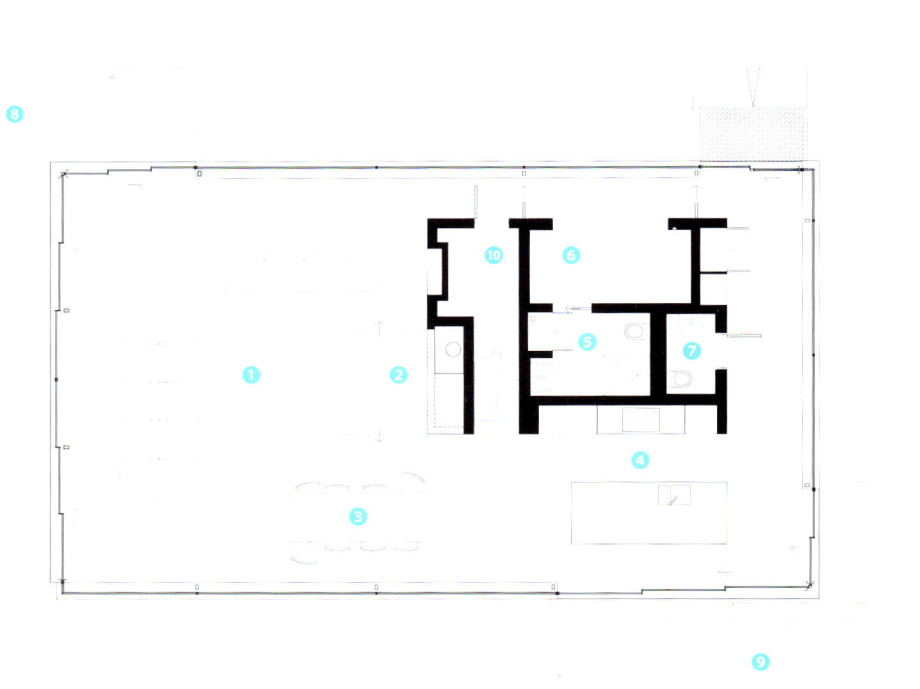

1. Living room
2. Sunken fireplace
3. Dining area
4. Kitchen
5. En-suite
6. Day bed
7. Bathroom
8. West terrace
9. East terrace
10. Plant room

First-floor plan

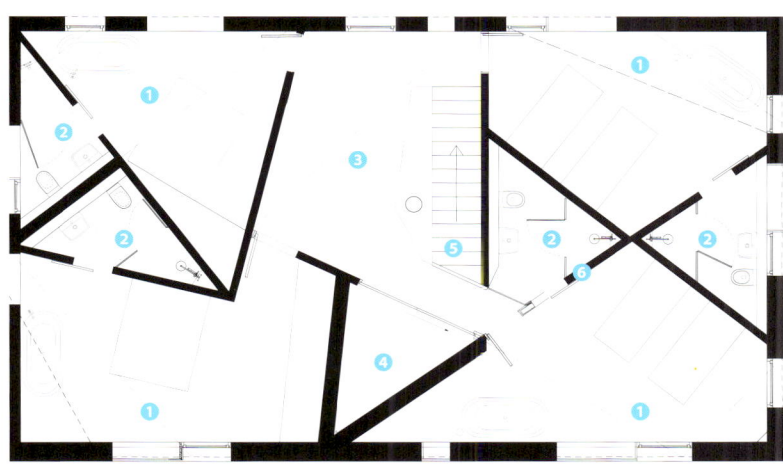

Second-floor plan

1. Bedroom
2. En-suite
3. Library
4. Roof terrace
5. Stairs
6. Walls and window

08 / Bedroom facing sea
09 / En-suite

Location /
Sun Moon Lake, Taiwan, China

Area /
7470 square feet
(694 square meters)

Architecture and design /
De-Sign Interior Design Studio, Chen Cheng-Che

Photography /
Liang Video Studio, Mark Image

Doris Home

Doris Home is a little world where cats and travelers can live together, which began receiving guests from around the world in 2005.

In 2017, it moved to a new premise and the new guest house is designed on the basis of a cat-friendly concept with the aim of being 'a guest house with a warm sense of design.' Its façade, with simple lines, uses black to highlight the white floors.

Walking from the courtyard full of flowers and plants into the first floor of the guest house, people will see a hall that features various elements designed for cats, such as stairs on walls, secret walkways inside ceilings, a big cat paw print on the ceiling of the open kitchen, and the ceiling lamp above the dining table is made of cats' favorite corrugated paper.

People can follow the cats' steps and walk up the solid wood stairs supported by steel structures—the stairs run from the first floor to the third floor, with a transparent daylight roof above the end of stairs. The sunlight at noon spills through wooden barriers, and the flickering light and shadow will bring people an ever-changing experience.

The interior design is unfolded from the world of cats: people can put some small objects on shelves that can be used for cats to jump, and hang up backpacks and clothes on cabinets with high penetration. Cats' favorite scratching posts and little houses for cats to stare out of the window are added in some rooms for travelers with children. Additionally, large and comfortable couches are set for people to relax.

Cat elements can be found everywhere, even during breakfast. A ladder-like shelf hangs from the ceiling above the kitchen, which can also be used for storage. Next to the breakfast room is a hidden wooden display stand, where works of local artists are displayed and cats can bounce up and down.

All in all, Doris Home is not merely a guest house, but a holiday home full of characteristics of human beings and cats, waiting for 'cat-like' travelers to come quietly.

01 / Front façade
02 / Corner of guest house

03-05 / Bright lobby

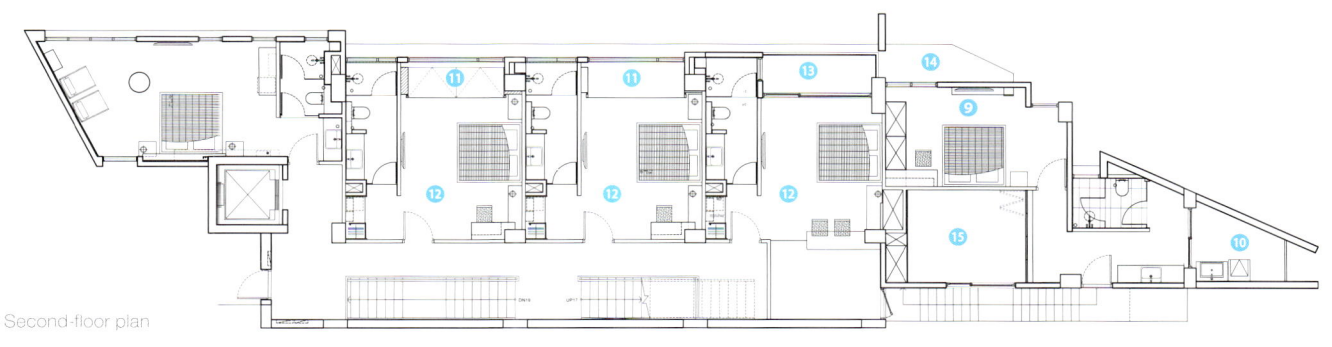
Second-floor plan

① Rest area
② Stairs
③ Reception area
④ Dining room
⑤ Kitchen bar
⑥ Storage room
⑦ Living room/dining room
⑧ Kitchen
⑨ Master room
⑩ Balcony for working
⑪ Couch
⑫ Double room
⑬ Balcony
⑭ Balcony for equipment
⑮ Guest room

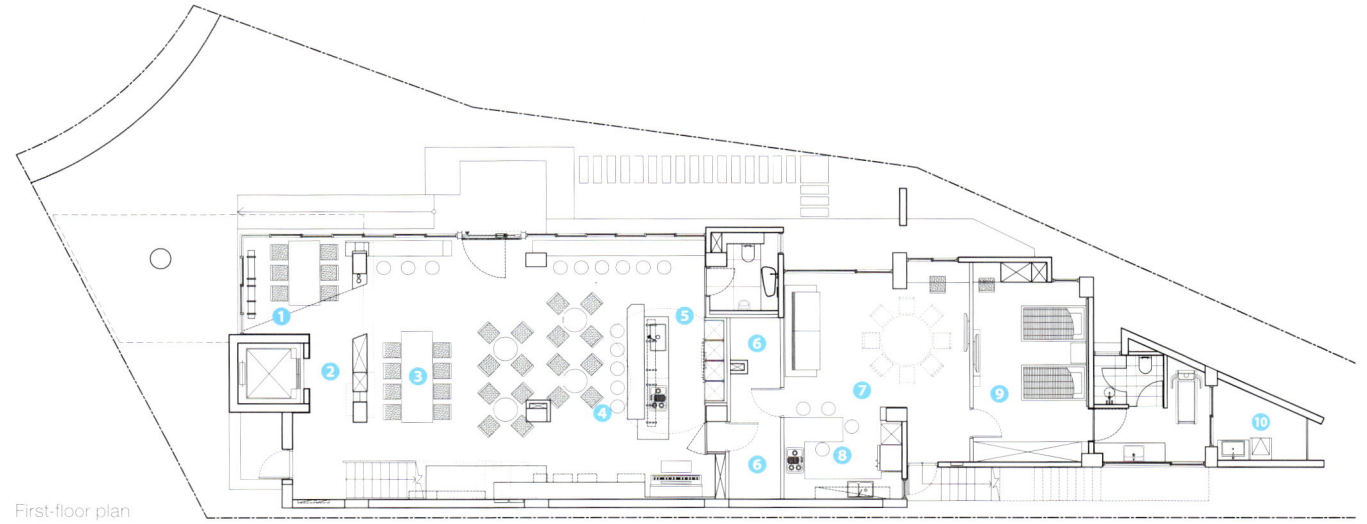
First-floor plan

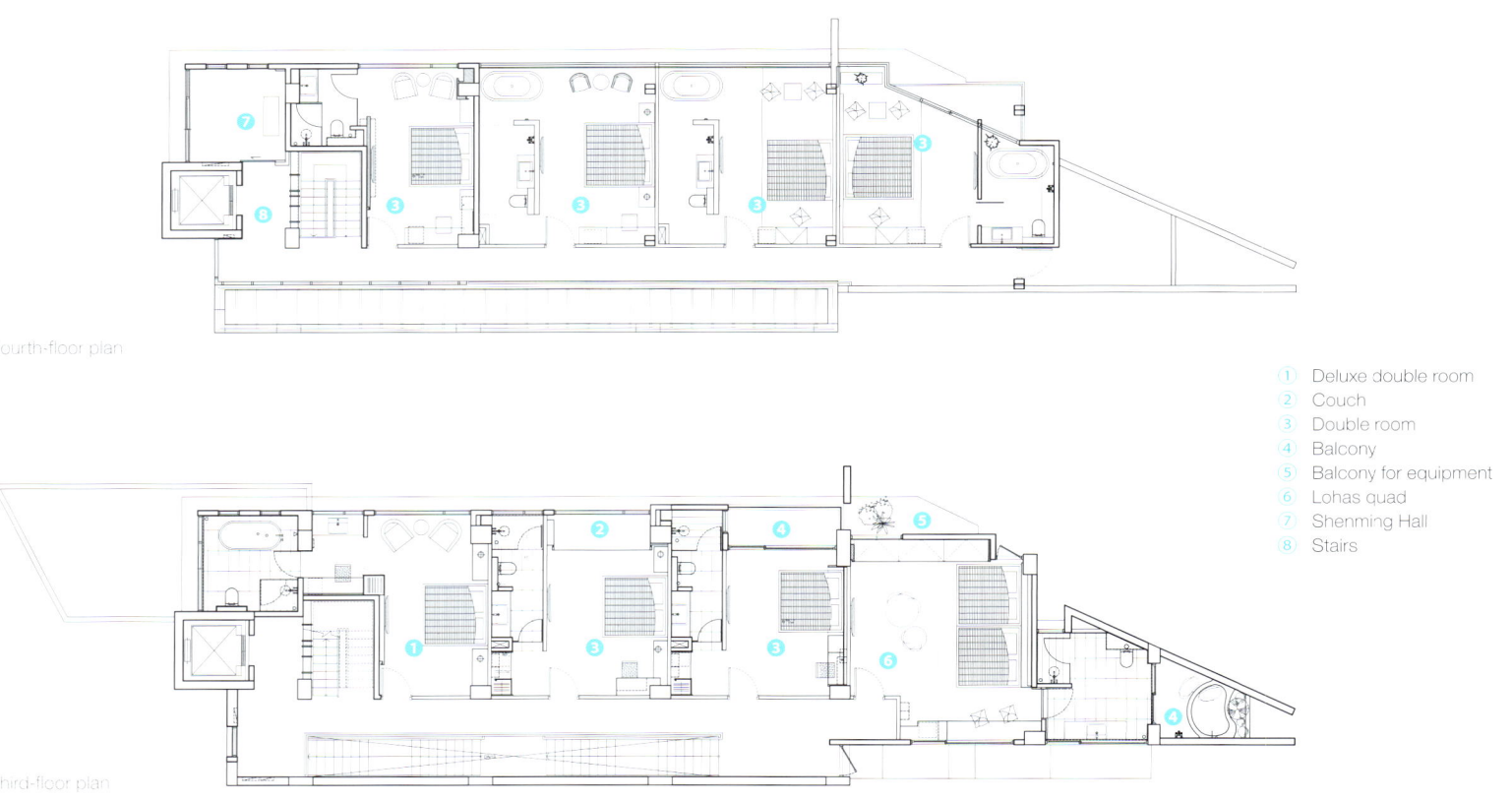

Fourth-floor plan

Third-floor plan

1. Deluxe double room
2. Couch
3. Double room
4. Balcony
5. Balcony for equipment
6. Lohas quad
7. Shenming Hall
8. Stairs

06 / Stairs leading from first to third floor
07 / Couch in guest room
08 / Guest room with mountain view

INDEX

APM / p 232
Tel: +34-971 69 89 00

ArchStudio / p 144
Tel: +8610 5762 3027

Bruno Lucas Dias / p 118
Facebook: www.facebook.com/Bruno-Lucas-DiasArquitecto-117690651912670/

bureau XII Ltd. / p 244
Email: office@b-xii.net

CAST Architecture, Tim Hammer / p 124
Tel: +1 206 256 9886

CCDI Grand Wisdom Interior Design / p 150
Tel: +86(10) 84266241

Chen Xi, Shanshui Boutique Hotel / p 138
Tel: + 86 15905595858

Chen Bo, Zhong Yun, Dengfeng Qingjing Lanshan Courtyard / p 66
Tel: + 86 18183723933

Chow I-Shin, The Bivou / p 58
Tel: +86 888 512 9449

Chuck Peterson Architect / p 256
Tel: +1 707 527 9091

De-Sign Interior Design Studio, Chen Cheng-Che, Doris Home / p 280
Tel: +886 49 2855221

Emil Eve Architects / p 184
Tel: +44 78 1545 3778

Franken Architekten Gmbh / p 158
Tel: +49 69 297 283 0

G&S Design / p 164
Email: gs_team@163.com

GEM Architects / p 50,266
Tel: (210) 6838118

Hostem Limited / p 200
Tel: +44 (0) 20 7033 6788

Hyndman Taylor Architects Ltd. / p 104
Tel: +64 3 451 1992

Ibiza Interiors / p 260
Tel: +34 697 757 494

IDO (Init Design Office) / p 22
Tel: +86 13452819918

Jarmund Vigsnaes Architects and Mole Architects / p 274
Tel: +47 22 99 43 43; 01223 913012

Jieyufeibai Studio, iii_house / p 170
Tel: +86 18629262607

Kostas Zouvelos + Kassiani Theodorakakou, Tainaron Blue Retreat / p 110
Tel: +30 2733 300461

Lime Deco pp 42, 98
Tel: +30 210 722 3157

Lin Weiping Interior Design Co., Ltd, Qingyan Guest House / p 78
Tel: +86 13957806100

ORA Atelier Znojmo / p 192
Tel: +420 776 760 280

PAD Studio Ltd. / p 208
Email: Wendy@padstudio.co.uk

QPdesign research office / p 250
Tel: +86 15168237791

reyes ríos + larraín arquitectos / p 220
Email: info@reyesrioslarrain.com

Shanghai Kun Yu Decoration Design Co. Ltd / p 72
Tel: +86 021 659 881 22; +86 0577 881 297 99

Snorre Stinessen / Stinessen Arkitektur / p 30
Tel: +47 91 58 09 77

Studio FARSETTI & BOSCHERINI associati / p 238
Tel: +39 0575 605047

Temp Architects / p 90
Email: info@temp-arch.com

TS Adams Studio, Architects, Inc. / p 178
Email: info@tsadamsstudio.com

UMMO Estudio / p 84
Tel: +34 634 522 578

Valentina Gianpiccolo and Giuseppe Minaldi, Mangiabove Guest House / p 36
Tel: +39 334 930 0441

Yan Lefeng, Haitian Zuoshe Guest House / p 16
Tel: +86 15705775577

Yang Ying, Shuimo Chanjing Lake View Holiday Inn / p 10
Tel: +86 15812218080

Yaoliang Architecture and Space Design Office / pp 214, 226
Tel: +86 177 0677 0531

Zhu Shouyao, Bushe Hotel / p 130
Tel: +86 15605591889

Published in Australia in 2018 by
The Images Publishing Group Pty Ltd
Shanghai Office
ABN 89 059 734 431
6 Bastow Place, Mulgrave, Victoria 3170, Australia
Tel: +61 3 9561 5544 Fax: +61 3 9561 4860
books@imagespublishing.com
www.imagespublishing.com

Copyright © The Images Publishing Group Pty Ltd 2018
The Images Publishing Group Reference Number: 1485

All rights reserved. Apart from any fair dealing for the purposes of private study, research, criticism or review as permitted under the Copyright Act, no part of this publication may be reproduced, stored in a retrieval system or transmitted in any form by any means, electronic, mechanical, photocopying, recording or otherwise, without the written permission of the publisher.

 A catalogue record for this book is available from the National Library of Australia

Title:	Romantic Escape: Designing the Modern Guest House III
Author:	Wendy Perring [Ed.]
ISBN:	9781864707991

Printed by Toppan Leefung Packaging & Printing, in Hong Kong/China

IMAGES has included on its website a page for special notices in relation to this and its other publications. Please visit www.imagespublishing.com

Every effort has been made to trace the original source of copyright material contained in this book. The publishers would be pleased to hear from copyright holders to rectify any errors or omissions.
The information and illustrations in this publication have been prepared and supplied by Wendy Perring and the contributors. While all reasonable efforts have been made to ensure accuracy, the publishers do not, under any circumstances, accept responsibility for errors, omissions and representations, express or implied.